KU-460-892

Wild Things

MATERIALIZING CULTURE

. . . .

Series Editors: Paul Gilroy, Michael Herzfeld and Danny Miller

Barbara Bender, *Stonehenge: Making Space*

Gen Doy, *Materializing Art History*

Laura Rival (ed.), *The Social Life of Trees: Anthropological Perspectives on Tree Symbolism*

Victor Buchli, *An Archaeology of Socialism*

Marius Kwint, Christopher Breward and Jeremy Aynsley (eds), *Material Memories: Design and Evocation*

Penny Van Esterik, *Materializing Thailand*

Michael Bull, *Sounding Out the City: Personal Stereos and the Management of Everyday Life*

Anne Massey, *Hollywood Beyond the Screen: Design and Material Culture*

Wild Things

The Material Culture of
Everyday Life

UNIVERSITY OF WOLVERHAMPTON
LEARNING RESOURCES

2275889

CONTROL
1859733646

DATE
10. AUG. 2001

CLASS
306.
4
ATT

SITE
DY

JUDY ATTFIELD

BERG

Oxford • New York

First published in 2000 by
Berg
Editorial offices:
150 Cowley Road, Oxford, OX4 1JJ, UK
838 Broadway, Third Floor, New York, NY 10003-4812, USA

© Judy Attfield 2000

All rights reserved.
No part of this publication may be reproduced in any form or by any
means without the written permission of Berg.

Berg is the imprint of Oxford International Publishers Ltd.

Library of Congress Cataloging-in-Publication Data

A catalogue record for this book is available from the Library of
Congress.

British Library Cataloguing-in-Publication Data

A catalogue record for this book is available from the British Library.

ISBN 1 85973 364 6 (Cloth)
      1 85973 369 7 (Paper)

Typeset by JS Typesetting, Wellingborough, Northants.
Printed in the United Kingdom by Biddles Ltd, Guildford and
King's Lynn.

For Ray, Robert and Jordan

Contents

List of Illustrations

Preface

O ne of the most formative realisations of my academic career was noticing how my design students were always ahead of the game. They always seemed to know instinctively what the latest trends in academic thought were, without necessarily being able to articulate their ideas very clearly. It was as if fashion had some sort of advance warning system to sus out the next hot topic in cultural theory. Their intense interest in identity, and in particular individuality, went with an aggressive assertiveness that clashed with any attempt to contextualise the impetus for self-expression as a social symptom. The only aspect of cultural studies which sparked any interest in them were transgressions of the order imposed by sociological analysis. They were impatient and dismissive with interpretations that explained the way certain styles arose at specific historical moments; they just wanted *to do it* – to be innovators.

In retrospect I partly put their insight down to their professional design training, which requires the development of a good 'nose' for fashion trends. The necessary survival kit for any designer who wants to succeed in the face of a very competitive market must include an arrogant self-regard for their own originality, a liking for risk taking, together with sufficient narcissism and technical expertise to publicise themselves. The art school ethos encourages a strong sense of self-identity and requires students to make presentations and defend their creations in 'crits' where they are open to criticism from their tutors and peers. Design students' almost instinctive awareness of the issues of the moment only made the fashion phenomenon more intriguing to me.

Except for the supremacy of innovation and originality, all the lessons of modernism with reference to 'fitness for purpose' and 'form follows function' etc., were lost on the generation of design students who I was addressing. Ever since I started lecturing in design history after a first career as a designer, I had noticed with increasing unease that students were bored by the fundamental principles of 'good design' derived from the moralising values of nineteenth-century idealists. History was for plundering any good ideas that they could recover and make their own. Style was what excited them. They were also interested in ethical issues such as recycling, 'green', fair trade and 'environmentally friendly' design, but seemed completely unmoved by the virtues of 'good design' which in many ways had similar aims for the betterment of society, but via universal solutions to suit a notional 'majority', subsuming both the designer and the user into an anonymous mass where individuality could not find a home.

But how to formulate the 'individuality' phenomenon beyond the narcissistic indulgence for which it could so easily be mistaken, took a while longer to crystallise into a convincing area of enquiry. At first, legitimisation posed one of the main problems, since it required a certain amount of courage to fly in the face of the totally 'politically incorrect' notion of individuality which apart from psychoanalysis is not allowed to exist in any serious field of enquiry except as a social construct related to the issue of identity within a cultural context. The second problem was how to research 'individuality' when the whole notion completely defies categorisation. But what intrigued me was how to find a way of overcoming what increasingly appeared to be a prejudice against the necessary 'attitude' that ultimately sustains most creative acts, and not just confining the definition to the realm of design; but what must be one of the most fundamental of all the life-enhancing acts – that of creativity. The evasion that it was too narcissistic a topic to contemplate, no longer seemed to hold since for the last twenty-five years postmodernists like Jonathan Raban in *Soft City* (1974) and sociologists like Anthony Giddens had been theorising personal identity as conditional and malleable. I found that a material culture approach offered an alternative that dealt with the designing process and its products. In avoiding the duality between art and design it took on issues of materiality and experience, and drew them away from the circular discussions that otherwise always revolve around the high/low culture debate.

My project has been to attempt to understand individuality in order to be able to explain why it is such a central feature of the contemporary modern mentality and consequently so wrapped up in the material culture of everyday life. The way people objectify that desire in the making, unmaking and remaking of their material worlds is a pervasive activity in people's lives one way or another; but which designers are more consciously involved in than most. I therefore make no apology for concentrating on the *particular* and the *specific*, both words that I know are over-used in the text. But there are only so many ways one can express in language that quality of versatility which is so much more aptly demonstrated in the vast array of things that testify to the importance of the sense of unique difference and individuality which activate people's sense of agency. At the same time I have exploited theory for what it has to offer in opening up material culture, a field that has turned out to be particularly unamenable to discourse. The only way to tackle this combination of the everyday and abstract theory has been to adopt a style of tacking back and forth between rhetorical questions, theoretical devices, items taken from the personal minutia of everyday life, and illustrative case studies. My style is inconsistent – from theoretical and detached to meditative. On many occasions my own research seemed to foreshadow news items while at other times they sparked off a line of thought I hadn't planned.

My attention to individuality like my interest in fashion should not be misunderstood as a superficial interest in style. Whether academics admit it or not we are all susceptible to the dynamics of fashion as a cultural engagement with the new. And it is in an attempt to discover the fundamental impulses that drive it as a means of objectifying the desire for innovation and social change that a large part of this work is dedicated. Nor should my interest in the deeply felt reality of the search for, and the belief in a true self be seen as somehow undermining feminist political strategies to question the so-called 'natural' definitions of sex and gender or indeed the decentring critique of power dynamics that challenges the very category of identity itself. It is the mismatch between theory and practice which brings such fundamental questions into the real world of lived experience, the only place where change can actually be effected.

The endeavour of this study has been to examine at close quarters the sense of identity gained both as an individual and a member of a group, through the process of designing and making the material world, not only among professional designers and makers, but that more amorphous vast public who also participate in its design and construction. This project has therefore been to consider the designer's, the maker's *and* the user's perspectives in the context of the same conceptual playing field in order to recontextualise design within the more general location of the material culture of everyday life. A number of inspirational authors to whom I draw attention in the text provided the final incentive which I needed to take this on as a project. The impetus in this study has therefore been to address the question of identity with particular reference to individuality within a cultural context that can take account of the subtle specificity of its imponderability.

This book is the result of many years of reflection as well as research into a varied and, at first glance what might appear to be, incongruous disparate range of sources, fields, disciplines and case studies. The questions I am asking of design arise from defining it as a common activity and only could have sprung from locating it as a practice of modernity, rather than from the disciplinary parameters that otherwise restrict it to a narrow exclusive professional practice. This is not to denigrate the work of designers, but on the contrary to contextualise it within an expanded cultural field of study that enhances the practice and enlivens the significance of the world of things.

I see this volume as a first step in establishing a theoretical starting point which I hope can contribute to a larger project in the investigation of the material culture of everyday life. It is not a project that I can or want to claim as my own because, as my secondary sources show, it is one engaged upon by many academics in a wide range of different fields in the arts and sciences. Although material culture does not conform to one definition, the varied and broad constituency of academics pursuing studies related to the field testifies to its dynamism and health at this moment when it appears to provide a useful frame of reference from which to address questions of contemporary interest.

In many ways I have set myself an impossible task rather like 'the hitchhiker's guide to the galaxy' – to try to understand the material universe and every 'thing'. But my task has not been to construct a definitive theory for the study of the material culture of everyday life because I have yet to be convinced that it is possible to totalise the subject in a theoretical manner. Nor is this an anti-theory work. The theories recruited in this endeavour have provided essential interpretative tools in the understanding of abstract concepts which form an intrinsic aspect of the study of the social meaning of things. My main intention has been to open up some ways of thinking about the meaningfulness of things in the context of everyday life, the location that sociologists call 'on the ground' and consumption scholars call 'in the street'.

As I complete the book it still feels like an open-ended unfinished project that I have only just started to explore. Apart from providing me with a platform for future projects, my aspiration for this volume is that it may encourage others to contribute to the search for an understanding of design as an aspect of the material world as a social place. There is so much to learn not only from the things we value but from the rubbish, detritus and discarded things. Most of all I hope that readers will find references and avenues to explore for themselves as well as much to argue with and discuss.

There are a number of colleagues, family, friends and students to whom I owe a debt of gratitude for different kinds of help at various stages along the way, especially Jeremy Aynsley, Barbara Burman, Cora and Maurice Clarke (dec.), Dinah Eastop, Michael Evans, Roberto Feo, Lu Firth, Tag Gronberg, Rosario Hurtado, Pat Kirkham, Keith Leaman, Eva Londos, Alex McCowan (dec.), Daniel Miller, Lesley Miller, Francisco Santos, Penny Sparke, Brandon Taylor, Julian Thomas, Joanne Turney, Lynne Walker, Suzette Worden, and my students on the MA Oral History project and the Material Culture of Everyday Life unit. I would like to thank those copyright holders of pictures used to illustrate this book who have given permission for reproduction, as well as those who, in spite of all my efforts, I did not manage to trace. I am also very grateful for the sabbatical leave granted by the History of Art and Design Division of Winchester School of Art, Faculty of Arts, University of Southampton, and the helpful co-operation of my colleagues and the staff in the Division which enabled me to complete the writing of this book. I would like to acknowledge the help and co-operation of all my interviewees, the staff of various archives and libraries consulted in the course of research, in particular Serena Kelly at the Archive of Art and Design, Victoria and Albert Museum and the Library staff at Winchester School of Art, and the two anonymous referees for their helpful suggestions. Very special thanks to Kathryn Earle of Berg Publishers for her enthusiasm for the project, her encouragement, patience, and understanding, and to Ray Attfield for his constant interest, difficult and challenging questions, and the many helpful discussions that helped me throughout this project.

Introduction: The Material Culture of Everyday Life

This is a contradictory project, because although its main focus is on the material object it is not really about *things* in themselves, but about how people make sense of the world through physical objects, what psychoanalytic theory calls 'object relations' in the explanation of identity formation, what sociology invokes as the physical manifestation of culture, and anthropology refers to as the objectification of social relations.[1] Thus this study is situated at the dynamic point of interplay between animate and inanimate worlds in order to look beyond the material world of mere things in themselves and reconsider their complex role in the relationship between objects and subjects.

This is also an unashamedly hybrid book. In academic terms it uses a post-disciplinary approach to the study of design and its history as an aspect of material culture in order to extend it beyond the framework which has largely confined design studies to the work of professional designers. The project here is to discuss the interactive role of physical manufactured objects in the making of the modern world into a human place. It is post-disciplinary, in as much as that although it deliberately starts from the sub-disciplinary base of studies in the history of design, it then goes on to breach the conventional borders of the specialism to draw from a range of fields; from social history, anthropology and archaeology to sociology, geography, psychoanalysis and general cultural studies. There was the time when such eclecticism would have been frowned upon as diluting and undisciplined, when to borrow was seen as a form of stealing, and the purity of the subject area was

1. These disciplines however, although helpful, in the main still fall short when it comes to dealing with physical things. For an exception see Miller, D. *Material Culture and Mass Consumption*, Oxford, Blackwell, 1987, Chapter 6: 'The Humility of Objects', pp. 85–108.

something to be defended. When, too, apologies would have had to be made to justify looking at objects, making sure to expunge any discussion that might be accused of fetishism, and (in more senses than one) that assumed such an association to be negative. However times have changed and in looking retrospectively at the progress of design history it is possible to explain both the narrowness and the unboundedness from which it has both suffered and from which it has developed and continues to grow. It is already apparent that what started as a small offshoot is developing into a healthy growth from which new lines of research will hopefully develop and flourish.

The definition of design history has also changed over time. It can now generally be agreed that the discipline came into being by default because the limitations of art history methods could not deal adequately with products of industrial mass manufacture. Therefore any project which sets out to use design history as a base line for the study of the material culture of everyday things needs to take its historiography into account in order to understand its conventional parameters and how they have expanded to encompass a more diffuse range of goods and a broader time band[2] to those with which it initially started out. Then, neither 'crafts' nor anything which might be mistaken for 'art' would have been considered a legitimate area of study under the aegis of design history. But what is of greater interest than attempting an exact definition which is bound to be partial, is to suggest an explanation for the changes it has undergone and what direction its impending shift might take in the light of new thinking on the subject. As the title suggests – design is just one aspect of the material culture of everyday life. The object of the exercise is to push the boundaries and explore the context to which design belongs. Having broadened the accepted range of artefacts that can be addressed by design however, what now needs serious attention is how to theorise such an endeavour to encompass a wider band of 'things'. And in spite of the more comprehensive parameters or maybe because of their tendency to blur the nature of the object, design critics and historians have become aware of the pressing need to challenge the constraints imposed by the discipline. To thus problematise the issue of interpretation, which is what I mean by 'theory' in this context, is not to favour any particular formulaic methodology, but rather to insist on the prioritisation of

2. Clifford, H. 1999. 'Introduction' to Special Issue: Eighteenth-Century Markets and Manufacturers in England and France, pp. 185–6. In *Journal of Design History*, Vol. 12, No. 3.

the importance of the questions that motivate research and enquiry into the cultural significance of things.

Though young, material culture is already a well established field of study[3] that has continued to talk across the boundaries between cognate disciplines within the humanities and social sciences. In association with design history it offers a more obvious place for the type of analysis that follows design products beyond the point of sale to examine how modern artefacts are appropriated by consumers and transformed from manufactured products to become the stuff of everyday life that have a direct involvement with *matters,* both literally and figuratively, of identity. So what I have called here 'the material culture of everyday life', acknowledges the physical object in all its materiality and encompasses the work of design, making, distributing, consuming, using, discarding, recycling and so on. But above all it focuses on how things have gone through all those stages as part of the mediation process between people and the physical world at different stages in their biographies.

Even though material culture does provide a most appropriate arena for the discussion of the social characteristics of design, nevertheless the starting point for this account commences within the field of design history; because it is from there that the project of this journey can best fulfil its purpose – to challenge visuality and aesthetics (good design) as a prime factor in the study of designed objects. Design history made a definite move away from its parent discipline – art history – some time ago. For in spite of the all-embracing attempts to integrate 'commercial art' and industrially mass-produced products in the 'new art history' of the eighties,[4] its subsequent re-categorisation as visual culture failed to consider its materiality and the most distinctive qualities which make design different from art in its relationship to the everyday, the ordinary and the banal. And significantly it is this relationship with the generic that has been the focus of exhibitions such as 'Material Culture'[5] at the Hayward Gallery in London in 1997

---

3. Some have argued that it is more than a field, but a discipline. See Prown, J.D. 1982. 'Mind in Matter: An Introduction to Material Culture Theory and Method'. *Winterthur Portfolio,* Vol. 17 No. 1. For a recent review see Attfield, J. 1999. 'Beyond the Pale: Reviewing the relationship between Material Culture and Design History' in *Journal of Design History*, Vol 12, No. 4, pp. 373–80.

4. Pointon, M. 1986. *History of Art: A Students' Handbook.* London: Unwin Hyman, pp. 14–32.

5. 'Material Culture: The Object in British Art of the 1980s and 90s' was shown in the Hayward Gallery, London from 3 April to 18 May 1997.

in which the curators sought to bring together the work of artists with a common interest in 'the object in itself, as raw material, found or functional thing and in relation to wider scuptural and artistic concerns'.[6] Similarly the increasing standing of the crafts in the expressive arts can in part be explained by the way they call attention to the skill and beauty of handmade processes. While at the same time we find design practioners, critics and historians currently showing an interest in ugliness and 'undesign' as seen in the recent 'Stealing Beauty' exhibition held at the Institute of Contemporary Arts (ICA) in London in 1999.[7]

Strictly speaking design is both the product and the process that conceptualises an aesthetic and functional solution to industrially produced goods – from garments to potato peelers and from cars to buildings. But that is not the end of the story. If it were, there would be little point in clearing a space to discuss design as producing a different type of object to that of art. In some contexts it could even be said to serve the same kind of expressive functions. It is more a matter of context. For engineers design has nothing to do with aesthetics, it is strictly operational. Design has tried, unsuccessfully to straddle aesthetics and engineering, resulting in an equivalent to two cultures, analogous to the art/science divide, with two very different definitions of design and a division of labour between the stylist who is in charge of the envelope for the works supplied by the engineer. This was made apparent in the Design History Society conference[8] held at the School of Design at Huddersfield University where the aim was to stimulate more contact between different types of practitioners, historians and theoreticians. In order to further that dialogue here, design is posited as the counterpart to art in order to challenge that divide. Whereas art enchants the ordinary object and makes it special, design disenchants it. Making design a 'thing' returns it from the display shelf, the collection, the museum or art gallery to the factory floor, the warehouse shelf or the forgotten corner at the back of a cupboard where it forms

6. 'Material Culture: The Object in British Art of the 1980s and 90s', Hayward Gallery leaflet, 1997 (unpaginated).

7. 'Stealing Beauty: British Design Now' (exhibition catalogue) London: ICA.

8. The Design History of Society, founded in 1977, is based in Britain, has an international membership, publishes a quarterly newsletter and refereed *Journal of Design History*. It holds an annual conference in one of the many UK educational institutions that offer degree courses on design practice, history and theory. See http://www.brighton.ac.uk/dhs/

part of the physical effects belonging to an individual, a household, a nation, a culture, the world of goods. In the same way the once highly valued paintings by a painter who has gone out of fashion can be deposed from a position of honour in the academy to become a thing hidden away in the museum store room. The spotlight of academic or critical interest appears mainly to focus on the object as celebrity and spectacle, when it is 'new', popular, highly acclaimed, sensational and above all – visible; or at the moment of its downfall from grace when, for example, it is exposed as inauthentic. But what doesn't seem to attract much attention is that larger part of the designed object's biography when it is no longer sacred, when it forms part of the disordered everyday clutter of the mundane, and joined the disarray of wild things that don't quite fit anywhere – the undisciplined.

While the 'new' art and design histories, represented by journals such as *Block*,[9] have revised and problematised 'historical facts' by subjecting them to critical scrutiny allowing a contemporary gloss to be added so that it was no longer possible for historians to assert the authority of a heroic account of modern classics, the problem of continuing to see design as a visual medium remained unchallenged. Thus the tendency to study design as if it were the same as fine art, requiring an educated eye to appreciate its formal qualities, remained and remains embedded within the discipline. That is not to say that representation, and all that the practice of interpreting meaning from visual images entails, is discounted as a method of valuing design either functionally, aesthetically or purely as a conduit of meaning. The impact of foregrounding the language-like characteristics of the visual have contributed so greatly to its understanding that this study could not have been envisaged without the platform that those studies have provided.

At the crudest level the model of design history rooted in Ruskinian principles of the arts and crafts movement which has insisted that its duty lay mainly in considering 'good design', has not just omitted vast swathes of artefacts, increasing incrementally with the rising prosperity and economic ambitions of nation states, but disregards the social life of things that unfolds beyond the initial commodity stage. Recently sociology has taken on the investigation of consumption as a social

---

9. *Block* was a journal published between 1979 and 1989 by a group of academics in what was then the Department of Art History and Related Studies at Middlesex Polytechnic (now University of Middlesex), concerned with the strategies of cultural practice commited to a socialist agenda.

activity using the study of products such as the Sony Walkman[10] to provide concrete examples of the physical embodiment of culture in the form of manufactured goods. But there are still relatively few examples that reveal the impact of economic and educational institutions in the creation of products for the market that chart the complete biography of the object, following it as it passes through the retail check-out into everyday life.

The aim of this study is to present some critical perspectives and suggest some ways of theorising design to include the less well-ordered things that inhabit the material world, beyond interpretations that confine it to a catalogue of pristine aesthetic objects. To locate design within a social context as a meaningful part of peoples' lives means integrating objects and practices within a culture of everyday life where things don't always do as they are told nor go according to plan. Although the historical dimension is an important aspect of the project, this work does not purport to provide 'a history' nor a fully formulated theory. Its main intention is to offer a tool box with some tentative definitions (Part I), themes (Part II) and contexts (Part III) with which to get started in thinking about how to make sense of the clutter of things that humans make, exchange and surround themselves with on this crowded planet at the beginning of the third millennium.

Part I explores questions around the definitions of 'design' and 'things' in order to distinguish them from each other as different kinds of things, while also considering how they both form part of the same material world. Chapter 1 defines design as 'things with attitude' where the designer's intention is made apparent through a strong visual statement. The institutional conventions that have defined the principles of good design within the modern movement have tended to dominate the discourse of design drowning out the more 'everyday' type of things which form the greater part of the material world. Current changes that include a more 'material culture' approach can accommodate the type of things defined in Chapter 2 – 'design in the lower case'. Ordinary things do not depend quite so much on meaning thrust upon them for marketing purposes. Once they enter the realm of the ordinary they evade notice and become absorbed into peoples' lives where they are no longer 'a taste thing', but become part of an individual's personal possessions that go towards forming a sense of

---

10. du Gay, P., Hall, S. et al. 1997. *Doing Cultural Studies: The Story of the Sony Walkman.* London: Sage.

individuality within a group that share the same values. The rediscovery of 'things' by design theoreticians confirms the turn away from the immateriality encouraged by theories of representation that reduce all meaning to language. The last Chapter 3 in Part I discusses the dynamic character of artefacts used to negotiate change at a social and individual level positing design as a dynamic process.

Authenticity, the subject of Chapter 4 is discussed through a case study of reproduction furniture, a type of artefact well suited to demonstrate the way in which it only becomes an issue with modern design theory that insists on originality, a concept entirely foreign to trade practices where the design process was integral to the production process and depended on repetition. The importance given to historical specificity as a means of referring to authenticity and maintaining a link with the past, embedded in certain types of material artefacts like furniture, becomes particularly pertinent in a period characterised by rapid change. In contrast to the sense of continuity objectified in reproduction furniture, one of the types of artefact best suited to embody ephemerality providing a material means of keeping in touch with the present, is textiles and fashion – the subject of Chapter 5. 'Containment', the theme addressed in Chapter 6, looks at the way personal possessions form a conglomerate arrangement sometimes referred to as 'clutter'. It allows the study of things gone wild into an unruly accumulation as well as an orderly arrangements of things as a form of ecology of personal possessions, using as a case study the role of domestic things in materialising the construction of self-identity.

Moving from the particular case studies of the middle section of the book, Part III opens up three fundamental contexts, exploring the materiality of the everyday in terms of space, time and the body. Context is abstract insofar as it is used to locate or position a subject, nevertheless it is discussed here as a physical entity. Although each is treated in a separate chapter there is a close interrelationship between them. Chapter 7 on space takes on a number of popular phenomena such as 'spec builders' vernacular' in order to apply various different perspectives in the investigation of space as a social artefact. Chapter 8 concerns 'time' and the way in which people use things to establish a relationship to it to form their subjectivity. The book ends with a consideration of the changing relationship between things and the body, suggesting a transition with the passing of time from embodiment to disembodiment.

Part I

Things

Introduction

'Things' is one of those generic categories that, in spite of close scrutiny by philosophers over the centuries, seems neverthless to have eluded any precise definition. Simply, it can be said to be a term that stands for the basic unit that makes up the totality of the material world. But in recognising how culturally determined the manner in which the material world is formed and perceived, it becomes clear how impossible it is to arrive at an objective catch-all designation. In these days of postmodern uncertainty and cultural diversity, an awareness of difference and alternative interpretations is a much more achievable aim than trying to reach an ultimately conclusive definition. The first three chapters are therefore dedicated to establishing some working defini-tions of 'things' that start out as a conglomerate clutter of artefacts that make up the totality of the physical world not as a raw mass of matter, but as material culture with human associations in as much as it is informed by meanings as fundamental as identity, life and death. This is not to over-dramatise the role of things, since the choice to use this term was made on the assumption that, by definition, 'things' are non-special and mundane, but merely that which makes up the physicality of the everyday. As Henri Lefebre has written 'The everyday is the most universal and the most unique condition, the most social and the most individuated, the most obvious and the best hidden' (Lefebre 1987: pp. 7–11). At the same time even though 'things' described in this way are unobtrusive and escape attention, they are nevertheless instrumental in the literal and grounded sense of mediating the link between people and artefacts and therefore between the human worlds of the mental and the physical.

Figure 1. Woodwork bench with milk bottle (Birmingham Museums and Art Gallery, photo: Mike Coldicott).

Figure 2. 'Designer' cheddar cheese.

The Meaning of Design:
Things with Attitude

The rise of Material Culture as a specific field offers a place for the study of the history and theory of design that refuses to privilege it as it is customarily seen, as a special type of artefact. By amalgamating design with the object world at large it becomes just one type of 'thing' among other 'things' that make up the summation of the material world – the objects of human production and exchange with and through which people live their everyday existence.[1] Therefore it is against that broader context that design can be considered, where it forms part of the wider material world rather than separated off, encapsulating a small exclusive array of special goods. But it is not the 'thing' in itself which is of prime interest here, even though it is positioned at the central point of focus. The material object is posited as the vehicle through which to explore the object/subject relationship, a condition that hovers somewhere between the physical presence and the visual image, between the reality of the inherent properties of materials and the myth of fantasy, and between empirical materiality and theoretical representation. The object therefore is both the starting point and the ultimate point of return, but overturning the usual interests of design practice by methodologically casting aesthetic visuality as subordinate to sociality. It is in the latter particularity that this project departs very distinctly from what could be characterised as conventional design studies which assumes 'design' to be at best a professional activity (designers know best) and at worst the result of a self-conscious act of

1. The term 'everyday' is used generically in this chapter (meaning 'common or garden', usual, informal, banal, unremarkable). But in the overarching project of this study 'the everyday' is given a particular significance, creating a specific context within which to discuss the meaning of things which are usually overlooked. For a definition see Chapter 2.

11

intentionality (as in do-it-yourself).[2] At worst, because the logic of design studies has been only to consider the 'best' examples along the conventions of modernist ideals of 'form follows function'.[3]

But design can be defined much more broadly as 'things with attitude' – created with a specific end in view – whether to fulfil a particular task, to make a statement, to objectify moral values, or to express individual or group identity, to denote status or demonstrate technological prowess, to exercise social control or to flaunt political power. Therefore in demoting design by recontextualisation and integrating it as one type of object among a more generalised world of goods that make up the totality of things, makes it possible to investigate the non-verbal dynamics of the way people construct and interact with the modern material world through the practice of design and its objectification – the products of that process.

This chapter will explore some of the various definitions that have been attributed to 'design' that have gone towards excluding it from 'things' – the totality of entities that make up the material world and divided it off by hierarchical order and generic category to distinguish design as a privileged type. The object of the exercise, in more ways than one, will be to dislocate design from the habitual aesthetic frame devised by conventional art and design historical and theoretical studies, to present it as just one of the many aspects of the material culture of the everyday. But before setting out to explore the wilder outer reaches beyond design's own territory, this chapter will first review as a starting point the more circumscribed definitions of

2. There are a sufficient number of exceptions to this generalisation, to safely predict that they belong to a growing trend, to which this volume aims to contribute. For a recent exposition of the fear that Design Studies might stray away from design practice as a primary concern, see Richard Buchanan's review of Jonathan M. Woodham's *Twentieth Century Design* (Oxford University Press, 1997) in *Journal of Design History*, Vol. 11, No. 3, 1998, pp. 259–63. For an earlier stated perspectival view that defined design beyond the narrow scope of professional practice see Attfield, J. 1989. 'Form/Female follows Function/Male' pp. 199–225. In Walker, J.A. 1989 *Design History and the History of Design*, London: Pluto Press.

3. Although it is now generally accepted that 'functionalism' represents a narrow form of determinism now largely discarded in design practice, the particular aesthetic it produced is enjoying a resurgence of interest, and the search to find ethical solutions to design problems continues to have pertinence. See Attfield, J. (ed.) 1999. *Utility Reassessed: The role of ethics in the practice of design*. Manchester and New York: Manchester University Press.

design,[4] its history, and some of the literature that has established it as a certain type of object and process. It will then redefine design so as to be able to accommodate more popular forms and ordinary objects to establish a more level playing field in which the interrelations between extra-ordinary designed objects can be considered alongside ordinary 'undesign'. This more inclusive redefinition of design will be used to frame the discussion within the 'culture/nature' framework that distinguishes cultural artefacts, such as chairs, from natural things like trees. The pairing of chairs and trees is particularly apposite in that chairs have traditionally been made out of trees, transformed by the process of design from organic entities into material culture. Design is the touchstone of modernity that differentiates between ubiquitous vernacular forms, tools and craft practices that have evolved gradually and unconsciously over thousands of years, and the spirit of innovation that has animated designers to turn away from the habitual traditional materials and modes of making to objectify new technologies and social change.

The conventions of design studies[5] have established a simplistic frame of reference based around the concept of 'good design' in opposition to 'bad' design that has tended to act as an automatic diagnostic censor to pluck out any subject considered beyond the pale. Therefore a prime task for this chapter will be to critique and locate the 'good design/bad design' debate within a specific historical context in order to extend and redefine design as a non-generic common process and thus to integrate it into the larger material world of goods.

When modern products termed 'design' are recontextualised as an aspect of material culture they lose their visibility to become part of the 'everyday'. The aim is to expand the definitions of design so as,

---

4. The context for this study is British design within the context of Western culture referring mainly to British design with some reference to design in Europe and the United States.

5. 'Design studies' is used here to include the history and theory of design in the context of the current debate that contests the limits placed upon it according to whether it is contextualised within practical or academic frameworks of enquiry. The position taken here is that there is an inextricable intellectual link between practice, history and theory but that there are institutional realities in terms of weight and emphasis given to any such division according to its appropriateness to specific courses. For the purpose of analysis there is also some advantage to be gained from keeping the theoretical and historical study, where and if possible, separate from the pressures of particular design practice interest groups in order to gain a more objective view.

not only to include its more usual role of 'things with attitude', but also to include a consideration of it as a process through which individuals and groups construct their identity, experience modernity and deal with social change.

Chairs Don't Grow on Trees: Defining Design

> The chair (which assists the work of the skeleton and compensates for its inadequacies) can over centuries be continually reconceived, redesigned, improved, and repaired (in both its form and its materials) much more easily than the skeleton itself can be internally reconceived, despite the fact the continual modifications of the chair ultimately climax in, and thus may be seen as rehearsals for, civilization's direct intervention into and modification of the skeleton itself.[6]

Somehow there is something quite natural about 'things'. Things seem always to have been there, defining the world physically – through such objects as walls that determine boundaries separating spaces and doors that give or prevent access. Things are ubiquitous like furniture that gives support to our bodies when we sit down, and paths that direct our feet where to walk, vehicles that transport us as we travel about on the daily round. Things lend orientation and give a sense of direction to how people relate physically to the world around them, not least in providing the physical manifestation, the material evidence of a particular sense of group and individual identity. Things don't necessarily call attention to themselves and are only noticed if not there when really needed. Their presence is incontestable; yet it is only in the naming of things – 'chair', 'car', 'coat', 'toothbrush', 'escalator' – that they assume a particularity that makes them stand out as individual entities from against the background of the general physical environment, as seemingly 'natural' as the very ground we walk on. This rather basic definition does not mean to ignore the literature that attends to the definition of the perceived world such as Ludwig Wittgenstein's philosophy of mind. Particularly valuable in this context is his preoccupation with 'the important questions of everyday life' as represented in his *Philosophic Investigations*[7] which concentrated on the role of language in the perception and expression of the relationship

---

6. Scarry, E. 1985. *The Body In Pain*, Oxford: Oxford University Press, p. 254.
7. Kenny, A. [1973] 1993. *Wittgenstein*. Harmondsworth, Middlesex: Penguin, p.10.

between the objective world and human thought. Wittgenstein's interest in philosophical propositions which set out to define reality drew a direct correlation between words and tools as instruments of meaning, giving greater importance to the process of language in the context of space and time than attempting to arrive at essentialist definitions.[8] But although the meaning of the object world is elucidated by such studies, just as semiotics has done so much to increase our knowledge of visual culture, the non-verbal nature of the material world referred to in this project cannot entirely be explained through language.

But the 'thing' as made-object is not natural, although it may appear so because there is nothing very special about it. It's presence alone does not lend it visibility, rather like the mystery of Poe's 'Purloined Letter', it eludes detection while staring the searcher in the face because it is 'too self-evident'. You have to be looking to find it. In Poe's famous short story, the compromising document was only found when the searcher 'came with the intent to suspect'.[9] 'Thing' is a term so obvious it needs no definition and can therefore ostensibly stand in for absolutely anything. Yet in so doing it might also be alleged that 'things' means absolutely nothing. But because things have no special attributes, their ubiquity defies definition and makes them appear natural. 'Thingness' lends artefacts an elusive quality through which it is possible to start to examine the particularity of the significance of the object world within the context of the social world. What then distinguishes 'things' from 'design'? Although design is a noun denoting things, it is also a verb – a self-conscious activity devoted to creating new forms of artefacts and therefore a conceptual as well as a manufacturing process that arose from a modern mentality that turned its back on the past and believed in the possibility of progress through change.

Things do not have the high-profile visuality of 'design'. It is only when a thing acquires a name that an artefact announces and thereby calls attention to itself. But in so doing, it also becomes a representation which distances the thing from its meaning. Thus the central problem of studying material culture – the social meaning of the physical world of things – necessarily revolves around the unresolved relationship between the object and its meaning, a relationship that is most

8. Wittgenstein, L. [1953] 1968. *Philosophical Investigations*. Oxford: Blackwell.
9. Poe, E.A. 1986. 'The Purloined Letter'. In *The Fall of the House of Usher and other writings*. Harmondsworth, Middlesex: Penguin, p. 331.

succinctly defined by the term – the object/subject relationship that focuses on the dynamic interplay between the object and its social meaning, not resting entirely on either one as determining the other. If this should sound like evading the issue it is in order to set the scene for the investigation into 'the nature of things', that renders the physical banality of the everyday invisible and thus hides its role as the physical embodiment of culture behind an apparent anonymous inevitability that raises no questions.

This account refutes scholarship that reduces artefacts to a form of visual imagery that can be decoded so that an object becomes a sign system by virtue of its style, thereby dematerialising it and thus denying it the reality of physical thingness. That is not to say that theories of culturalism and representation are not vital in the understanding of the contingent status of meaning on the object world. But concentrating exclusively on trying to decipher what an object means detracts from an understanding of its materiality even if by doing so it defines its contingency according to its context. Furthermore the fact that the interpretation of Marxist analysis that has attached negative connotations to 'fetishism', and thereby refused to consider it as productive of knowledge, has worked against the study of the object as if it has no a priori existence to its interpretation. Uncoupling the thing from its meaning, while elucidating the ideological roots of its cultural production, also runs the grave danger of dematerialising it altogether. Although sophisticated methods of visual analysis derived from an environment drenched in media imagery has undoubtedly increased our knowledge and understanding of the object world, the missing ingredient increasingly becomes the object itself so that the discussion revolves around the meaning divorced from its objectification. What primarily occupies this study is the dynamic relationship between people and things, referred to above as the object-subject relationship.

Things like chairs are not natural in the organic sense, they do not grow on trees; they are the result of design, human thought, manufacture and distribution processes based on detailed and strategic calculations. They are also the accumulation of hundreds if not thousands of years of experience and skill in how things are made and put together from different kinds of materials. What distinguishes modern design from traditional forms as in vernacular buildings and furniture, tools and utensils that continue to be reproduced in similar forms to their ancient predecessors, is the impulse to innovate, to create something new that responds to different circumstances. They are part of an economic system. Most books on design assume that designed objects are automatically highly visible, primarily making themselves felt through the style and 'look' that heightens their fashionablility (desirability) or their user efficiency (function). Even in the case of individuals training to be designers, conditioned to be aware of the *physical* properties and forms of design, it is highly unlikely that they will have had direct physical contact with many of the icons of the modern movement. More often than not the awareness of a design as a highly stylised visual experience is encountered through seeing it first as an image so that the *real thing* only becomes so through the mediation of a photographic representation. Nevertheless there are many other less self-conscious encounters with the object world which are not accounted for unless the physical reality of things is acknowledged. And in considering that physical reality by engaging with materiality as human endeavour (design) it is possible to understand what Elaine Scarry has described so vividly, as the way in which 'the object is only a fulcrum or lever across which the force of creation moves back onto the human site and remakes the makers'.[10]

The experience of engaging in the act of designing is not confined to professional designers, nor amateur do-it-yourself activities such as home decorating, it is something that most people do everyday when they put together a combination of clothes to wear or plan a meal. It is soon learnt that certain elements 'don't go' together – that chocolate sauce does not go with pasta. But the cultural specificity of such distinctions is revealed by considering, say the Mexican use of chocolate in savoury dishes. The non-visual senses learn about these cultural conventions much less self-consciously than the eyes. Designers who depend on the visual appeal of their designs to announce themselves and sell their work, find themselves in an increasingly catch-22 situation – while they aspire to creating the ideal classic design to blend into the artefactual landscape and be absorbed into the everyday, they also want their designs to bear their name through an instantly recognisable form: a sort of visual signature.

A recent exhibition of design at the Institute of Contemporary Arts (ICA) in London – 'Stealing Beauty',[11] sub-titled 'British Design Now' – expressed the eternal dilemma of the modern designer. By the time this is published the 'now' will have become 'then' and the fashionability of the slightly skewed versions of furniture designs meant to

10. Scarry 1985. *The Body in Pain.*

11. 'Stealing Beauty' was on show at the Institute of Contemporary Arts (ICA), London, between 3 April and 23 May 1999.

make the viewer look at ordinary things in a new way by making them a bit 'strange', will be just as dated as the 'fabulous mid-century design icon or the very latest thing from Philippe Starck'[12] given as examples to indicate the tired old passé designs of the previous decade. And the point of the exhibition to distance design from the 'super-slick, high-gloss world of consumption' that is supposed to deny the 'materiality' (here meaning commercial value) of the exhibits, depends on the metaphysical concept that beauty cannot be bought and sold but is for 'stealing'. However in this case the 'stealing' is on the part of the designers, attempting to 'reappropriate' the ordinariness of things which have managed to evade the contamination of 'designer' gloss. It would seem a last-chance-saloon stand against the dictatorship of the style police, while at the same time covertly disguising the aspiration to be in the avant-garde, illustrated by one of the design groups that took part in the exhibition significantly calling itself 'El Ultimo Grito'.[13] (see Figure 3)

The interest in 'undesign' is not exclusively English, nor is it a phenomenon exclusive to the 1990s. There are Italian precedents in the 'anti-art' design movement in Italy initiated more than two decades earlier with the establishment of design practices like Studio Alchymia of Milan in 1979[14] and Ettore Sottsass's Memphis.[15] Of the same generation, the now New York-based Italian architect Gaetano Pesce still shows his skeptisim in 'the search for "beauty" or formalism in today's architectural output'[16] prioritising the need for low-tech design and the role of architecture as 'a vehicle of communication' that is able 'to become a record of "our" time and therefore a reflection, or image of life and culture in the street'. The Dutch design group, Droog, also have affinities with the British 'Stealing Beauty' generation through their interest in recycling low-tech products.[17]

12. Roux, C. 'You're sitting on a work of art'. In the *Guardian*, 6 April 1999, pp. 10–11.

13. A Spanish expression meaning 'the last word'.

14. Sparke, P. 1986. *An Introduction to Design and Culture in the Twentieth Century*. London: Allen & Unwin, p. 199–202.

15. Sparke, P. 1982. *Ettore Sottsass Jr*. London: Design Council.

16. Pesce, G. 1995. '18 questions on architecture today'. In *Domus*, No. 768, February, p. 1.

17. *Droog Design 1991–1996*, Utrecht: Utrecht Centraal Museum; Ramaker, R. and Bakker, G. 1998. *Droog Design: Spirit of the Nineties*. Rotterdam: 010 Publishers.

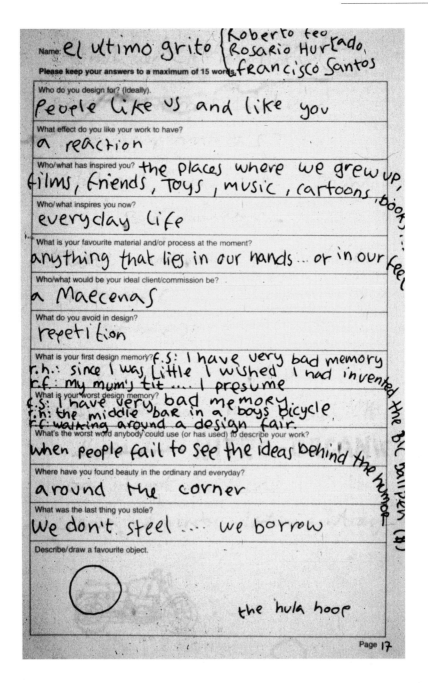

Figure 3. Statement made by *El Ultimo Grito*, one of the design groups exhibited in the 1999 'Stealing Beauty' exhibition at the Institute of Contemporary Art in London. (ICA)

Much of the accounts of the history of design, whether through texts, museum displays, or exhibitions, are directed at attracting their publics to look intensely and learn to appreciate and understand the visual qualities of well-designed objects. So what is the value of analysing design as mere 'things'? The intention is to question rather than reduce design to a category within an ordered framework that positions it in terms of aesthetic value, so that it can be considered as a meaning-making process which does not merely produce unique products but encompasses the materialisation of the physical world as a human project of creation. Anthropologists call this process 'objectification' defined as a dialectic and not to be confused with objectivism, the negative association so often attributed to materiality that determines objects according to a fixed rule-based system.[18]

The body of design history literature which has largely determined how design is valued foregrounds the cult of 'good design'[19] based on modern aesthetic principles derived from the concept of utility and placing the interests of society above those of the individual. 'Good design' also continues to hold an equivocal relationship to machine and hand production through which the conflict of identity formation is played out. On the one hand, craft has represented the stand against alienated labour imposed by the Fordist system of industrialised production à la William Morris; but at the same time it has also become a secondary form of fine art representing the cult of the individual in an age of mass production.[20] While on the other hand, machine production was favoured by advocates of modernist design reform for its allegiance to the social ideal of the accessible paradigm – the multi-reproducible prototype that could mass-produce a good design.[21]

Things with Attitude

Tracing its historiography explains how design was conferred a place in the history of the modern movement and how that position has

18. See Miller, D. 1987. Part I: 'Objectification' pp. 1–82 and 'The Limits of Objectivism' pp. 163–7. In *Material Culture and Mass Consumption*. Oxford: Blackwell.

19. See Sparke, P. 1986. 'Good Design' pp. 67–9. In *An Introduction to Design and Culture in the Twentieth Century*, London: Allen & Unwin.

20. See Dormer, P. 1990. 'Valuing the Handmade: Studio crafts and the meaning of their style'. In *The Meanings of Modern Design*. London: Thames and Hudson.

21. Heskett, J. 1980. *Industrial Design*. London: Thames and Hudson.

been informed and even dominated by the 'good design' critique.[22] It is quite simple to say that the history of design is just another field of history, but *that* too has to be contextualised within the changes which have occurred across the history front generally.[23] A useful consequence of postmodern thought has resulted in the acknowledgement of the under-representation of certain social groups in conventional historical accounts as well as the introduction of different critical methods and types of sources to aid the investigation of areas formerly not considered by design historians.[24] Within design history studies the implications of postmodern approaches that questioned the basis of 'good design' and its concomitant valuing of functionalism, produced critiques like John Thakara's 'Beyond the object in design'[25] prioritising meaning over materiality. While the implications, for example of treating an artefact as a historical document rather than an aesthetic object, do not require it to have passed the 'good design' test in order to qualify as a viable subject for investigation. A more critical awareness of the process of historical research also brings with it a greater consciousness of the kind of questions that can be tackled in the pursuit of an understanding of the process of design, the nature of things produced by that process and its role in the making of the human world.

Design History (as distinct from the field – the history of design) is the common name for the discipline by which it is referred to institutionally as in, e.g. the *Design History Society*, the *Journal of Design History* and so on. This is not to say that design history should be considered a discrete subject area, because its institutional, educational and cultural constitution links it inextricably with the theory and practice of art and design as well as with its trade traditions and nineteenth-century art education roots.[26] Nevertheless design history has been acknowledged as having an identity of its own although it isn't that long since the debate shifted away from defining it according to its difference

22. E.g. MacCarthy, F. 1972. *All Things Bright and Beautiful*. London: George Allen & Unwin. In 1979 published under the revised title: *A History of British Design 1890–1970*.

23. For example Jenkins, K.1991. *Re-thinking History*. London: Routledge; Rees, A.L. and Borzello, F. 1986. *The New Art History*, London: Camden Press.

24. Woodham, J.M. 1997. *Twentieth Century Design*. Oxford: Oxford University Press. See 'Introduction', pp. 7–9.

25. Thakara, J. (ed.) 1988. *Design After Modernism: Beyond the Object*. London: Thames and Hudson, pp. 11–34.

26. For a background to the history of design history see Walker 1989. *Design History and the History of Design*.

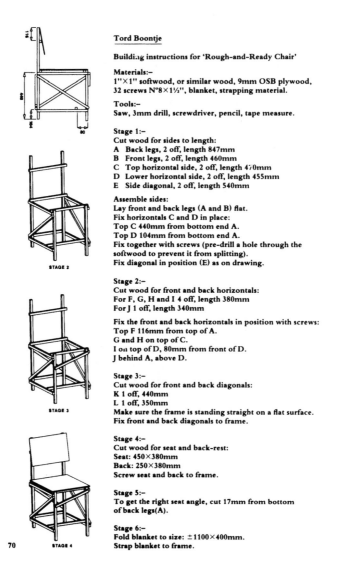

Tord Boontje

Building instructions for 'Rough-and-Ready Chair'

Materials:–
1"×1" softwood, or similar wood, 9mm OSB plywood,
32 screws N°8×1½", blanket, strapping material.

Tools:–
Saw, 3mm drill, screwdriver, pencil, tape measure.

Stage 1:–
Cut wood for sides to length:
A Back legs, 2 off, length 847mm
B Front legs, 2 off, length 460mm
C Top horizontal side, 2 off, length 470mm
D Lower horizontal side, 2 off, length 455mm
E Side diagonal, 2 off, length 540mm

Assemble sides:
Lay front and back legs (A and B) flat.
Fix horizontals C and D in place:
Top C 440mm from bottom end A.
Top D 104mm from bottom end A.
Fix together with screws (pre-drill a hole through the
softwood to prevent it from splitting).
Fix diagonal in position (E) as on drawing.

Stage 2:–
Cut wood for front and back horizontals:
For F, G, H and I 4 off, length 380mm
For J 1 off, length 340mm

Fix the front and back horizontals in position with screws:
Top F 116mm from top of A.
G and H on top of C.
I on top of D, 80mm from front of D.
J behind A, above D.

Stage 3:–
Cut wood for front and back diagonals:
K 1 off, 440mm
L 1 off, 350mm
Make sure the frame is standing straight on a flat surface.
Fix front and back diagonals to frame.

Stage 4:–
Cut wood for seat and back-rest:
Seat: 450×380mm
Back: 250×380mm
Screw seat and back to frame.

Stage 5:–
To get the right seat angle, cut 17mm from bottom
of back legs(A).

Stage 6:–
Fold blanket to size: ±1100×400mm.
Strap blanket to frame.

Figure 4. 'Rough and ready chair' designed by Tord Boontje exhibited in 1999 in the 'Stealing Beauty' exhibition at the Institute of Contemporary Art in London. (ICA)

from art history. In Adrian Forty's seminal book he argued strongly against Stephen Bayley's assertion that 'Industrial design is the art of the twentieth century'.[27] The genre of objects now encompassed by the discipline has diversified beyond the stricture which only allowed it to deal with the useful and the product of mass industrialised production. More recently the debate taking place between American and British academics concerned with design history, would appear to have been prompted by struggles over academic boundaries that distinguished between design *history* and design *studies*.[28] Although 'material culture' is still identified with the decorative arts and museums where objects are their main raison d'être, the increasing popularity of material culture studies now often includes design within its parameters. And because 'material culture' is linked to museology the two fields are often subsumed. The principal concern of institutions with arte-factual collections has been the need to rethink how to collect, display and educate in the light of such cultural changes as the advent of post-colonialism. Since the publication of John A. Walker's *Design History and the History of Design* in 1989, which introduced a selection of methodologies based on a Marxist critique of history, the trend in design studies has been led by the theory of representation treating design as one field among many within the collectivity of the visual arts.[29]

Design history, just like art history, continues to redefine itself in the light of the needs of education and from within the various institutions in which it operates, and not least in relation to the historical period in which it finds itself. The effects of training designers as artists in the current climate of post-industrial Britain has placed greater value on rapidly disappearing skills and crafts which were a common place in the trade schools, such as the art of cutting and dress-making.[30] The climate has also stimulated the desire on the part of designers to fashion their own type of self-reliant practice along the

27. Forty, A. 1986. *Objects of Desire: Design and Society 1750–1980*. London: Thames & Hudson, p. 7.

28. Margolin, V. 1992. 'Design History or Design Studies: Subject Matter and Methods', *Design Studies*, Vol. 13, No. 2, April; Forty, A. 1993. 'Debate: A Reply to Victor Margolin' pp. 131–2. In *Journal of Design* History, Vol. 6, No. 2; Woodham, J. 1995. 'Resisting Colonization: Design History Has Its Own Identity' in *Design Issues*, Vol 11, No. 1, Spring, pp. 22–37.

29. See Walker, J.A. and Chaplin, S. 1997. *Visual Culture: An Introduction*. Manchester: Manchester University Press.

30. Reynolds, H. 1997. *Couture or Trade. Chichester, West Sussex: Phillimore.*

same lines as fine artists, in preference to the traditional constraints of
the industry which disallows autonomy and undervalues the work of
designers.[31]

Design historians have always relied on literature beyond the borders
of their own specialised field of the history of design, not only because
Design history, the discipline, hasn't had enough time to acquire more
than a start-up body of literature; but because design, by its very nature,
is an androgynous hybrid discipline, poised between art and science
with a foot in both camps.[32] In her handbook for students on the
History of Art which first came out in 1980, Marcia Pointon was already
acknowledging that design history was 'a discipline within its own
right', noting that 'a specialised literature in connection with the subject
is growing fast'.[33] But twenty-five years on it cannot realistically be
concluded by any stretch of the imagination, that the literature *has*
grown to quite the predicted extent. There are many reasons for this
which have nothing to do with a lack of interest in the subject matter.
Probably the most important has been the limitations of a field that
has confined research and enquiry within rather restricted parameters
imposed by 'good design' criteria. Not that the lack of experimentation
or theoretical thrust in their own field has gone unnoticed by design
historians who habitually attempt to reconsider history in the light of
such developments as postmodern critiques of élite culture, or the
change of perspective in economic/social history produced by the study
of the history of consumption.[34]

31. As Angela McRobbie identifies so insightfully in her recent book on *British Fashion Design* (London: Routledge, 1998), the individualism encouraged by art education has created a new breed of fashion designers who are reshaping the industry into 'a new kind of rag trade' defining design as a form of cultural production disassociated from the élitism of traditional haute couture.

32. Attfield, J. 1984 'A tale of two cultures' and 'Design for learning'. *The Times Higher Education Supplement,* 10 August, p. 13.

33. Pointon, M. 1980. *History of Art: A Students' Handbook*. London: Unwin Hyman, p.15.

34. The assumptions of conventional design history were questioned by for example: Attfield, J. 1985 'Feminist Designs on Design History' in *Feminist Art News* Vol. 2, No. 3: pp. 21–3 cited in Buckley, C. 1986 'Made in Patriarchy: Towards a feminist analysis of women and design'. *Design Issues* Vol. 3, No. 2, Fall, pp. 3–14, acknowledging popular culture studies and feminist analysis in the study of the history of design because of the emphasis such studies placed upon the relationship between people and things. John A. Walker included J. Attfield's 'Feminist critique of design' as a postcript to his student handbook *Design History and the History of Design* first published in 1989 (Pluto Press)

Arguably the maintenance of design history as a discrete discipline has given it a place to pursue studies which previously only occupied the margins of parent disciplines. But once having acquired a distinct identity, it has benefited more from its inter-disciplinary alliances and cross-border dialogues rather than from operating within the confinement of strict disciplinary boundaries. The most fruitful alliance has been with the field of material culture studies which has enabled the study of the history of design to grow beyond narrow limits of period and subject which first defined design history as only dealing with mass-produced objects in a modern aesthetic, reluctantly allowing 'craft' to be included as an acceptable democratic compromise.[35] In recent years it has been increasingly common to see 'material culture' replacing 'design history' in titles of courses and departments, indicating an engagement with theoretical issues of cultural value that question the interpretation of visual and material culture. This can be taken as an acknowledgement that history is not an exact science and that the practice of interpreting the production and consumption of design is not merely a matter of discovering the 'facts'. Institutions responsible for collection and conservation of the nation's material heritage are particularly sensitive to the importance of a more socially inclusive policy to that which was exercised in the past. The critique of con-sumerism assumed by the 'good design' approach which aspired towards the production of perfect design solutions through design history studies does not address the issue of the vast exponential growth of goods that has proliferated since the nineteenth-century. Material culture studies may prove a more fruitful approach towards the understanding of the phenomena of modernity by taking a less biased position in approaching the material world as the objectification of social relations.

It was clear from the start in about 1970,[36] that the emergence of design history as a distinct discipline was instigated by the desire to

---

which questioned the 'good design' criteria as a basis for the study of the history of design. Subsequent reviews of design history and theory studies have continued to cite these sources to indicate affiliation to the concept of reforming approaches to the study of design history. See e.g. Doordan, D.P. 1995. *Design History: An Anthology*. Cambridge, Massachusetts: The MIT Press, 'Introduction' pp. Ix–xiv and Woodham, J. M. 1997. *Twentieth-Century Design*, Oxford University Press, 'Introduction' pp. 7–9.

35. See Attfield, J. 1999. 'Beyond the Pale: Reviewing the relationship between Material Culture and Design History' in *Journal of Design History*, Vol. 12, No. 4, pp. 373–80.

36. For an account of the establishment of Design History as a discipline see Walker, 1989, *Design History and the History of Design*, pp. 15–19.

break off any connoisseurial associations that it might have retained from a relationship to conventional art history, where design, by being defined as 'applied arts and manufactured objects',[37] was automatically relegated to a lower position in the hierarchical scale of value in relation to fine art. But even once a seemingly value-free space was cleared for the specialism, there have continued to be border skirmishes about what type of objects could legitimately be included under the heading of 'design'. Some historians only accepted 'mass produced objects'[38] with an emphasis on production, as suitable for study under the heading of design history, a claim repudiated by feminist design historians who saw the study of consumption as a legitimate area of research because it acknowledged the contribution of women particularly in the role of consumers. Some Modernists did not consider craft a valid category of design because it evolved from traditional vernacular practices and relied on hand production. But once 'contemporary craft' distanced itself from rural traditions, 'trade' and vernacular practices, it took on a modern form and was taught as 'design' in colleges of art and design.[39] Meanwhile 'design' became a neutral banner under which, what William Morris would have called the 'lesser' arts, consisting of objects like ornamental metalwork, ceramics, jewellery, textiles and furniture, could include a range of historic decorative arts alongside twentieth-century, industrial, serially produced items in new techniques and materials like plastic. This is exemplified by the Victoria and Albert Museum's recognition of the importance of its collections of modern artefacts with the opening of its most recent of its two twentieth-century galleries in 1992 in which the display includes both industrially produced design and contemporary craft objects.

Similarly there have been discussions about whether the history of design could be mapped from the activities of particular named designers or whether it was more realistic to plot the story of anonymous design via the evidence supplied by such documents as patent records.[40] In his seminal study of the history of design, Adrian Forty

37. Pointon 1980. *History of Art: A Students' Handbook*. p. 15.

38. See C. Buckley and L. Walker's letter to the *Design History Society* Newsletter, No. 21, April 1984, p. 5 for an example of the disagreement over the exclusive definition of design history that confined it to the 'study of mass-produced objects'.

39. See Dormer, P. 1990. *The Meanings of Modern Design,* London: Thames and Hudson, Chapter 6:' Valuing the handmade: Studio Crafts and the Meaning of their Style', pp. 142–69.

40. As in Giedion, S. 1948. *Mechanization Takes Command,* New York: Oxford University Press.

attributed the 'poor showing' of design historians in accounting for 'the causes of change in the design of industrially-made goods' to 'the confusion of design with art'. [41] Forty based the distinguishing characteristic of design on his refutation that the design process, unlike that of art, involved much less, if any degree of autonomy, and was not motivated by self-expression. Such questioning addressed a range of possible agencies from the primacy of technological determinism, 'good design' ideology and therefore the need only to document excellent examples as models, or the contextual importance of social history. In this vein the project of design history has consistently been to consider the particularity of design as both referring to a specific genre of artefact as well as a certain type of practice bent on innovation and change, and quite distinct from the works and practices of fine art.

The development of design history has grown out of various institutional needs resulting in the different character of the specific courses and reflecting the internal concerns of various interest groups. It thus makes sense that centres of architectural education have bred theoretical courses that serve the interests of architecture, and object-centred museum courses, focused around museology and display, have grown out of very specific collections like those of the Victoria and Albert Museum in London or the Cooper-Hewitt in New York. Both these museums call themselves 'the national museum of design' but their collections largely consist of objects categorised as crafts and decorative arts. While some educational and commercial establishments have concentrated on design as a commodity and specialise in training connoisseurship to produce experts for the markets in antique decorative arts and the more recent so-called 'modern design classics' which ostensibly includes industrially produced products.

Critics and historians who take a sociological perspective, refuse the concept that creative works of art or design hold autonomous transcendental qualities, asserting that they are the product of specific socio-historical conditions.[42] Even where the 'social production of art' type of theoretical analysis sensitively fends off the tendency of reductionism, acknowledging that 'the relative value of different works is determined within the discourse of art and aesthetics and is not amenable to appropriation by different discourses",[43] it does not

41. Forty, A. 1986. *Objects of Desire: Design and Society 1750–1980*. London: Thames and Hudson, p. 7.

42. Buck, L. and Dodd, P. 1991. *Relative Values: or What's Art Worth?* London: BBC Books.

43. Wolff, J. 1981. *The Social Production of Art*. London: MacMillan.

recognise the fact that design is not just about aesthetics, nor does it accept the way design has indeed been appropriated by 'the discourse of art and aesthetics'. The more recent emergence of the field of 'visual culture', which alongside fine art includes mass and electronic media, performing arts and arts of spectacle, crafts and design, emphasises visuality above any of the other senses. But while Walker and Chaplin acknowledge that in the case of design it 'ought not to be judged on aesthetic or stylistic grounds alone', in the last analysis they resort to the outdated functionalist view that the criterion on designed products should be based on 'performance ... on how well they fulfil the purposes for which they were designed'.[44]

'Design discourse', a term introduced by the field of design studies, even while recognising the communicating role of design, continues to rely inordinately heavily on the determinist definition that 'design is what all forms of production for *use* have in common' (emphasis added).[45] What most of these definitions of design *do* have in common with art studies is the refusal to be associated with the object in its commodity phase where it is seen as 'degraded' once it is located within the sphere of consumption and thus deemed 'commercialised'. Among theoreticians associated with 'design studies',[46] a particular distinction is made between the 'user', referring to a knowing critical audience who can make the 'correct' judgements of what constitutes a 'good design' based on the utility of an object 'fit for use',[47] and the 'consumer' who is characterised as an acquisitive creature who is likely to be taken in by weak and sentimental 'gimmicks', desiring objects for the fulfilment of possession rather than for their practicality. The fictitious characterisations of the 'user' and the 'consumer' do not help to clarify the definition of design nor its practice beyond that of adhering to a particular 'good design' ideology which sets up impossible ideals. Such theorising does not help to explain why the public has not responded to so-called good design in quite the way designers might have hoped,

44. Walker and Chaplin 1997. *Visual Culture*, p. 24.

45. Buchanan, R. 1985. 'Declaration by Design: Rhetoric, argument and demonstration in design practice' in Margolin, V. (ed.) *Design Discourse: History/ Theory / Criticism*. Chicago and London: The University of Chicago Press, p. 108.

46. Characterised by the American journal *Design Issues*, between 1984 and 1993 edited and published by the School of Art and Design at the University of Illinois at Chicago and then edited by the Department of Design at Carnegie Mellon University and published by the Massachusetts Institute of Technology Press.

47. Ibid., p. 107.

and equally why new designs do not always necessarily 'take', however sophisticated the built-in prediction factor. Yet the aspiration to attain the perfect design classic sustains the practice of designers and complements the belief in progress through technological innovation.

The critical position that locates aesthetic value in a different order to that of commerce, attributing capitalism with the corrupting effects of inflating the commodity value conferred upon fashionable 'collectibles' has quite understandably dismissed connoisseurial design history as 'train spotting'. While the type of study suggested by this book, that design is just one type of 'thing' among the collectivity of material culture in general, does not even call upon aesthetics as a major arm of analysis, but uses a material culture framework in which things are referred to as the objectification of social relations. This type of stance makes a strong case for the sake of academic objectivity and rigour of keeping the study of design history and theory separate from specific interest groups so that it does not have to serve any one master. Nevertheless it is precisely within the type of institutional context committed to the obligations of conserving and displaying an existing collection, or 'servicing' a particular area of design education, from where design history and material culture studies have emerged.

The effect of home-grown histories of design adapted to the exigencies of a particular museum collection of costume, or responding to the specific field of graphic design education, has tended to produce a fragmented and somewhat diffuse body of knowledge. Changes of structure in museums and education since the 1980s have given research higher priority so that in theory more top-down strategies, unencumbered by departmental limitations, can be devised to encompass broader cultural issues at a more interdisciplinary level. There is clearly a logic to taking into account the distinctions between object types as different as cars and apparel. But for obvious reasons these differences are based on traditional media- and technique-based practices directly related to the trades and industries from which they originally derived. Many classifications such as 'woodwork' and 'industrial design' have been superseded by new technologies, management strategies and historical circumstances so that defining boundaries can become limiting barriers. The interdisciplinarity encouraged by a material culture approach can prevent the conventional pocketed system of design classifications from forming intellectual backwaters as an effect of research that turns material culture to reductive static object analysis with no reference to the social life of things beyond the train spotter's collection or the museum archive. It also attends to the mismatch that occurs between the real thing in the real world against the aspirations of modern design theory about the democratisation of luxury goods through mass production or theories that support the prioritisation of socially motivated ethical and ecological values over those of profit. There is nothing quite like focusing on the object itself to discover the specificity of its materiality and how that particular form objectifies sociality at a more general level of analysis.[48]

More recently the genre of objects called 'design' has diversified to encompass many new regimes of things well beyond the strictures which only allowed the useful and the product of mass industrialised manufacture. The debate between British and American academics concerned, would now appear to be centred over the boundaries that distinguish design *history* as a purely academic field from design *studies* which links theory to practice.[49] The current post-industrial climate in Britain has seen a change of attitude in design education, turning away from training designers to serve a rapidly contracting, almost defunct national industrial sector, to treating them more like international fine artists, placing greater emphasis on self-motivation to prepare them for freelance work in the global market. And among the media-based design training aimed at producing designer/makers with a fine art ethos of individuality and creativity, there is also an increasing awareness placed upon the value of maintaining disappearing craft-based skills which were a commonplace in the trade schools of the nineteenth and first half of the twentieth centuries.[50] But even more important than the disappearing differences between fine art and design education, has been the shift away from the concept of designer as hero. So that now in 1999 designers like Geoff Hollington, commenting on a recently published celebratory book on the design 'pioneers' of the twentieth century can write:

> I do personally wonder if, from our *fin de siècle* perspective, it really is useful to look at design history that way [. . .] Today much of the most successful and influential design comes from in-house design teams [. . .] or from international design firms which have the resources to assemble multi-disciplinary creative teams [. . . the] image of the [designer] as hero with a sketchpad is simply out of date.[51]

48. See Miller, D. 1998a. *Material Cultures: Why some things matter.* London: UCL Press.
49. See Note No. 28 above.
50. McRobbie 1998 *British Fashion Design.*
51. Hollington, G. 1998, referring to Sparke, P. 1998. *A Century of Design: Design Pioneers of the 20th Century* in *Design* (Michael Beazley). In *Design 1,* Summer, p. 62.

But can design historians take up Hollington's challenge on the brink of the new millennium – to 'devise a new way to analyse and chart the design? If design history can only attend to accounts of the professional activity of designers, be they individuals or teams, working as consultants to industry or from within innovative multinational manufacturing firms creating design-led branded products, that would still only form a very small constituent of the history of the material culture of the twentieth century to which design undoubtedly belongs as an integral part.

Another question which has troubled the design historian and helps to explain the emphasis on the practice of design as a pure activity separated off by professionalism from the world of commerce, has been the consideration of consumption as a determining factor. But does giving due consideration to consumption actually need to implicate the historian as biased against the profession? This fear was expressed by Richard Buchanan's recent review of Jonathan Woodham's book, *Twentieth-Century Design*,[52] when he wrote: 'this approach', referring to the acknowledgement of 'consumer behaviour', 'is not only hostile towards but contemptuous of design practice'. He then went on to ask: 'Does the author seek to reorient design history within the framework of cultural studies, focused on material culture?' Whether or not Woodham's account does in fact actually prioritise consumption over other factors is highly questionable anyway. But the reason for mentioning the accusation is not to refute it, but in order to present an example of the awareness within design history/theory circles of the cultural significance of design on a much broader front. It also shows up the understandable discomfort such an approach still appears to provoke among those who give their main allegiance to the education of designers and see the practice of design directed unproblematically at 'users'. While the importance of the status given to material culture in studies of the history of design may be equivocal, it does reveal a lack of full-hearted confidence in throwing design into the generality of 'things' as if it would somehow down-grade it in refocusing from celebration of the 'pioneers' to the 'real thing'-ness of the designed object.

History of design has until now implicitly separated the 'good' from the bad and the ordinary, and the disciplined from the wild. But now it would seem that it has to acknowledge that there is something out there called 'material culture' that can no longer be ignored even

---

52. See Richard Buchanan's review of Jonathan M. Woodham's *Twentieth-Century Design* (Oxford University Press, 1997). In *Journal of Design History,* Vol. 11, No. 3, 1998, p. 261.

though it removes the privileged categorisation design has enjoyed so far. Perhaps the fear is that in thus acknowledging design and becoming associated with *mere* ungeneric 'things', demystification would displace design from a special category of goods and throw it into the flotsam of everyday life – leaving it to swim along with the rest of the plethora of things in general. This study sets out to test the consequences of embracing design as an aspect of material culture as a way of contextualising what has habitually been seen as special, within an area much more amenable to theorising the significance of things. In his review of the state of design history in 1984 Clive Dilnot expressed the hope that design history would dedicate itself to the larger intellectual project of exploring the significance of design as a fundamental human activity, rather than just a particular form of professional practice.[53] And although a number of design historians have concurred with this view there is still very little fruit of this type of research in published form. So in releasing design from the definition of a type of object with a particular 'good design' aesthetic, and from the disciplinary corral of design history which has accorded it that status, it is possible to home in on the particularity that makes a design object into a social thing within a dynamic existence in the material world of the everyday.

Identity and Agency in the Practice of Design

But once having placed 'design' in the lower case in the more generalised context of material culture, the task is to reconstitute it as a particular type of practice objectifying sociality rather than reduced to a particular type of artefact in a recognisable style. The characteristic which distinguishes design in this sense, is the practice that produces 'things with attitude', the material culture of innovation driven by a vision of change as beneficial. It is a larger project than tracking a history of periodisation that categorises objects according to their conformity with a particular aesthetic form, be it the 'streamline', the 'machine aesthetic', minimalism or any of the other nomens given to distinguish products of one decade from another. Thus modernity is seen as the articulation of a particular type of attitude towards change in which the focus shifts from attempting to reconstruct the past to creating a new type of future, as the only temporal space where it is possible to bring agency to bear in material form. Design as a practice

---

53. Dilnot, C. 1984. 'The State of Design History – Part I: Mapping the Field' pp. 4–23. In *Design Issues*. Vol. 1, No. 1, Spring.

of modernity signifies the possibility of social change, rather than the visual style associated with the history of the modern period. Such a view only makes sense when the concept of modernity is relocated beyond the aesthetic moralising frame that restricts the incursion of any versions which do not conform to the canon of 'good design', the term synonymous with 'modern' that has until very recently been the only qualification needed to allow objects entry through the gates of conventional design history. Thus it is necessary to include, rather than exclude objects that defy the definition of good design – those 'things with attitude' that don't fit into the description of 'good', that disreputable wild and dangerous rabble of 'objects that talk back'.[54] The type of things that import 'poor taste', badly behaved 'trifles', fancy goods, the kitsch, the fetish, the domestic, the decorative and the feminine, the bric-a-brac that exudes unashamed materiality.

The foundation of the material culture view referred to above is based on the concept of hybridisation – that objects are cultural and therefore cannot be classified within fixed categories such as 'good design' or captured and held within the correct relationship to each other as in a 'well-designed' interior. This is in distinct contrast to that of, say, the modernist architect who could only accept certain objects on sufferance if they didn't fit in with his vision of the correct ensemble, who defined his wife's Victorian plant stand and his children's plastic toys as 'rogue elements', invading his well-ordered contemporary home.[55] And by the same token the modernist design historian would not have metaphorically countenanced giving house-room to anything other than 'good design', except as a rhetorical example all the better to make the point. It is only in acknowledging the whole ensemble of things that make up an environment, 'rogue elements' and all, that it is possible to envisage the material world, whether consciously 'design', mere 'things' without any particular attitude, or more realistically – a promiscuous mixture of both.

The cultural analysis of things is more like a vehicle for dialogue between people and objects than a classificatory exercise. This depends

54. See Pels, P. 1998. 'The Spirit of the Matter: Fetish, Rarity, Fact, and Fancy'. In Spyer, P. (ed.) 1998 *Border Fetishisms: Material Objects in Unstable Spaces*. London: Routledge, p. 93.

55. Penny Sparke also invokes Nicholas Barker's television series *Signs of the Times* (1992) in *As Long As Its Pink: The Sexual Politics of Taste* (London: Harper Collins, 1995: 1) citing the same interviewee – an architect who only 'permitted' curtains in the children's bedroom.

on discarding the outdated concept of causality characterised by 'influence'-as-determining so neatly refuted by Michael Baxandall[56] who shows influence to be a one-way process which assumes a hierarchy, a dominant agent, with no room for a more reciprocal encounter. This more fluid approach does not mean that, for the purposes of analysis, it is not possible to pause to consider the object as animate, not only to question the discourse of representation now criticised for depending on idealism,[57] but to make the pause long enough to reflect on the 'thingness' of things. The blatant contemplation of the material presence of things, with no alibi that transfers the object into cultural identity or social relation, runs the serious risk of being accused of fetishism. If the pause is long enough to hear 'objects talk back' it is just as feasible to propose that design is *things with attitude*, implying the intentionality that sets design apart from the generic-less object that best describes the nature of things. But things like chairs are not natural, they do not grow on trees and it is not only designers who enliven objects with intentionality. There is life beyond the design phase when the object moves through what Arjun Appadurai refers to as different 'regimes of value' in which objects are enlivened by various types of human transactions in the course of their existence.[58]

Roland Barthes described the dilemma of attempting to interpret the meaning of things in his summary of the object/subject relationship in *Mythologies*, as a form of dynamic in which:

> we constantly drift between the object and its demystification, powerless to render its wholeness. For if we penetrate the object, we liberate it but we destroy it; and if we acknowledge its full weight, we respect it, but we restore it to a state which is still mystified.[59]

Barthes' insight into the dangers of reductionism in the study of material culture still holds and has particular pertinence here. His observation explains the main problem of materiality as a way of thinking about design and things. It is even more pertinent today than

---

56. Baxandall, M. 1988. *Patterns of Intention: On the Historical Explanation of Pictures.* New Haven and London: Yale University Press, pp. 58–60.

57. Pels 1998. 'The Spirit of the Matter', p. 113.

58. Appadurai, A. (ed.) 1986. *The Social Life of Things: Commodities in Cultural Perspective.* Cambridge: Cambridge University Press. See 'Introduction: commodities and the politics of value' pp. 3–63.

59. Barthes, R. [1957] 1981. *Mythologies.* London: Paladin, p. 159.

when he originally wrote the essay in the mid-1950s, now that physical experiences seem increasingly to be reduced to the virtual, where the representation all too readily replaces the real thing.

Material culture has several definitions – in short, it can, and often does, just mean the study of objects, or the specialised study of object collections as in museum studies, and more specifically and how I use the term: the integration of artefacts into the social world beyond the empirical study centred on physical features, through the acquisition of social meaning within specific cultural/historical contexts.

To explain further – probably the most usual and self-evident definition derives from the use of the term 'material culture' in museum studies, where it refers to the study of artefacts specifically within the ideological context and physical confines of museum collections. That is to say a type of analysis that bring into questions the role of the museum in conferring value through such institutional regimes as acquisition and conservation policy, display design, the impact of state funding, of private patronage, and the sensitivity of issues concerning authentication and ownership of imported art objects in a post-colonial period, and so on.[60]

To plot its development it should be noted that although Material Culture has multidisciplinary connotations it has been adapted from social archaeology,[61] where it is in the process of being redefined and theorised to apply to modern society. A substantive body of research has emerged in the Anthropology Department at University College, London University (UCL) around the work of Daniel Miller who has recruited material culture as a theoretical frame to discuss mass consumption as a modern cultural process.[62] This approach lends itself to design history in dealing with consumption as a social process engaged in by active consumers,[63] in contra-distinction to the critique of consumerism that assumes the public has no taste and is duped by marketing to purchase poorly designed goods. Thus it has been possible to move on from the circular so-called 'failure of modernism' argument

60. For example see Coombes, A.E. 1988. 'Museums and the Formation of National and Cultural Identities' pp. 57–68, Vol. 11, No. 2; Jones, M. (ed.) 1990. *Fake? The Art of Deception.* London: British Museum; Phillips, D. 1997. *Exhibiting Authenticity.* Manchester and New York: Manchester University Press; Tunbridge, J.E. and Ashworth, G.J. 1996. *Dissonant Heritage: The Management of the Past as a Resource in Conflict.* Chichester and New York: Wiley.

61. Tilley, C. (ed.) 1990. *Reading Material Culture.* Oxford: Blackwell.

62. Miller 1998a *Material Cultures.*

63. Miller, D. 1987. *Material Culture and Mass Consumption.* Oxford: Blackwell.

which invariably ends up with the depressing conclusion that designers' attempts to elevate the standard of design remains unrecognised. I characterised this argument in an article about the role of design in the twentieth-century British furniture industry which exposed the mismatch between the aspirations of the advocates of so-called 'good design'[64] and traditional trade practices. The furniture tradesmen resented the critical incursions on their design procedures by a small élitist middle-class group by what they regarded as untrained self-appointed experts arrogantly assuming that they knew best.

The move in the last decade or so that has seen design history turn from a strong focus on production to consumption, concentrating on the stage at which a product is distributed, sold and appropriated, coincided with development of material culture studies. Through the medium of the *Journal of Material Culture,* material culture has defined itself as a field that has released itself intentionally from the rigidity of disciplinary affiliations. It rejects the barrenness of purity that prohibits consorting with any subject it wishes, and allows, encourages even, excursions across borders into disciplines such as psychology, history, and the cultural studies branch of sociology. It is pragmatic in its approach to method using techniques derived from ethnography to analyse and interpret the social meaning of the object world, rather than profess to 'reveal' its history as if it were a natural phenomenon out there waiting to be discovered. And most importantly its objective, posited on the concept that meaning is culturally constructed, is to discover the meaning of things. It provides a framework which does not exclude regimes of ordinary everyday goods alongside more exclusive classes of goods such as decorative arts located within a privileged domain of art and connoisseurship.

Nor does material culture segregate art from science, a separation which has remained part of the heritage of English design since the inception of the English national museum of design – the Victoria and Albert Museum in London. Nowhere is that failure to combine art and industry more apparent than in the half-century of unsuccessful attempts to effect the union under one roof of what is now the Victoria and Albert (V & A) Museum. Between 1857 and 1899 when the progenitor of the V & A – first called the South Kensington Museum – progressed from a few disparate buildings on its present site to the

64. Attfield, J. 1996. '"Give 'em something dark and heavy": The Role of Design in the Material Culture of Popular British Furniture 1939-1965' pp. 185-201. *Journal of Design History,* Vol. 9, No. 3.

building it is today, the attempt to accommodate art alongside science was never resolved. It is significant to note the progress of its seed collection which started as an adjunct to the newly established School of Design and Ornamental Art set up in 1837.[65] When the premises became too cramped from the augmentation of 'scientific' as well as ornamental exhibits acquired from the Great Exhibition of 1851, the collection was moved to Somerset House where it became the Museum of Manufactures and was joined a year later by the School of Design. With the final move to its present site at South Kensington in 1857, the School of Design changed to the Art School which survives to this day as the Royal College of Art, with plans for new museum premises progressed in fits and starts over a period of over fifty years.[66] The decision to remove the scientific collections to new dedicated premises on the opposite side of the road from the arts collections housed on Exhibition Road[67] were already determined in 1884. But it was only after the dissolution of the South Kensington Department of Science and Art,[68] that the foundation stone for the V & A was finally laid in 1899. The main objective in the arrangement of the Museum as expressed in 1908 by Robert Morant, the Secretary of the Board of Education, was its 'direct practical purpose of stimulating the craftsman and manufacturer and inspiring the designer and student who is engaged in the production of objects of modern manufacture'.[69] Yet the final severence from any connection with science or industry was made when the building was finally completed in 1909, just before the official opening when it was decided, with Morant's agreement, to restrict the name 'Victoria and Albert Museum' to the Art Museum although when Queen Victoria had bestowed the name it was assumed to also apply to the Science Museum.[70]

65. Cocks, A.S. 1980. *The Victoria and Albert Museum: The Making of the Collection.* Leicester: Windward.

66. Physick, J. 1982. *The Victoria and Albert Museum: The history of its buildings.* London: Phaidon, see Chapter I: 'The genesis of the Museum', pp. 13–18.

67. Ibid., p. 179.

68. Ibid., p. 206.

69. Ibid., p. 235.

70. Although John Physick in his history of the Victoria and Albert Museum, interprets Morant's objective as 'giving to technology precedence over art' (Physick 1982: p. 235), the latter's ready agreement to restrict the name of the Victoria and Albert Museum to the Art Museum would seem to contradict any such intention, and point instead to the wish to sever all connections between industry and art.

Art and science do not normally consort comfortably within academia because of the divide established by the conventions of Western philosophy that imposes a separation between the sciences and the humanities. But the products of design, once they leave the factory and the high-street shop check-out to form part of everyday life are not that well ordered, and it is not possible to disconnect nature from culture in separate mental compartments. No such orderly commensurability is assured and, as Bruno Latour has observed , the propagation of hybrids continue to proliferate.[71] This is not a difficult concept for a design historian to grasp. Design has always had an androgynous character poised between art and science, with a foot in both camps. In spite of Pointon's assertion quoted earlier, the extent of design history literature is far from vast, nevertheless its research has flourished by referring to an eclectic range of sources and methods from business, economic and social history to technology, and from anthropology to semiotics, psychoanalysis and popular culture, pragmatically selecting the most appropriate to the area of enquiry.

As for the type of object that can be studied – at one end of the spectrum a material culture approach to the history of design can refer to the interpretation of small and seemingly inconsequential items like plastic food containers,[72] the products of home craft production,[73] sea shells, cooking utensils and other found objects as souvenirs,[74] or the mini football strip car mascot,[75] with no particular high aesthetic value, but culturally representative of a particular group of people. And at the macro-level it can refer to a mixed array of artefacts located within a geographical setting like a whole town or community. My study of post-war house interiors in Harlow New Town[76] dealt with a gendered

71. Latour, B. 1991. *We have never been modern.* New York: Harvester Wheatsheaf.

72. Clarke, A.J. 1999. *Tupperware: the promise of plastic in 1950s America.* Washington D.C. and London: Smithsonian Institution Press.

73. Burman, B. (ed.) 1999. *The Culture of Sewing: Gender,Consumption and Home Dressmaking.* Oxford and New York: Berg.

74. Naylor, G. 1999. 'Modernism and Memory: Leaving Traces' pp. 91-106. In Kwint, M., Breward, C. and Aynsley, J. (eds) 1999. *Material Memories: Design and Evocation.* Oxford and New York: Berg.

75. Dant, T. 1999. *Material Culture in the Social World.* Buckingham and Philadelphia: Open University Press, pp. 5–7.

76. Published under the title of *'Pram Town'* was integrated into an anthology jointly edited with Pat Kirkham entitled *A View From the Interior* about women and design, first published by The Women's Press in 1989, second edition: 1995.

perspective of design as well as with issues of popular taste contextual-ised against the 'good design' debates of the late 1950s in contrast with the lived experience of inhabitants of one of the first totally designed new towns. Through this study it was possible to explore the social significance of space, the dynamic relationship between people and things and observe the ways in which people order or were ordered by objects. As the variety and quantity of goods continues to proliferate towards the end of the twentieth century the study of the world of goods becomes ever more complex and the wish to escape materialism through the search of authenticity and individuality ever more acute. Material culture has proved an effective method of analysis where the 'good design' measure does not operate to restrict the enquiry, and going much further towards gaining an understanding of how people manage the transformation from alienation to appropriation.

Consumption needs to be highlighted as a vital ingredient in the study of material culture. In the last decade or so design history has seen a shift of focus from the study of the history of production, recog-nising consumption as a neglected area of study. This was precipitated by the awareness that it is was not possible to study the material culture of industrialised societies without giving due consideration to the process of consumption. As noted above, the emphasis on consumption has been criticised for allegedly concentrating on the degradation of quality brought about by mass production and the weak giving in to commercial values. But scholarship in the history of consumption has taught us what such a perspective can contribute to the history of design. While recent works like Ben Fine and Ellen Leopold's *The World of Consumption*[77] and Leora Auslander's *Taste and Power*[78] have shifted away from the crude opposition between production and consumption to look at the overall interactions between designers, makers, distrib-utors and consumers.

One of the confusions that sometimes arises in the definition of 'material culture' has been between the empirical and more abstract types of cultural analysis. The empirical is associated with a very precise type of object analysis that seeks to document the concrete particu-larities of the form, materials, and making processes that result in a specific manufactured product and don't necessarily engage with its meaning or its social relation. This approach, usually associated with

77. Fine, B. and Leopold, E. 1993. *The World of Consumption*. London: Routledge.

78. Auslander, L. 1996. *Taste and Power: Furnishing Modern France*. Berkley: University of California Press.

the deterministic model which explains form as deriving directly from economic processes, has been fiercely critiqued by material culturists who have championed consumption as a more appropriate point of entry into the cultural study of objects.[79] Although object analysis does usually include some socio-economic contextual considerations, it does not necessarily attend to the subtle dynamics of the changes of use and meaning an object undergoes in the course of its post-production existence except as a generalised nod in the direction of 'reception'. Material culture while focusing on the material object also has broader interpretative connotations beyond the object itself, homing-in much more acutely on less stable territory – on things and places where the interrelationship between people and the physical world at large is played out.

There are also a number of givens which are often found to operate around a borrowed idea of 'material culture' as a method of analysis that does not appear to proceed from a theoretical foundation but seems entirely based upon the literal interpretation of the premise that objects can 'speak for themselves'. This is exemplified in Joan Severa and Merrill Horswill's assertion that 'the costume artefact [. . .] may be expected to reveal evidence of attitudes, belief systems and assumptions which shed light upon a culture'.[80] Equally misleading is Alexandra Palmer's suggestion that material culture analysis is a simple 'reconciliation' between 'object analysis' and further contextual research based on 'theory [that] can be deduced from the objects themselves'.[81] Although she may be justified in accusing theoreticians of using objects to support their theories, the above-mentioned type of over-literal 'object analysis' asserts a pragmatic position which refuses any kind of theoretical grasp of the material object. It also fails to deal with the concept of things as intermediaries between people and the physical world at large, the dynamic and complex non-duality of the object/subject relation which lies at the centre of the study of material culture. A more self-conscious situating of the object within that kind of dynamic lends a better understanding to things as a form of physical articulation, a non-functional practice negating the 'utility' sense of use, such as that recognised by artists like Neil Cummings, repositioning their practice

79. See Miller, D. (ed.) 1995. *Acknowledging Consumption*. London: Routledge.

80. Severa, J. and Horswill, M. 1989. 'Costume as Material Culture'. In *Dress* Vol. 15, p. 53. cited by Palmer, A. 1997. 'New Directions: Fashion History Studies and Research in North America and England' in *Fashion Theory*, Vol. 1, No. 3, Sept, p. 301.

81. Ibid., Palmer p. 303.

from within the 'autonomous sphere' of art to the 'wider realm of *things*', that is to say – material culture.[82]

The debate between the insubstantial superficiality, as against the concrete reality of 'material', has particular resonance in the existential world view which pervades a period in which the loss of faith in religion throws the onus on the individual acting in the present moment, characteristic of the sense of modernity. Thus if the focus is shifted from defining the nature of things as inevitable by means of the irrefutable characteristics which determine that, say 'wood can't melt', to the materiality of things as the physical manifestation of making, it is then possible to envisage change 'by design' as agency – a self-aware process.

There has been a recurring debate encapsulated in the critique of consumerism concerning 'material' as denoting mere physical matter that is seen as distorting the reality that emanates from authentic experience. Thus in an article decrying the insubstantiality of high fashion (artifice) when juxtaposed with the 'real' body (nature), Julie Burchill can ridicule the importance given to 'glorious frocks' by exclaiming in the quaintly old-fashioned disapproving tone typical of the affluent person who has already 'made it', that 'It's just material!'.[83] While Judith Williamson, a writer who has consistently criticised consumerism, mounting one of the earliest and most sophisticated critical exposés of the false promises made by advertisements,[84] attributed the appeal of Madonna's stardom to her 'ordinariness' as 'not just another unattainable sex symbol for men' but her identification with 'women struggling to make it in a material world'.[85] Thus the adoption of frivolous fashion in Madonna's case is characterised as a process of self-production that the more self-assured person with a strong sense of their own subjectivity can refuse because they already possess a definite vision of their own identity.

82. Cummings, N. 1993. 'Reading Things: The alibi of use'. In Cummings, N. (ed.) *Reading Things*. London: Chance Books, p. 27.

83. Burchill, J. 'Material boys'. In *The Guardian Weekend*. 3 October 1998, p. 3.

84. Williamson, J. 1978. *Decoding Advertisements: Ideology and Meaning in Advertising*. London and Boston: Marion Boyars.

85. Madonna recorded the hit song 'Material Girl' in 1985. See Williamson, J. 'The Making of a Material Girl', pp. 46–7. *New Socialist*, No. 31, October 1985.

Cummings' Parachute and a Case Against the Theory of Representation

Turning the focus back on material things as the meeting point between design, as a common or 'everyday' making practice, and the realities of everyday life, returns the view to the certainty of the real world. Some objects have no meaning if they don't work. This is not to justify the crude 'use value'/ 'exchange value' dichotomy that forms the basis of the critique of materialism often presented as consumerism, but to challenge theories of representation which talk up the importance of the sign over that of thing itself. The example of Cummings' parachute makes it all too apparent that whatever the thing may look like, the moment of truth is when it 'either works or it does not' and the jumper either plummets to earth and dies, or survives the fall.[86]

A material culture perspective de-emphasises the importance given by the theory of representation that prioritises meaning over matter through the interpretation and explanation of ideological cultural codes that are seen to reside behind the false front of appearance conceived as a 'system of signs'.[87] While theoretical studies of representation have done much to explain and interpret the material world so that it is no longer possible to 'take it as given', it has also dematerialised it to the extent that we can no longer 'believe our eyes'. Representation theory is concerned primarily with deconstructing the image and does not account for visual encounters that take place outside the critical frame. In the context of the 'everyday' the casual visual encounter may well evade or distort the intended sign-value in an insignificant and direct act of consumption. Nor does design as a common practice conform to the concept of the thing as 'fetish' in the context of crude consumerism critique which relies on a negative state of 'false consciousness'. To conceptualise design as a practice of making meaning material suggests an enabling process in reconstituting and situating those aspects of life such as identity and authenticity, that have become destabilised as a result of rapid social, economic and political changes.

The so-called 'invention of tradition' type of mythology that characterises representation theory, uses debates around language that destabilises

---

86. Cummings 1993. 'Reading Things', p. 23.

87. See Hall, S. ed. 1997. *Representation: Cultural Representations and Signifying Practices*. London and Thousand Oaks, California: Sage. For a critique of cultural studies that relies on theories of representation see McRobbie, A. (ed.) 1997. *Back to Reality? Social Experience and Cultural Studies*. Manchester and New York: Manchester University Press.

the meaning of things and makes objects insubstantial. This type of analysis that only deals with the visual image through the medium of language and text is not sufficient in the project to elucidate the meaning of things. It will be argued that only dealing with the visual features of artefacts, obscures the work of designers, makers and users as all involved in the making of meaning through things.

two

The Meaning of Things:
design in the lower case

In Chapter 1 design was characterised as things with attitude and distinguished from things in general as found in the context of everyday life. Whole universes of difference lie between conceptualising the world and making it into a physical reality. There are so many ways in which design can change between the original idea and its final realisation according to an infinite and undefinable range of contingencies, not to speak of the natural laws, physical materials and technologies selected for its execution. This chapter will discuss some of the features that distinguish specialised professional design and craft practices from that of the unclassifiable random processes that also operate in the physical construction of the material world. The aim is to characterise a variety of perspectives on design and skill from the inside of particular disciplines and as defined by critical practices.[1] Design as 'things with attitude' is compared against a less obrusive 'lower case' form of things, framed within the more generalised context of 'the everyday' as examples of how meaning is objectified or made material.

What particularly concerns the project of this book to include design as an aspect of material culture, is to explore how people's relationship to the object world has evolved and changed in the last half century. The modern mentality[2] has seen an increased sense of

1. The description does not claim to give more than a schematic representation based on a generalisation of the changing face of design education, institutional and commercial patronage in order to locate some of the more important debates which have concerned professional industrial designers and craft makers.

2. 'Mentality' is used here to acknowledge the importance accorded by historians to the analysis of forms of consciousness, the more subjective areas of social life not touched on by social and economic history. See Schöttler, P. 1995 'Mentalities, Ideologies,

social responsibility not only felt by practising designers,[3] theorists and critics who see themselves as decision makers, but also by a more environmentally and socially aware consuming public. But beyond the group of self-aware designers there is also a contingency of makers who do not see themselves as designers but nevertheless contribute to the physical substance of the material world. Deskilling – the corollary of modernisation, which has changed the meaning and value of design and craft techniques previously considered the exclusive prerogative of a highly trained group of specialists – has also popularised and given access to a public that would otherwise have been excluded from these practices by a lack of savoir faire. Thus deskilling of design and craft enables the non-specialist to gain a greater sense of agency through direct involvement in the physical construction of the material world.

The traditional routes and class divisions established by nineteenth-century craft training and design education[4] were not as applicable by the mid-twentieth century that saw the entry of a new breed of art-school-trained designer-makers with creative aspirations.[5] New approaches entailed changes in the way that designers positioned themselves in relation to the economic and moral economy of their own times, to their public and to the object world. Design as a new profession in the post Second World War period[6] evolved from a pragmatic practice to one with a more sophisticated awareness of aesthetics exploring the relationship between form and function that

Discourses on the "third level" as a theme of social-historical research' pp. 72–115. In Lüdtke, A. (ed.) 1995. *The History of Everyday Life: Reconstructing Historical Experiences and Ways of Life*. New Jersey: Princeton University Press.

3. The term 'designers' is used here very generally to refer to any kind of designer who conceptualises but does not actually *make* the products and buildings they design. They could be architects or town planners, or might have any of the following qualifying prefixes to their title: fashion, landscape, furniture, film set, industrial, textile, automotive, ceramic, interior, costume, graphic, etc.

4. Gloag, J. 1944. *The Missing Technician in Industrial Production*. London: Allen and Unwin; Gloag, J. 1947. *Self Training for Industrial Designers*. London: Allen and Unwin; Macdonald, S. 1970. *The History and Philosophy of Art Education*. London: University of London Press; Sutton, G. 1967. *Artisan or Artist? A History of the Teaching of Art and Crafts in English Schools*. Oxford: Pergamon; Pevsner, N. 1940. *Academies of Art*. London: Cambridge University Press, see Ch 4: 'The revival of industrial art and artists' education'.

5. Piper, D.W. (ed.) 1973. *Readings in Art and Design Education*, 2 volumes: *1. After Hornsey, 2. After Coldstream*. London: Davis Poynter.

6. Sparke, P. 1983. *Consultant Design: The history and practice of the designer in industry*. London: Pembridge Press.

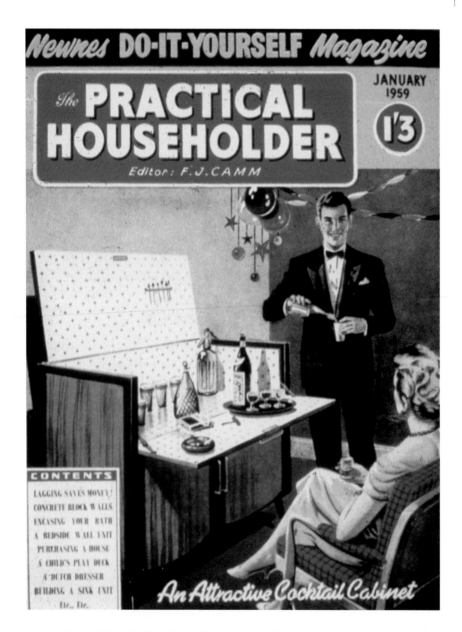

Figure 5. A DIY cocktail cabinet illustrated on the cover of *The Practical Householder,* 1959. (Newnes)

had formed part of the education of the type pioneered by the Bauhaus School in Germany.[7] But as design became a commodity it was seen as a system of representations that could be utilised by producers in the dissemination of goods and by consumers in the formation of personal and group identity.[8] Trends since then have been driven much more by the market place and state institutions concerned with design as a marketing tool have been much more aware of the power of the image.[9]

Designers with a conern to contribute to the human environment are increasingly conscious that the material world is part of a fragile holistic ecological system as well as a complex network of political and social relations.[10] There is little room for individuality among designers working for an anonymous public. And while craft workers had at one time to carry out designs to clients' requirements, today many choose the maker's route into design in order to be able to exercise their own creativity rather than have to conform to set specifications, producing works without an individual client in mind. And although most professional designer-makers work to commission their primary concern is the fulfilment and sense of independence gained from being in command of their own productions and running an autonomous practice.

The recognition of the embodiment of meaning in objects – through material culture studies – rather than reading meaning into form through the designer's intentions, has a direct application to the interpretation of the artefactual world in the twentieth-century Western American/European context as well as to 'other' design histories.[11] The

7. Baynes, K. ed. 1969. *Attitudes in Design Education.* London: Lund Humphries; Benton, T. & C. 1975. *Form and Function: A Source Book for the History of Architecture and Design 1890–1939.* London: Granada; Sparke, P. 1986. *An Introduction to Design and Culture in the Twentieth Century.* London: Allen and Unwin, see ch. 10 'Educating Designers'.

8. Shields, R. ed. 1992. *Lifestyle Shopping: The Subject of Consumption.* London and New York: Routledge.

9. Whiteley, N. 1991. 'Design in Enterprise Culture: Design for Whose Profit?' pp. 186–205. In Keat, R. and Abercrombie, N. (eds) *Enterprise Culture.* London and New York: Routledge; Woodham, J.M. 1999. 'Design and the state: post-war horizons and pre-millennial aspirations' pp. 245–60. In Attfield, J. ed. *Utility Reassessed: The role of ethics in the practice of design.* Manchester and New York: Manchester University Press.

10. This summary of changing attitudes to design is intended as a simplified framework for the purposes of analysis and is not meant to suggest that all designers would somehow fit into such categorisations.

11. For example see Fry, T. 'A Geography of Power: Design History and Marginality', pp. 204–18. In *Design* Issues, Vol. 6 No. 1, Fall 1989.

Figure 6. Kaffe Fassett, designer/maker, knitting in his studio,1981.

Figure 7. Carpet designer at work in the Brinton carpet factory studio, Kidderminster, 1982.

use of material artefacts as the objectification of relations between people and the world at large can be seen reflected in the latest debates on design theory. These are exemplified in the concept of creating 'eternal' designs,[12] meaning durable from an ecological perspective, rather than 'classic' in the stylistically timeless sense. Similarly design discourse increasingly attempts to produce designs that 'engage' the user at a deeper level than that of superficial visual attraction. The question that remains concerns the extent to which design can actively meet the user's needs and desires and effectively produce a comprehensible platform to enable user participation.

The main aim of this chapter is to step out from the controlled environment of design theories which try to conceptualise a better more beautiful world that will weather the transference into real things and places, and move from the circumscribed shelter of the craftmaker's studio, back into the disordered wild world of things, the everyday. But before proceeding to consider the changing perceptions of the designer's and the maker's role this is a good place to define 'the everyday' as it forms the backdrop against which these practices are discussed.

The Everyday is not a Taste Thing

The term 'the everyday' (lower case intended) – that which does not get recorded in the history made up of important 'events' – is contradictorily distinguished by the same lower caseness as 'the thing' in Chapter 1. Neither 'things' nor 'the everyday' call attention to themselves nor bear any distinguishing marks to differentiate them from their antitheses. Even to enclose 'the everyday' in inverted commas changes its meaning too much by plucking it out from the commonplace of the given. Until now the term 'the everyday' has been used in this text in the generic sense meaning ordinary, common or garden, usual, informal, banal, unremarkable. It also has a very particular meaning in the literature of recent cultural politics which has been annexed by contemporary architectural design theorists and is used here as an important part of the theoretical framework of this study. It is things, as opposed to design or craft, product or commodity, that make up the materialisation of the everyday. Everyday things have nothing to

12. The Eternally Yours Foundation based in The Hague, the Netherlands, is just one of a number of 'eco-design' initiatives. See: http://www.ecomarket.net/EternallyYours/index,html

do with the 'low' aesthetic of 'high/low'[13] culture that has allowed the popular to infiltrate the prestigious art gallery in order to affiliate it to art. Susan Sontag's 1964 essay 'One Culture and the New Sensibility'[14] is representative of a certain type of American critique which posited a new approach to contemporary culture that could transcend the separation that once divided art from science. She claimed that the

> most interesting works of contemporary art are adventures in sensation ... experimental – not out of an élitist disdain for what is accessible to the majority, but precisely in the sense that science is experimental. It reflects a new, more open way of looking at the world. It does not mean the renunciation of all standards: there is plenty of stupid popular music as well as inferior and pretentious "avant-garde" paintings.

Since Sontag's defence of cultural pluralism, 'low' in the context of the art gallery has taken on a sophistication that has come to be associated with de rigueur irony to demonstrate a superior knowingness, an adeptness that dematerialises and reduces artefacts to a language of signs. A similar strain of ironic awareness has migrated to fashion in the high street with the adoption of highly stylised retro-chic references like the recycling of 1970s flares in the late 1990s, celebrating bad taste and popular culture.

'The everyday' has a distinct place in historiography based on a political position that acknowledges the importance of taking into account the more mundane aspects of life which are ignored by official histories that only give the dominant point of view.[15] It is therefore not surprising that much of the serious theorisation of the history of everyday life – *Alltagsgeschichte* – has arisen out of studies of the Nazi regime that have revealed the extent of the 'shared experience' of fascism. The so-called 'historian's debate' threw doubt on the view that individuals and groups were not mere 'cogs in the machine' but active

13. Varnedoe, K. and Gopink,A. 1991. *High & Low: Modern Art and Popular Culture.* New York: Museum of Modern Art.

14. Sontag, S. 1994. *Against Interpretation.* London: Vintage, see 'One Culture and the New Sensibility' [1961] pp. 293–304.

15. One of the manifestos of the cultural revolution that erupted in Paris in May 1968 – *Traité de savoir-vivre a l'usage des jeunes générations* by Raoul Vaneigem, was first published in English in 1983 as *The Revolution of the Everyday* by Left Bank Books and Rebel Press (London).

Figure 8. Guggenheim Modern Art Museum, Bilbao designed by Frank Ghery, 1998. (photo: Keith Leaman)

accomplices in the making of history.[16] There are many parallels in working-class history,[17] feminist[18] and Marxist critiques of history[19] which in charting aspects of the history of everyday life uncover how different peoples have 'appropriated' their own worlds. It has been argued that an anthropological, self-aware, decentred standpoint is more conducive to uncovering those 'hidden' histories that are not revealed by the top-down view of the historian working towards a unified concensual generalisation. It follows from such a perspective that in discussing the appropriation of the everyday as a cultural practice that the artefactual world would offer a particularly appropriate vehicle for the exploration of that more unconscious domain much less amenable to matching the grand theories of conventional history. So histories of the everyday investigate cultural practices within social structures of work, home, play, education, the body and so on.

Moreover in the object/person relation that defines material culture, the thing becomes a covert manifestation in a physical form not necessarily perceived at an intellectual level. Thus in referring to the everyday rather than the field of studies known as 'popular culture' the intention is to separate the project from the critique of populism. Cultural populism assumes a critical stance against the dangers of passive consumption of mass-produced poor quality goods which permeates the literature of critical theory and tends to stop at a general-ised crude interpretation before reaching the evidence of lived experi-ence. Although the arguments for and against popular culture debates inform this study they are not part of the context that frames it. Taking a broad perspective the cultural differences that exist between British and American cultural criticism continue being rehearsed in cultural studies literature,[20] at a theoretical level without actually engaging in the cultural practices of the everyday. While British cultural studies attempt to redefine a cultural practice of resistance,[21] the American

16. Lüdtke 1995. *The History of Everyday Life*, pp. 4–5.

17. Thompson, E.P. 1963. *The Making of the Working Class*, Harmondsworth: Penguin; Thompson, P. 1988. *The Voice of the Past: Oral History*. Oxford: Oxford University Press.

18. Rowbotham, S. 1973. *Hidden from History*. London: Pluto.

19. Samuel, R. 1994 and 1998. *Theatres of Memory*, Vols. I and II. London and New York: Verso.

20. For example see Storey, J. 1997 *An Introduction to Cultural Theory and Popular Culture*. London & New York: Prentice Hall Harvester Wheatsheaf; Strinati, D. 1995. *An Introduction to Theories of Popular Culture*. Manchester University Press.

21. Willis, P. 1993. *Common Culture*. Milton Keynes: Open University Press.

trajectory has identified 'the popular' as the repository of authentic American cultural identity.[22]

The Rediscovery of Things [23]

A recent feature of design discourse has been the conscious shift of attention from process in professional design practice back to the material product. Peter-Paul Verbeek and Petran Kockelkoren, two design theoreticians in a recent article on the philosophy of technology, declared 'Things have been rediscovered',[24] countervailing Abraham A. Moles's assertion exactly ten years earlier – 'An immaterial culture is emerging'[25] – predicting a shift in the future of design practice that would have to deal with an 'artificial reality' generated by the technology of a post-industrial society.[26] And it was in the same year, 1988, that John Thakara attempted to contextualise a new approach to design within a virtual world 'beyond the object',[27] suggesting that 'design's crisis lies in the broader political and cultural context, the "postmodern condition" of a society, full of proliferating images, which has lost confidence in the idea of progress, and in which "technoscience" seems to have taken on a life of its own'.[28] Thakara attributed artificial intelligence with creating an alienating gap between design and experience that could be bridged by the designer delegating a major share of the creative act to the user. Thakara's vision coincided with

22. Carson, C. 1997. 'Material Culture History' pp. 401–28. In Smart Martin, Ann and Ritchie Garrison, J. (eds) *American Material Culture: The Shape of the Field*. Winterthur, Delaware: Henry du Pont Winterthur Museum.

23. This section relies on providing a synthesis of broadly drawn attitudes to design practice based on debates in design theory discourse in the last twenty years for the purposes of explaining the particularity of the current significance given to classifying design as an aspect of material culture. It does not set out either to 'cover' all the various tributaries of design methodologies or is any critical evaluation implied or stance taken at this point.

24. Verbeek, P.P. and Kockelkoren, P. 1998. 'The Things That Matter' pp. 28–42. In *Design Issues*, Vol. 14, No. 3, Autumn.

25. Moles, A.A. 1988. 'Design and Immateriality: What of It in a Post Industrial Society?' pp. 25–32. In *Design Issues*, Vol. 4, No. 1–2 (Special Issue 1988).

26. See also Lyotard, J-F.1985. *Les Immatériaux* [exhibition catalogue] Paris.

27. Thakara, J. (ed.) 1988. *Design After Modernism: Beyond the Object*. London: Thames and Hudson.

28. Ibid., p. 29.

the concept of the product as some kind of 'illusion'[29] obsessing theoreticians attempting to free themselves from the strictures of modernism's 'form follows function'[30] that no longer made sense in an age when information technology required a 'participating user' rather than a passive consumer. One of the concerns of designers, conscious of the so-called 'failure of modernism', was how to conceive of a 'design' as an unintrusive, non-aesthetic entity that enabled the user to enter into the creative act of designing.

The conscious retreat of the designer from the role of an autonomous creative agent to a more social stance that prioritised the needs and tastes of the consumer, coincided with an awareness that providing 'choice' was an economic imperative that ruled designers practising in the commercial sector during the 'designer eighties'.[31] That period also saw architects lose authority and credibility through the popularisation of conservative reactionarism to radical modern designs. This was exemplified through such interventions as Prince Charles's royal pronouncements in 1984 on the planned extension to the National Gallery in London, criticising the winning entry as 'a monstrous carbuncle on the face of a much loved and elegant friend'.[32] The concomitant loss of self-confidence among British architects saw many of them agreeing with the reactionary attack mounted on their own profession instigated by Prince Charles's claim to be giving voice to the majority view. Significantly, and contrary to the usual class distinctions that are said to mark different types of taste, his representation of the so-called man-in-the-street's perspective coincided with the anti-modernist stance of the Royal Fine Art Commission, bringing

29. Mitchell, T. 1988. 'The product as illusion' pp. 208–15. In Ibid.

30. The slogan that has come to encapsulate the principles of rational modernism derive from an essay written by the American architect Louis Sullivan working at the turn of the century and particularly renowned for his designs of multi-storey buildings. See Sullivan, L. 1896 'The Tall Office Building Artistically Considered' p. 13. In Benton, T. & C. with Sharp, D. (eds) 1975. *Form and Function*. London: Granada.

31. See Gardner, C. and Sheppard, J. 1989. *Consuming Passion: The Rise of Retail Culture*. London: Unwin Hyman, p. 69.

32. For an account of the National Gallery extension from its inception in 1959 to the completion of the Sainsbury Wing in 1993 see Amery, C. 1991. *A Celebration of Art and Architecture*. London: The National Gallery. For the popular-versus-modern politics of the architectural debate see Hebdige, D. 1989 'Designs for Living'. In *Marxism Today*, October 1989, pp. 24–7.

populist and élitist status quo views together.[33] The 'carbuncle' episode culminated in the appointment of the American firm of Scott Brown and Venturi to design the new wing of the National Gallery in the form of a neo-classical façade that referred stylistically to the existing building. But at the same time that architects suffered loss of confidence and status, group design practices servicing the advertising and retail industries flourished during the 1980s.[34]

The changes the designer's role has undergone in the last twenty years or so is reflected in the shift of importance accorded to design as the formal synthesis of ideal form; and from a very visual high-fashion image to a return to the physicality of design as material objects. This is illustrated in the difference between this century's 'modern' and 'postmodern' architectural styles. The former relied on abstraction to express basic principles of design contrasting starkly against the flamboyantly rule-less postmodern revivalist designs that flourished at the height of the monetarist climate of the 1980s. The worst of postmodern architecture produced a superficial expendable fashion-ability from unfettered reference to historical and other culturally familiar sources derived from scenarios reminiscent of suburbia and Disneyland. By entering the commodity system architecture changed from a professional establishment practice to producing leaders of taste and popular styles with the attendant consequences of the short-lived attraction of fashion that requires constant change and renewal to keep its credibility.

Currently there is a sense of a revived back-to-reality concern with producing designs that 'work', and rethinking everyday things for the benefit of the user. Thus Donald Norman, a design critic, writes: 'people feel guilt when they are unable to use simple things, guilt that should be not theirs but rather the designers and manufacturers of the objects'.[35] Norman's contention that no device need be difficult to use if the designer heeds the needs of users and the principles of cognitive psychology, is directly in line with 'good design' principles. This immedi-ately raises questions around how this renewed sense of responsibility for making designs that work, is *different* from the straightforward modernist faith in functionalism that has been so thoroughly shown

33. Bourdieu, P. 1984. *Distinction: A social critique of the judgement of taste*. London: Routledge and Kegan Paul.

34. Rawsthorn, A. 'Lutyens, Starck and the barrow boys: design and the economy in a post-Thatcher world', pp. 14–16. In *Issue*, Spring 1991.

35. Norman, D.A. 1998. *The Design of Everyday Things*. New York: Basic Books, p. xii.

to have failed and condemned as crudely deterministic by latter generations of design critics. But there is a strong difference in attitude between the 'good design' ideal that relied on an aesthetic form to produce and prove the correct relationship between form and function, and the much more focused attention given to prioritising fundamental qualitative material properties. Thus the design group Eternally Yours[36] gives precedence to 'durability' above other qualities and assumes that form is in fact a *function* of a well-designed object, although not necessarily the *result* of its function. While the necessary feature of 'engagement' that Verbeek and Kockelkoren refer to, formerly assumed to be provided by design that was 'fit for its purpose', now demands a participating user who will get involved with, and 'work' the design, rather than be automatically regulated by it, passively contemplate it, or not even notice its existence.

Another symptom of the current socially responsible approach to design practice, reminiscent of 'good design' principles, albeit in a different form, was evident in the Cooper-Hewitt National Design Museum exhibition 'Unlimited By Design' that opened in New York in 1998, displaying current design theory represented in the work of contemporary design practices. It promoted a single type of 'universal design' that 'seeks to enhance the routine activities of the *greatest number of people*' (my emphasis) rather than foster a particular style as the obvious promoter of functionality. This may be a conscious rejection of the international style[37] promoted several decades earlier to foster an easily importable democratic form, supposedly devoid of cultural references to make it universally applicable. However, its association with a featureless corporate style of architecture, characterised by Mies Van der Röhe's Seagram building in Manhattan and celebrated by Henry-Russell Hitchock and Philip Johnson,[38] became the object of criticism by later generations of architects and critics who perceived the international style as a form of alienating cultural imperialism based on capitalism and technocracy.

36. Verbeek and Kockelkoren 1998. 'The Things That Matter', pp. 29–30; Eternally Yours web site: http://www.ecomarket.net/Eternally Yours.

37. Philip Johnson and Henry-Russell Hitchcock's exhibition, *The International Style* at the Museum of Modern Art in New York in 1932, gave the name to a phase of the Modern Movement in architecture.

38. Hitchcock, H-R. and Johnson, P. 1966 [1932] *The International Style*. New York and London: Norton and Co.

An additional factor in the thinking of socially aware designers is the growing demand for 'sustainable' and socially responsible design. This is an outcome of ecological awareness and the ethical duties that fall on designers working at the concept stage where they may be able to influence some of the decisions that can make the difference between sustainability and waste, socially responsible design and speculative development. For example, architects have to work within the confines of laws governing planning regulations ultimately controlled by the political interests of the government in power. The deregulation of city planning controls brought in by the British Local Government Planning Act (1980) under the Thatcher regime, allowed the indiscriminate proliferation of speculative commercial development in certain privileged urban areas in order to stimulate monetarist-style 'economic revival', to the detriment of public sector development. Therefore the financial and political pressures that restrict what designers can actually determine are such that they can rarely, if ever be held fully responsible for a design.[39] This may not be a bad thing if it discourages the kind of monumental mistakes that have resulted from pursuing an ideal aesthetic or an unquestioning belief in that mythical figure, the individual creative 'genius'. So it would be naive to suggest that non-commercial design is more than, although a growing, minority concern. Only some design practices pursue a 'green' policy and those protocols that govern professional codes of conduct are few and far between.[40]

Since 1980 architects were no longer barred by their professional body, the RIBA (Royal Institute of British Architects), from involvement in speculative development or from advertising.[41] It is now recognised that designers offer a service and operate within a commercial environment in which their name is similar to a product 'brand' or label representing their reputation. The hype surrounding big names and practices that specialise in signature designs, however, together with a surfeit of 'product clutter' and several recessions later, has resulted in a jaded cynicism fed from too much 'choice' and baroque over-elaboration. A

39. Ravetz, A. 1986. *The Government of Space: Town Planning in Modern Society*, London: Faber and Faber.

40. For example the British professional designers' body, The Chartered Society of Designers, specifies that the primary responsibility of the designer is to the 'client and employer' ignoring the consumer and user, and giving no mention to ethics in terms of the social responsibility that falls upon the profession. See Whiteley, *Design For Society*, 132–3.

41. Lyall, S. 1995. *Architects' Journal Centenary Issue*, Vol. 100, 9 March, p. 171.

healthy backlash to over-design has manifested itself in a revival of interest in a pared-down style reminiscent of modern functional good design. But whereas minimalism was once an exclusive minority taste it is now a popular style, testified by its appearance in one of the largest middle-market international chain stores retailing clothes and household goods, defining the 'minimalist' lifestyle as the type who is 'not into clutter'.[42] And although 'utility chic' may be a contradiction in terms it is widely used by fashion commentators and signals a popular recognition of the benefits of a more rational approach to consumption of fashions that for example combine leisure and workwear, and cosmetics that combine two applications in one. At street level it may not indicate anything more than the usual 'new' product marketing technique, but at the same time it echoes the more politically motivated groups among those with ecological concerns such as ULS (Use Less Stuff), a lobby that does not consider recycling radical enough but advocates the rationalisation of the number of goods produced through what could be termed a form of voluntary ethical rationing.

If what young avant-garde designers like the exhibitors at the 'Stealing Beauty: British Design Now'[43] exhibition at the ICA are doing is indicative of the cutting edge, it should first be noted that they would reject the appellation if not the status of 'avant-garde'. Their recognition that 'over the past few years design has offered an instant passport to a sophisticated image: you spend your money and you get the look', positions their practice as a critique of consumerism. But their alternative claims to 'a new kind of beauty' inspired by things in everyday use, is clearly aligned with an urbane élitist lifestyle based on an aesthetic practice. It is much more to do with being able to *choose* an 'objet trouvé' in preference to a more pragmatic practice born out of necessity of making do with ad hoc second-hand goods. Stealing Beauty's critique of cosy suburban armchair consumption included a similar project to 'grunge', a style of dress based on recycling old clothes, an anti-fashion derived from punk sub-culture.[44] But Stealing Beauty's version only produced a nostalgic revival with none of the subversive

42. 'The best of both worlds' in *M&S Magazine*, Marks and Spencer, Summer 1999, p. 118.

43. *Stealing Beauty: British Design Now* [exhibition catalogue] ICA, 1999.

44. What started out as a subcultural style was made respectable by its inclusion in the Street Style exhibition at the Victoria and Albert Museum in London in 1996 and its adoption by high fashion designers like Versace who included garments made from recycled materials in his collection.

intent. An earlier example of a design practice with a similar philosophy to that of Stealing Beauty is the Italian-based international association of designers, Memphis. Established in 1981 under the directorship of Ettore Sottsass,[45] it developed a distinctive style based on the ironic rejection of good design drawing on sources ranging from popular Americana to classicism. If we take designers such as those exhibited in Stealing Beauty as characteristic of current forward thinking, what distinguishes them from those that preceded them in the 'anti-design' tradition, is the value placed on the elusive qualities of materials with a previous life acquired through time and use. The reuse of things with a particular biography is not in the parsimonious spirit or shabby heroism of wartime make-do-and mend, but an attempt to capture a form of authenticity that 'the look' alone cannot provide. Having lost faith in the modernist concept of originality that is supposed to emerge from their own tabula rasa imaginations, contemporary designers seem to be more interested in finding authenticity outside themselves in the materiality of 'thingness' that resides in the real world.

The Maker's Perspective

In considering the maker we turn from the type of professional designer who is mainly involved at the point of the conceptualisation of a product or site, prior to its manufacture or construction, to the type of designer who engages directly with the object of their design through the process of making. The physicality of manufacturing an artefact necessitates a range of technical knowledge and expertise which has traditionally been identified with working-class trades. These were usually carried out in a specific material that required expert knowledge of its properties, used skilled hand technology, specialised tools and operated within a particular craft culture with its own training system, affiliation procedures, vocabulary and restrictive practices. Wood, for example has traditionally been associated with carpentry, joinery and furniture making carried out in factories or building sites. Even once the existence of machinery largely deskilled the trades a new group of studio designer-makers emerged who refuse the separation of head from hand and make their own designs using craft skills. Through the physical control of the production process it was possible to retain immediate control over their designs by seeing them through all the stages of manufacture to the final form of the product. The operative

45. Sparke, P. 1982, *Ettore Sottsass Jr.* London: Design Council.

Figure 9. 'Utility chic', a 1999 version of the austere fashion of the 1940s that stripped away all unnecessary detail. (*Independent*, photo: Neil Massey)

word here is 'studio' as opposed to 'factory', implying that the new type of 'craftperson' created by the establishment of the Crafts Council in 1973 associated craft with art.

As Christopher Bailey has observed 'there are three principle sites of craft production: the factory, the studio and the home'.[46] But barring a few exceptions, most academic attention has concentrated on the studio or *fine* crafts for obvious reasons of patronage,[47] and class distinction associated with taste.[48] Tanya Harrod in her history of twentieth-century crafts reveals that Michael Cardew, one of Britain's most distinguished ceramists, found it necessary to justify his work being masculine in the world of studio pottery then perceived to be feminine.[49] His was not an unusual attitude among that generation of male designers who considered themselves modernists.[50]

The relatively new profession of industrial designer, created by the division of labour between head (designer) and hand (worker), imposed by the industrialisation of manufacture and the invention of new materials such as plastic,[51] gave the designer the responsibility of being an innovator. It was no longer possible to rely on traditional forms and craft processes. The designer's brief was to create new types of products for new types of manufacturing and distribution technologies as well as new types of markets consisting of an anonymous homogeneous mass of consumers. This contrasted sharply with craft production dependent on an entirely different economy based on small batch and

46. Bailey, C. Editorial, *Journal of Design History*, Vol. 2, Nos. 2 and 3, 1989.

47. Note that Harrod's compendious tome on twentieth-century crafts (see below) is sponsored by the Crafts Council of Great Britain and the Bard Graduate Centre of Decorative Arts in New York.

48. See for example the special issue on the crafts of one of earliest editions of the *Journal of Design History* Vol. 2, Nos. 2 and 3 mentioned above, and the two more recent special issues on craft, *Craft, Culture and Identity*, Vol. 10, No. 4, 1997 and *Craft, Modernism and Modernity*, Vol. 11, No. 1, 1998. There is a certain amount of social history literature that attends to craft-associated trades in working-class history in a more sociological context. See for example Samuel, R. 1977. 'Workshop of the World: Steam power and hand technology in mid-Victorian Britain', pp. 6–72. In *History Workshop*, Vol. 3, Spring; Berg, M. 1985. *The Age of Manufactures*. London: Fontana Press.

49. Harrod, T. 1998. *The Crafts in Britain in the Twentieth Century*. New Haven and London: Yale University Press, p. 123.

50. Reed, C. (ed.) 1996. *Not At Home: The Suppression of Domesticity in Modern Art and Architecture*. London: Thames and Hudson.

51. Gloag, J. 1945. *Plastics and Industrial Design*. London: George Allen and Unwin.

bespoke production. Craft training derived from traditional manual skills passed down through the generations by means of specialised occupational apprenticeship institutionalised through the guild system. Skills were gained through working with a master craftsman who jealously guarded 'the knowledge' through a form of restrictive trade practice to ensure that his livelihood was not forfeited. He initiated and guided the apprentice through a series of phases, only releasing technical know-how in gradual stages in order to keep control over the dissemination of his precious skills. This form of training was not uncommon even after 1960 with the creation of the Diploma of Art and Design that was eventually to replace the National Diploma of Design (NDD).[52] The gentrification of design through changes in the education system finally made a separation between design and manufacturing, prioritising the conceptual process over that of making as the appropriate education to produce professional designers for industry.

The case of a third-generation furniture maker, Laurence Clarke, typifies the experience of the last of the trade designers with a craft-based training. Though graduated with a National Diploma of Design (NDD) in 1966, he needed traditional skills to work in his father's furniture factory. His experience explains the mismatch between an education intended for training design professionals and the more conservative sector of the post Second World War furniture industry that could see no need to separate design from making and still valued craft skill above technological innovation.

> [At college] we were mainly designing modern furniture, [. . .] we were using all sorts of modern techniques – plastics, laminations and anything we could virtually think of, which was completely different to the background I was brought up in. When I started in [my father's] firm . . . I worked on the benches [. . .] I used to fill in where there was a gap. We only had, say two machinists, two or three makers and two polishers. [If one was] away it made quite a big hole in the production. Most of our workers were fairly old, and we found it difficult to replace them. If anyone did retire or was ill I used to fill in and take their place. I picked up some wonderful skills.

52. The NDD, instituted in 1946, to channel a branch of art education specifically to producing designers for industry, still integrated design with making techniques. J. Attfield 1984 'Design for Learning', p. 13. *Times Higher Education Supplement*, 10 August.

I worked with a hand polisher for several years and it took me a long time to actually learn his techniques because he wouldn't actually tell anybody what he was doing. He was one of the old school and [. . .] it was a long time before he told me all his secrets. But in the end he did, fortunately. They wouldn't write anything down [. . .] it would all be in their heads. I suppose they were jealous or afraid of losing their jobs to somebody else. I did several years under him polishing, several more in the making-shop learning to shape things by hand, assemble things and machining as well [. . .] all of which have been quite useful to me even now. I picked up more at Clarkes than I did at college.[53]

The impact of industrialised manufacture, however, made much of the type of craft production referred to above, redundant just after the War. The resultant scarcity of crafted goods that changed the value of handmade artefacts, transforming them from ordinary objects to luxury goods, made it possible for Clarkes to survive until 1970 by upgrading their production of everyday furniture for the middle market to high-quality expensive pieces.[54]

But there is a blind spot in design history accounts which refuses to acknowledge traditional trade skills as a category of craft still active in the second half of the twentieth century. Design historians dedicated to the modern period seem for the most part to have preferred to either chart the progress of industrialised production or to concentrate on the more privileged sector of art school trained studio crafts. And for all the attempts to draw in the morally cleansing and philanthropic craft activities of the Woodcraft Folk movement and the Women's Institute as eccentric variants from the 'norm', such comparisons would appear to be used as a platform all the better to legitimate the modern aspects of the studio crafts.[55] One need only look just beyond the text to understand the need of museums like the Victoria and Albert Museum, whose collections are largely constituted of craft objects, to augment its symbolic value through the creation of a literature of history and criticism that valorises the decorative arts alongside fine art rather than tracing it back to its working-class trade roots, in spite

53. J. Attfield 1992, 'The role of design in the relationship between furniture manufacture and its retailing 1939–1965 with initial reference to the furniture firm of J. Clarke' (unpublished doctoral thesis) Brighton: University of Brighton. pp. 161–2.

54. Ibid., p. 171–2.

55. Greenhalgh, P. 1997. 'The history of craft' p. 37. In Dormer, P. (ed.) 1997. *The Culture of Craft: Status and Future*. Manchester: Manchester University Press.

of the fact that the provenance of the major bulk of its holdings actually derives from it. It will be significant to note where the V & A's collection of Windsor chairs[56] will be positioned once the British Galleries reopen in 2001. Until their closure in August 1998 they had lurked rather uneasily on the landing just outside the entrance to the Galleries as if waiting after all these years to be integrated into the main collection.

The term 'craft' should not be read here as meaning the rejection of machines in the stereotypical Luddite or pro-Morris sense. It does not literally imply manual manufacture in the precious 'handicraft' sense. Ever since powered hand tools and machinery have been available craftworkers have been using them. The high degrees of skill and intelligence required to keep control of design by following it through into the process of production is what has distinguished the contemporary practice of craft. Its élite expensive version is characterised by evidence of good quality materials and fine 'workmanship'.[57] But perhaps more fundamentally, contemporary craft provided in theory the opportunity for an individual designer to work autonomously, to be creative on their own terms and produce uncommissioned work for sale through art galleries and craft fairs in a similar way to that in which fine artists operate. In practice, of course designer-makers just like fine artists do work for client patrons and are often dictated to by the galleries and commissioning agencies who take them on and charge a percentage of commission when they sell their work.

There is no need to repeat the debates between tradition and modernity discussed through numerous accounts of the arts and crafts movement that have variously sought to denounce craft production as retrogressive or to preserve it as a precious inheritance about to disappear. The romantisisation of craft production has patronisingly represented the apprenticeship system as a communal 'sharing' of experience and hand-crafted products as having an inherent quality of 'elegance' unobtainable in machine-made products. The reality however was not quite as ideal as middle-class utopian aspirants such as William Morris and later generations of design theorists liked to

56. In England the Windsor chair was a genre of country furniture produced by a cottage industry for ordinary everyday use and originally destined for the cottage or the tavern, rarely if ever infiltrating the quarters 'above stairs' in the grander type of house. Sparkes, I. 1973. *The English Country Chair*. Buckinghamshire: Spur.

57. Pye, D. 1968. *The Nature and Art of Workmanship*. Cambridge: Cambridge University Press.

imagine.[58] Not all hand production was of good quality, nor were the conditions of work under the guild system always satisfactory.[59] Much of William Morris's success has been attributed to his business ability, without which his designs, however good, would have been unable to reach the public.[60]

With the creation of the Crafts Advisory Committee (CAC)[61] in 1971 the crafts were given a state-funded body of their own, separate from the Design Council, to promote hand production.[62] The government's drive to encourage industrialisation after the War had previously seen the crafts subsumed under the umbrella of 'design'. Thus the creation of a separate body – the Crafts Council, which grew out of the CAC – to attend to the crafts as a special category of design, product and making process, showed a recognition of the quality and value of the handmade. It also announced the seemingly contradictory wish, at the root of the controversy that still pertains to craft in the present day, to both preserve ancient craft techniques while at the same time to develop a contemporary aesthetic and a critical language with which to evaluate it on equal terms with fine art. Designers in search of skilled artisans to execute their designs by means of traditional fine craftsmanship or to incorporate the principles of the arts and crafts movement into their buildings were disappointed by the CAC's insistence on cultivating an ethos of craft as a form of art.[63]

By the mid-1980s the continuing prejudice against the 'crafts' that associated handmade objects with traditional rustic trades, was seen to be tarnishing the image of the work of the new breed of maker-designers emerging from the degree courses on design established a decade earlier. The risible image of 'craftspersons' as a band of eccentric

58. For example see Percy, C. and Triggs, T. 1990. 'The Crafts and Non-verbal Learning', pp. 37–9. In *Oral History*. Vol. 18, No. 2, autumn.

59. See for example the type of goods and conditions existing in the furniture trades. Kirkham, P. et al. 1987. *Furnishing the World: The East London Furniture Trade 1830-1980.* London: Journeyman.

60. Harvey, C. and Press, J. 1991. *William Morris: Design and Enterprise in Victorian Britain.* Manchester University Press.

61. To become the Crafts Council in 1973.

62. For the history of the other important craft institution in Britain, The Crafts Centre, see White, J.N. 1989. 'The First Craft Centre of Great Britain; Bargaining for a Time Bomb', pp. 207–14. In *Journal of Design History*, Vol. 2, Nos. 2 & 3.

63. Harrod 1999. *The Crafts in Britain in the Twentieth Century.*

'amateurs' was a persistent one seen by the new craft establishment to be disadvantaging its commercial potential. A concerted campaign was fought to transform the public's perception of crafts from 'brown lumpy' things to a more up-to-date vocabulary to indicate their connection with art, is evident in the self-conscious way the Crafts Council represented itself through its exhibitions and publications. For example in 'The Raw and the Cooked', an exhibition of contemporary ceramics, we see how carefully the Council disassociated the medium from the term 'pottery' or any hint of functionality, referring rather more pretentiously to 'empty vessels' and 'new work in clay' indicating an ambitiously intellectual, cultural and aesthetic project.[64]

So craft, initially defined as a separate category of object to differentiate the handmade from the industrially produced, never quite acquired the respectability intended by the CAC. To those critics who saw craft as a retreat from innovation, modernism and progressive design, the bid was to elevate its status by redefining craftwork as a 'creative' art and 'craftsmen' as designer-makers with a right of entry into the circle of respectability enjoyed by fine artists.[65] The aspiration for fine crafts to gain acceptance as art was to remain unrealised. But it does in part explain why the revival of interest in the crafts in the 1970s coincided with a resurrection of interest in the 'decorative' and 'applied arts', bringing those terms back into the language of art and design to link them to fine art.

Another significant symptom of the phenomenon of self-transformation undergone by the craft establishment was the change of name in 1986 of the British Crafts Centre to Contemporary Applied Arts (CAA).[66] Situated in the heart of London its main aim was to provide a gallery for the sale and promotion of the best of British crafts. The change was instigated by the awareness that, unlike the artisans of the 1960s and 70s, young makers graduating from 3D design courses in the 1980s did not want to be 'craftsmen' nor did they necessarily want to go off and live in the country 'to avoid commerce and competition' in search of 'the alternative good life'. To help them survive the harsh economic climate of the market, the CAC set out to provide a well-organised

---

64. Britton, A. and Margetts, M. 1993. *The Raw and the Cooked*. London: Crafts Council.

65. As characterised, for example, by Swengley, N. 'Very Arty Crafty' in the *Observer*, 5 July 1987, pp. 40–3.

66. Hill, R. 'How the country craftsmen became contemporary applied artists'. *Guardian*, 15 January 1987.

agency to obtain commissions and generally promote artesanal work through a more sophisticated 'arty' image.[67]

Also in 1987, the state-funded Crafts Council organised an exhibition entitled 'The New Spirit in Craft and Design' to change the 'corn dollies and macramé' image of 'crafts' to a more up-to-date relevant representation that would promote designer-makers and their work. The association of crafts with traditional country trades had been assumed and encouraged until then by the Council for Small Industries in Rural Areas (CoSIRA) who funded the setting up of small out-of-town craft workshops to create jobs and boost the rural economy. CoSIRA promoted small workshop enterprises that were no longer considered relevant in an industrial era, only succeeding in turning crafts from rural working-class occupations into middle-class, almost leisure pursuits that could only survive with help from government funding bodies upholding the principle that like the arts, crafts were worth subsidising.[68]

There is a distinct separation between fine crafts produced in studios and the craft skills employed in engineering workshops, or exercised on most building sites like bricklaying or joinery.[69] There is also a difference of prestige perceived in the sophisticated contemporary crafts that have aesthetic value but no functional purpose, in comparison with useful everyday utensils and implements like baskets, pots or hand tools. The latter category of vernacular crafted objects often derive their particular characteristics from regional contingencies such as available materials near at hand, climate and geographical phenomena. But traditional methods of manual manufacture no longer relevant in an industrial age take on a different significance when they are in danger of dying out. Crafts thus have also become associated with regional history as representative vernacular forms are valued when they became scarce and therefore precious. The interest in reproducing local crafts is not only for the pleasure in making, nor just for the intrinsic beauty

67. Ashwin, C., Chanon, A, and Darracott, J. 1988. *Education Crafts: A Study of the Education and Training of Craftspeople in England and Wales*, London: Crafts Council; Bittker, S. 1989. 'Report of a Survey of Recent Crafts and Design Graduates of Scottish Art Colleges', pp. 219–28. In *Journal of Design History*, Vol. 2, Nos. 2 & 3.

68. Swengley 1978. 'Very Arty Crafty'; *Craft Workshops in the English Countryside*, 1978, Salisbury: CoSIRA; Ashwin, C. 'Craft makes a comeback', *Times Higher Education Supplement*, 1 May 1987.

69. Coleman, R. 1988. *The Art of Work: An Epitaph to Skill*. London: Pluto, p. 43.

of the object, but in order to keep traditional skills alive as part of the national heritage.[70]

Peter Dormer's questionable definition of craft as a commodity representing unnecessary labour[71] would appear to have been derived from Veblen's late nineteenth-century critique of the middle class who could not afford to be leisured and therefore simulated it by means of the display of wealth through 'conspicuous consumption'.[72] This now outdated definition in part explains the traditional class-based distinction that places the artisan in a subordinate position in relation to the client. Yet today much craftwork can be deemed 'leisure' in that it is often carried out in the home, and frequently subsidised if not entirely maintained by other means of income. Craft is a precarious way to make a living and many designer-makers would be unable to survive without institutional funding from bodies like the Crafts Council. And just as Veblen observed that it was the woman of the middle-class household whose duty it was to represent leisure, so craft has, for many, been feminised and transformed from a working-class skilled occupation to a subsidised middle-class (leisure) activity.[73] The shift in status up to the middle class also means that craftworkers are no longer in a subordinate position in relation to their clients because they have a measure of self-determination and an expectation that their work should be enjoyable and fulfilling.

The intellectualisation of the crafts as a middle-class aesthetic practice alongside, but not quite equal in prestige to the fine arts, was finally legitimated in Britain by the education establishment instituting degree courses on design (ceramics, woodwork, metalwork, plastics, jewellery, etc.) in 1972.[74] These courses to train 'designer-makers' is a twentieth-century phenomenon that has developed out of the upgrading of craft activity from pre-industrial trades to the type of craft promoted by the

70. Putnam, T. 1990. 'The Crafts in Museums: Consolation or Creation', pp. 40–3. In *Oral History*, Vol. 18, No. 2; Williams-Davies, J. 1989. 'The Preservation and Interpretation of Traditional Rural Crafts at the Welsh Folk Museum', pp. 215–8. In *Journal of Design History*, Vol. 2, Nos. 2 and 3.

71. Dormer, P. 1990. *The Meanings of Modern Design*. London: Thames and Hudson, p. 142.

72. Veblen, T. [1899] 1934. *The Theory of the Leisure Class*. New York: The Modern Library.

73. Harrod 1998. *The Crafts in Britain in the Twentieth Century*.

74. Attfield, J. 1984. 'A tale of two cultures' and 'Design for learning'. *The Times Higher Education Supplement*, 10.8.84: 13.

Craft Council, conforming to a modern rather than a traditional aesthetic. The creation of the Fellowship in the critical appreciation of the crafts at the University of East Anglia first held by Peter Dormer (1996–1998)[75] and later by Tanya Harrod,[76] was the culmination of the concerted intellectual project to validate the crafts as a separate entity with its own specialised critical apparatus rather than to remain as a sub-group within the fine art camp and thus have to settle for second-class status.

The commercial context that determines the monetary value within the art market places higher value on fine art for its expressive content than on a craft piece executed with a high degree of skill. It may be because there is more prestige attached to craft work with a strong aesthetic quality that discourages some designer-makers from developing their skills as a major feature of their productions or from making functional objects. Evidence from studies of workers in the craft industries does suggest that one of the main motivating expectations on the part of 'artistic' craftpersons is the direct satisfaction derived from transforming materials, but maybe even more significantly, from the creative effects of making objects as individual personal statements.[77] In craft practice the artisan is in touch with the material object and in control of the design, even when carrying out another designer's concept. Contrary to Giedion's 'mechanisation takes command',[78] ultimately it is the expectation that the *maker* can 'take command'. And it is only through a thorough knowledge of their craft that they are able to do so. Craft, whether it is annexed to 'art' by being called 'applied arts', 'decorative art' or whatever, does not have same glamour or potential high returns as fine art. The expectation of fulfilment that craft practitioners hope to derive from the intimate relationship with their medium and making process, would therefore seem to be one of the main attractions in taking up such a hazardous livelihood.

75. Dormer, P. (ed.) 1997. *The Culture of Craft: Status and Future.* Manchester: Manchester University Press.

76. Harrod 1998. *The Crafts in Britain in the Twentieth Century.*

77. Ranson, B. 1989. 'Craftwork, Ideology and the Craft Life Cycle', pp. 77–92. In *Journal of Design History*, Vol. 2, Nos. 2 & 3.

78. Giedion, S. 1948. *Mechanisation Takes Command.* New York: Oxford University Press.

Retransforming the Extraordinary: Undesign and the Material Culture of Everyday Life

There is a whole swathe of uncategorisable non-professionally produced design and craft activities and objects, mainly produced in the home, the garden shed or the adult education evening class, which go unaccounted for in the history of design. Although it is beyond the scope of this volume to rectify this omission, part of the project is to address the way in which ordinary things objectify or make material the everyday. What makes the difference between what is categorised as 'design', 'craft' or uncategorised 'thing' is the way that craft and design objects are separated out from the mere, banal, cluttered collectivity of goods in general. The categories and criteria which define these terms can be explained through the examples selected by the institutions which collect, house and represent the nation's material culture.[79]

The recognition that different research methods are needed to access working-class history where there are few or no documentary sources inspired the development of oral history techniques for the study of the history of crafts. Tapping the 'oral tradition' has resulted in the creation and housing of recorded interviews with people working in the crafts that have been deposited in national and regional sound archives.[80] There is also much material evidence in regional social history museums that have collected and preserved local craftwork from lace to vernacular building techniques, agricultural and household implements and utensils, tools, and the contents of whole workshops and retail shops.[81] It is only recently that the idea of integrating research sponsored by various institutions discussed the use of creating documentary sources in the form of audio recordings to augment evidence relating to material artefacts in order to document the crafts. The consciousness of the past, or of the memory of an 'imagined past' which has been such a feature of post-industrial 'heritage' culture has seen the survival and gentrification of traditional crafts through demonstrations in open-air museums, transforming them into middle-class leisure pursued through weekend and evening classes and hobby

79. See Bourdieu. P. 1993. *The Field of Cultural Production*. Cambridge: Polity Press.

80. In 1989 the Oral History Society held a conference – 'Oral History and the Crafts' – at the Central School of Art (now Central St Martins, London Institute) as part of an initiative to record and collect interviews with people working in the crafts.

81. Such as in the Castle Museum in York.

activities. The advent of more widely accessible means of making audio-visual recordings has made it is possible to record craft techniques that cannot easily be transmitted orally or through static photographs.

There have been many utopian initiatives which characterised craft as beneficial and fulfilling in the drive to ennoble work during periods when exploitation was considered a serious social problem and the quality of products perceived to be degraded by machine production. In the nineteenth century there were a number of bodies directly aimed at women, such as the Home Arts and Industries Association (founded in 1884) and the National Federation of Women's Institutes[82] started in 1915 and still active today, with agendas to promote the crafts as a means of educational and moral elevation. The crafts were also promoted for their supposed therapeutic propensity by early twentieth-century arts and crafts educators like W.R.Lethaby who added to the feminised reputation accruing to the crafts by annexing domestic activities normally associated with women, such as breadmaking, dressmaking and housework.[83]

The site which has been most neglected apart from the attention accorded to it by feminist historians,[84] is craft production which takes place in the home.[85] The reason for its neglect can be accounted for by the low status or invisibility of domestic production and the failure of its products to conform to the quality judgement of experts, presenting a particularly difficult problem when considering its value within an aesthetic frame of reference. This is certainly the case with the group engaged in popular or 'hobby' craft, not made for profit but to keep or give away, or sold informally through church bazaars, WI-type charity events, and semi-amateur craft fairs all over the country.[86] This type of informal production, however, cannot be overlooked since

82. Andrews, M. 1997. *The Acceptable Face of Feminism: The Women's Institute Movement.* London: Lawrence and Wishart.

83. Lethaby, W.R. 1923. *Home and Country Arts.* London: Home and County.

84. Such as Broude, N. and Garrard, M.D. 1982. *Feminism and Art History.* New York: Harper & Row; Elinor, G. et al. 1987. *Women and Craft,* London: Virago; Parker, R. and Pollock, G. 1981. *Old Mistresses: Women, Art and Ideology,* London: Routledge & Kegan Paul; Parker, R. 1984. *The Subversive Stitch: Embroidery and the making of the feminine.* London: The Women's Press.

85. Current post-graduate research in progress is being undertaken by Joanne Turney on British Crafts in the Home (Winchester School of Art, University of Southampton).

86. With the notable exception of Kirkham, 1995. 'Women and the Inter-war handicrafts revival', pp. 174-83. In Attfield, J. and Kirkham, P. (eds) 1995. *A View From the Interior. Women and Design.* London: The Women's Press.

it is of the very stuff that gives substance to the material culture of everyday life. The male counterpart of home crafts, DIY, is an aspect often mentioned in passing but still not accorded much attention by design historians.[87] So it is not only the professional design or crafts practitioner who needs to be considered in discussing the designer's role or the maker's perspective. It has been recognised by historians researching working-class and women's history that the craft production that goes on in locations other than the studio and workshop needs more attention. Even within the home, there is a significant difference in the meaning attached to craft in terms of class and gender depending on where in the home the craft is carried out – in the interior, in the garage or outbuildings of the house, whether it is regarded as work or leisure, what type of tools and machines are used, and if the activity of making is for reasons of thrift, to clothe the family, to enhance the home, for gifts, for profit, therapy, charity or for the sheer pleasure of making with no particular concern over its ends.

In *Consumer Culture and Postmodernism* Mike Featherstone describes the aestheticisation of everyday life as a postmodern phenomenon. The heightened awareness of the visual in a period of mass media is construed as part of an historical continuum with antecedents in the carnivalesque of the medieval fair where the world was turned upside down enabling the populace to experience cultures not normally accessible to them. But from being a once-a-year occasion in which meanings were destabilised and rules broken in a controlled environment, the postmodern condition has been characterised as one in which meaning is in a permanent state of flux, conditioned by the multiplication of opportunities availed by sites of mass consumption such as shopping malls, theme parks, media and tourism. Spectacular forms of design, exemplified by clothing fashion and avant-garde architecture dominate contemporary visual culture giving precedence to eye appeal rather than substance. The same is even more true of contemporary art. One exhausted art critic, faced by the 'pervasive futility' of the 'Abracadabra' exhibition of installation art at the Tate (July 1999) complained: 'We've all seen too much', putting art's 'identity crisis' down to the fact that '[a]rtists can become part of the mass media, but they can't compete with it'.[88]

87. While some social and economic historians have looked at the impact of 'self-provisioning' and DIY in particular, for example: Pahl, R.E. 1984. *Divisions of Labour*. Oxford: Blackwell, pp. 98–105; Samuel 1994. *Theatres of Memory*, Vol. I, pp. 51, 72–3.

88. Searle, A. 1999. 'Cheap tricks, bad jokes, black magic', pp. 12–13. In the *Guardian*, 13 July.

So far the focus has mainly been on the category of things called 'design' and 'craft' that derive their meaning from their obvious visual presence and their link to art. In contrast to 'things with attitude', that which forms the bulk of the material culture of everyday life – things in the lower case – are much more elusive and less easy to categorise. Once objects escape the boundaries of categorisation they become wild, and like the wild cards in a pack of cards, can be used to take on different values according to the state of play of the game. The next chapter will attempt to provide a way into understanding why certain types of things that might appear quite ordinary in appearance, actually take on the role of mediators in both adapting and resisting social change.

Things and the Dynamics
of Social Change

If, as suggested in the last chapter, we are to capture some sense of
the wild things, the material world of the everyday which escapes
the order of visual aesthetic categorisation, it is necessary to diagnose
features that give them value as vehicles of meaning through which
people negotiate their relations with each other and the world at large.
The features picked out for analysis are selected for their dynamic
qualities in negotiating issues of identity and social change. Thus design
can still be conceived of as a practice of modernity[1] whereby it is
deemed possible to effect change, albeit not in its original homogenis-
ing paradigm in the control of professional designers, but as a practice
of self-construction realised through consumption as well as in the
acts of making and living. Nor is the theory of design as a practice of
modernity to be mistaken for the crude functionalism of the ideology
of early modernism, that fatal unrealised ideal that envisaged the total
sweeping away of the past. Here it is referred to as a much more subtle
sensibility which has also to deal with the opposition to change that
creates an apparently intractable undertow pulling away from anything
new. Through the investigation of pragmatic practices of design, making
and using the artefactual world, rather than the matching up of such
practices to unrealisable utopian ideals, this section is an attempt to
provide a model through which to get in touch with the dynamic nature
of the material culture of everyday life.

This chapter will particularise three characteristics to be associated
in Part II with specific case studies of object types to illustrate examples
of the role of artefacts in the process of social change. The three

1. See Attfield, J. 1997. 'A case for the study of the coffee table: Design as a practice of
modernity' pp. 267–89. *Journal of Material Culture,* Vol. 2, No. 3, November.

Figure 10. The introduction of the home computer prompted this representation of it in 1982 in the *Observer* newspaper, as a domesticated household pet lying tamely on the hearthrug next to the master's slippers. (Topham Picturepoint).

characteristics – authenticity, ephemerality and containment (order) – are presented as representative ideational features of modern and contemporary everyday life. Authenticity as an idea manifested in domestic aretefactual forms such as the house, its environment, furnishings and equipment, poses issues concerning longevity, history, tradition and resistance to change. The materialisation of memory as a nostalgic construction of popular history, and of desire in the striving after an ideal condition, exemplifies the inevitably unfulfilled search for authenticity in unchanging 'non-material' values such as stability, freedom from strife, and happiness worked through in the material culture of the everyday.

At the other extreme, ephemerality encapsulates the transitory and the unstable, indicated by the fashion system as most obviously displayed in women's high-style apparel, and the way it increasingly infiltrated all types of mass-produced goods by the mid-twentieth century. Fashion, whether in couture, avant-garde art or any other artefactual form, embodies change on the move. The cycle of fast changes from one style to another, works as a metaphor of the passing of time visibly shifting focus, moods and meanings through the illogical mechanism that throws a new fashion 'out' no sooner it comes 'in'. The case of fashionable dress is particularly apposite in addressing questions of group and self-identity since it constitutes the layer of material that lies between the body and the outside world. As such, fabric mediates the relationship between the individual being and the act of being in the world at the most intimate level of social relations. An obvious example is Donald Winnicott's 'transitional object'[2] – the corner of a child's blanket which the infant uses as a transitional device with which to negotiate the separation from the mother. Moreover the homologous vulnerability of cloth and skin to the ageing process, explains the transition wrought by time in the banalisation of fashion, and differentiates individuals in generational terms not only at the level of kinship but within the larger time-frame context in relation to history.

The third feature selected to characterise modern material culture – containment or order- is proposed because it illustrates the central 'given' in design theory derived from modernism that still holds today. It assumes agency on the part of the design process to be able to predict and control how the product will be put to use within certain parameters of space and place. This raises questions around the positioning of the subject in the object/subject relation with regard to agency. In other words, how far can an individual or a social group have an impact on the physical environment that has been 'designed' for them, and at a macro level, on the power relations established by design controls imposed through planning and other forms of regulation? The pertinence of this question and the extent to which such a dynamic might be proposed, is conditioned by a large and imponderable gamut of historical circumstances that need to be seen against the backdrop of a

2. Winnicott, D. 1971. *Playing and Reality.* London: Tavistock.

postmodern critique which has undermined the concept of autonomy.[3] Conversely and most importantly, design as agency, also underwrites the possibility of the objectification of social change implicated by the modern mentality, that is – design as a practice of modernity.

Thus the metaphorical and physical limits of conceptual frameworks, definitions, hierarchical boundaries, and the cultural politics of locality, all aspects of order, need to be brought into play to contextualise the process that results in the physical manifestation of different cultural perspectives. This allows space for the discussion of the impact of social diversity acknowledged by postmodernism and social anthropology, and the problems of relativism that arise from considering different interest groups. Positionality also has a bearing on questions of power relations between the centre and the periphery, and the politics of the personal versus that of the so-called common good. Containment stands for the imagined space where debates take place, within which new worlds can be conceptualised that design tries to capture in physical form. The project envisaged here, rather than proposing an all-purpose model, sets out a series of cultural contexts as characteristic features of modern and contemporary everyday life to be discussed below under the headings of authenticity, ephemerality and containment, that will serve to introduce the themes illustrated in Part II.

Authenticity – a Matter of Course

Authenticity – the legitimacy of an object or experience according to established principles of fundamental and unchallengable 'truths' depends on particular, apparently unchanging belief systems of authoritative knowledge that distinguish the authentic from the inauthentic as a natural matter of course. Authenticity also implies a degree of authorial autonomy that conceives it possible for a person to originate and realise an entirely new idea unaffected by, or knowingly against the grain of the cultural context of their own place and time. This kind of transcendental view of the world has been exhaustively challenged by the very mentality which gave rise to the notion of the creative individual as autonomous in the first place and the modern concept of the avant-garde. It was only a modern mentality which could have envisaged a perfectible world effected primarily by human effort. And it was only a modern mentality which sees change as the motor of progress that questions established, seemingly unquestionable values

3. Benjamin, A. (ed.) 1992. *The Problems of Modernity.* London: Routledge.

and thus undermines the foundations of belief in order to enable innovation.

It is the belief in innovation which distinguishes the modern mentality from the deconstructionism of the postmodern way of thought that destroys the notion of intrinsic (authentic) value. Under postmodern critique authenticity, together with the other so-called 'meta-narratives'[4] which give meaning to the world we live in, has become an increasingly unstable concept. And as it recedes as a marker of stability and truth, the concept of authenticity has taken on a particular resonance and pertinence in relation to contemporary cultural sensibility which questions the very theory of origins from which it derives. Authenticity assures provenance and assumes origins – that the history of the conception and birth of an object, idea or particular individual or group identity can be traced back to a particular place and moment in time of coming into existence. Being able to identify the origins that formulate that subjectivity, establishes a bridge between the present and the past making it knowable by association. But as those historians who see writing history as a critical practice have demonstrated, the gloss of familiarity gained from tracing the roots of a 'tradition' that confers it with a credible 'history' does not automatically render an accurate representation of the past.[5] In establishing that it is rhetorical devices as much as historical 'facts' that render something 'authentic', what has to be recognised is the importance given by society in terms of value to certain aspects of authenticity. Brian Spooner's anthropological explanation for the popularity of the 'authentic' oriental carpet suggests that 'the evolving constellation of social relations in our complex society generates a need for authenticity, which leads people to cast around for cultural material on which to work out the obsession for distinction'.[6] Because the more authenticity is questioned by new and more exacting demands placed upon it, the more it is rendered unstable, and as it becomes rarer the more value is placed upon it. So what is it about authenticity that makes it so precious and sought after?

4. Lyotard, J.F. 1984. *The Post-Modern Condition*, Manchester: Manchester University Press.

5. Hobsbawm, E. and Ranger, T. (eds) [1983] 1992. *The Invention of Tradition*. Cambridge: Cambridge University Press.

6. Spooner, B. 1990. 'Weavers and dealers: authenticity and oriental carpets' pp. 195-235. In Appadurai, A. (ed.) *The Social Life of Things: Commodities in Cultural Perspective*. Cambridge: Cambridge University Press, p. 200.

Apart from establishing a direct connection with its moment of birth (origin) when an object is translated from an idea into a physical manifestation, authenticity is also associated with the state of originality – the uniqueness that comes into being at the moment of conception when a particular unreproducible concatenation of materials and conditions come together to produce a sui generis creation. The moment just prior to the act of materialisation is when the object is at its most pure, its most authentic state – that urstage before refinements and adjustments that inevitably compromise the ideal but make realisation possible.

Originality is one of the most highly valued attributes in a world where technology enables the effortless production of an infinite number of clones to be reproduced from the prototype. This explains the importance given to persons attributed with originality – the authors, artists and designers who are able to dream up new ideas particularly in the face of the constantly increasing number of new creations. It also accounts for the way the process of attribution used to authenticate the 'original' gives more value to the author of the idea rather than the maker. This is a problem that would not have arisen prior to the industrialisation of production when the conceiver was the same person as the maker and therefore, within the conventions and limitations of the particular materials and techniques used, had complete autonomy over the process of creation. The search for autonomy by enlightenment philosophers and enacted in the struggles for freedom and democracy since the eighteenth century is reflected in the material culture that underlies the pragmatic thinking that defined politics as the meeting between public and private interests and conceived it as 'the art of the possible'.

Following on from the question about what makes authenticity so precious and sought after, is the impossibility of capturing that unique moment of conception except as desire and reconciled in material form as a way of retaining some hold on it, however tenuous. Thus once the idea of attaining perfection is surrendered to the possibility of realisation, the abstract concept can begin to take shape in a sort of ur-existence – a primitive imperfect version that comprises its most authentic formulation. It is only modern design practice which expects a design to emerge fully formed first time round without reference to a type or the refinements of the evolutionary process.[7]

----

7. See the case study of reproduction furniture in Chapter 4.

Authenticity, like most profound concepts is contradictory and multifaceted. The facet that probably manifests authenticity most convincingly is its propensity to represent the real even though perfection is impossible to reproduce. An authentic antique is the 'real' thing, it doesn't just represent antiquity, it is a piece of it – you can touch it, feel it, own it and pass it down to your descendants. And materiality would seem to be more important than either perfection or uniqueness. So much so that visible imperfections and accidental flaws would seem to act as the evidence of authenticity by calling attention to the moment of bringing the concept into existence in the form of a material object. Thus authenticity calls to mind the sense of presence for which there can be no representation or substitute for the real thing.

Ephemerality – the Unresolved Moment of Truth

Just as authenticity in an artefact represents stability and longevity by referring to the perceived moment of origin some time in the far distant past, its antithesis, ephemerality, places emphasis on the present, that fragile evanescent moment that passes in a flash. It reminds one of the passing of time. But concentrating on that delicious moment of experiencing the ecstasy of existence can also hold the terror and danger of its end, putting one in mind of the inseparable link between life and death. Translated into things, the ephemeral can refer to valueless rubbish, not made to last for more than a day or two. It has no provenance, no foothold in the past or any destination in the future. Its main value lies in its consequence to the moment, a lifetime too brief to become substantive yet its very quality of impermanence can make a lasting impression in the same way that the death of a young person can often transform them into a hero.

Because of its inability to rely on permanence, ephemerality relates directly to the aspects of modernity that depend on innovation. Its apparent insubstantiality stimulates the special regenerative qualities that instigate change and transformation – that wonderful and terrible moment when 'all that is solid melts into air' as Marx described the experience of modernity, cited by Marshall Berman in his book of the same title on the paradoxes that pervade modern life.[8] The genre of things that best embodies the refreshing capacity of ephemerality to

8. Berman, M. 1983. *All That Is Solid Melts Into Air: The Experience of Modernity.* London: Verso, p. 12.

constantly come up with new ideas is that which comes under the dictates of the fashion system that formulates the cultural forms and mores deemed appropriate to the times. In common usage 'fashion' mainly refers to women's dress, a hierarchical regime managed by leading tastemakers – designers, media and personalities of the moment, who authorise what fashion followers will be wearing. Although I call on this definition below to illustrate and discuss some of the characteristics of ephemerality I am ultimately referring to fashion as a typicality of modern material culture – a phenomenon manifested in constantly changing forms that spill out into all corners of the artefactual world. The rate of change and relative importance between diverse genres of goods governed by the fashion system may vary – say between the seemingly trivial but very fast-moving high-fashion textile goods of which high-style women's wear only constitutes a very small segment, and the more ponderous but nevertheless shifting global trends in technology and urban planning that go to make the changing forms of buildings, towns and cities. Nevertheless they are subject to the same drive towards change, a mechanism that can be traced back to the dynamic relation between the physical world, the body and time. Fashion encapsulates the ephemeral nature of this abstract relation and translates the way that the awareness of time on-the-move, so particular to·the modern sensibility, is experienced in the world of the everyday.

Fashion, as stated earlier, most commonly associated with feminine high-style dress modes is a characteristic material manifestation of ephemerality. At one time it would have been royalty and the aristocracy who set the pace of fashion. During the first half of the twentieth century, fashion was dominated by the dictates of the Paris couture houses, an élite sector of the garment industry, subsidised and guarded by quality controls imposed by the French government. The couture houses depended on the fashion system which established them as leaders maintaining a position of authority that enabled them to dictate a fast turnover of changing styles for each new season. In this way they were able to foment markets and exercise their influence on fashion houses all over the world while at the same time jealously guarding their supremacy by controlling the distribution of their exclusive designs.[9] Since then sophisticated technological developments have changed what was an exclusive luxury trade to a vast industry in parallel with social changes, bringing fashion goods within the reach

9. Garland, M. 1962. *Fashion*. Harmondsworth: Penguin. See Chapter 3: 'The Construction of the High-Fashion Market', pp. 35–45.

of a much larger group of consumers so that few could escape its influence.[10] With modernisation fashion expressed innovation, change and individuality. Where once the royal family would have been the arbiters of fashion using a form of dress to indicate their social superiority, the challenging of the status quo made their formal style look old-fashioned and passé.[11] It was only the wild cards in the British royal pack – Mrs Simpson in the inter-war years, Princess Margaret in the 1960s and in the 1980s and 90s, Diana[12] who dared to be fashionably modern in defiance of being side-lined by the old guard. Of Mrs Simpson, Prudence Glynn wrote

> Even if further evidence were needed that Bessiwallis Warfield Spencer would have been quite unsuitable as Queen of England it could be supplied by the fact that she was obsessively chic.[13]

While the two rather tragic princesses who fashioned themselves as beautiful mavericks had the most to gain from the disestablishment of the monarchy. But although they ultimately lost out personally from their failure to conform, their efforts can be regarded as part of an emerging aggregation of symptoms of instability in the royal establishment which may well eventually build up into an effective movement of reform.

At a more general level fashion can be said to apply to all aspects of everyday life seen in the rise and fall of the popularity of particular styles of dress, food, music and so on. But here, in spite of its stereotipicality, dress in particular is referred to because it makes such an apposite example through which to discuss the way in which people use things to relate to time passing, and thereby to accommodate themselves to the fast pace of modern life. Fashion's seeming triviality hides profound meanings about life and value which get attached to garments through their intimate connection to the body putting people in touch with their age, peer group, generation, with rites of passage,

10. Fine, B. and Leopold, E. 1993. *The World of Consumption*. London: Routledge. See Chapter 9, 'The manufacture of the fashion system', pp. 93–137.

11. Beaton, C. 1965. 'Fashions of Royalty', pp. 265–6. In Roach, M.E. and Bubolz Eicher, J. *Dress, Adornment, and the Social Order*. New York: John Wiley.

12. Coleridge, N. 1989. *The Fashion Conspiracy*. London: Heinemann. See Chapter 7, 'Princess of Wales Check: the Palace Through the Looking-glass', pp. 158–66.

13. Glynn, P. 1978. *In Fashion: Dress in the twentieth century*. London: George Allen & Unwin, p. 111.

badges of office and countless other significant life experiences, and ultimately with their own sense of mortality.

From the growing amount of publications on fashion theory devoted to dress,[14] it appears to be a topic of increasing interest among academics, although apart from some notable exceptions,[15] few seem to have made the link between time and garments. Even though the parallel between fashion and modernity is repeatedly noted it is almost as an assumption made in passing usually in connection with the rise of the capitalist economic system and the imperative of commodity markets that require planned obsolescence. The other usual reference to the link between fashion and modernity is the self-referential definition of fashion as a 'sign of the times' – that keeping in fashion is to do with 'newness and nowness'.[16] Fashion has also been observed in the psychoanalytical sense as a means of spectacular self-realisation and aesthetic self-expression in the development of so-called 'modern individualism'.[17] Sociological analysis has proved to be the most pervasive and persuasive explanation of fashion reinforced by Thorstein Veblen's theory of the leisure class (1899),[18] Georg Simmel's emulative 'trickle down' theory (1904)[19] and latterly Pierre Bourdieu's analysis of taste (1979)[20] as the marker of social distinction. The branch of sociology that set out to investigate popular culture produced studies of the subversive use of style in the formation of sub-cultural groups[21]

14. For example the *Journal of Fashion Theory* launched by Berg in 1997.

15. For example: Wilson, E. 1985. *Adorned in Dreams: Fashion and Modernity.* London: Virago; Wilson, E. 1989. *Hallucinations: Life in the Post-Modern City.* London: Hutchinson Radius; Gronberg, T. 1998. *Designs on Modernity: Exhibiting the City in 1920s Paris.* Manchester: Manchester University Press.

16. Fox-Genovese, E. 1987. 'The empress's new clothes: the politics of fashion', pp. 7–30. *Socialist Review,* Vol. 7, No. 1, p. 11. Cited in Craik, J. 1994. *The Face of Fashion: Cultural Studies in Fashion.* London: Routledge, p. 6.

17. For example Wilson 1985. *Adorned in Dreams* mentions 'the development of modern individualism' in the 'Contents' page describing Chapter one 'The History of Fashion', but does return to expand on it any further in the actual text.

18. Veblen, T. [1899] 1934. *The Theory of the Leisure Class,* New York: the Modern Library.

19. Simmel, G. [1904] 1973. 'Fashion' pp. 171-191. In Wills, G. and Midgley, D. (eds) 1973. *Fashion Marketing: An anthology of viewpoints and perspectives.* London: George Allen & Unwin.

20. Bourdieu, P. 1984. *Distinction: A social critique of the judgement of taste.* London: Routledge and Kegan Paul.

21. For example Hebdige, D. 1979. *Subculture: the Meaning of Style.* London and New York: Methuen; McRobbie, A. (ed.) 1989. *Zoot Suits and Second-Hand Dresses.* Basingstoke, Hampshire: Macmillan.

making valuable contributions to the ongoing study of identity. The type of critiques that have taken a simplistic moral stance against fashion as one of the more extreme and ridiculous symptoms of conspicuous consumption[22] have been overturned by the raising of the importance of the meanings given to things which do not work according to the functionalist logic of use value, or the flip side that automatically confers the determining power of fashion to aesthetic genius. Interdisciplinary approaches to material culture emerging from within anthropology[23] and design history[24] have contributed to the burgeoning field of consumption studies by scholars who have resisted a single totalising explanation but seek more subtle approaches to a profound and complex cultural system which has much more to say about the object/subject relation than meets the eye.[25]

Notable among theoreticians who have made the link between the abstract notion of time as a cultural dimension are those in the academic traditions of existential philosophy like Martin Heidegger[26] and social anthropologists like Marcel Mauss[27] and Pierre Bourdieu who have all referred to its relevance to the experience of everyday through the material world. But few authors have referred to fashion as a material manifestation of time as an indication of cultural attitudes to social change, among whom Giles Lipovetsky[28] and Ted Polhemus[29] figure as exceptions. Lipovetsky's thesis poses fashion as the vanguard cultural force that manages more effectively than ideology to hold society together because of its particular propensity to deal effectively with

22. For example Veblen 1934. *The Theory of the Leisure Class;* Baudrillard, J. 1981. For a *Critique of the Political Economy of the Sign.* St.Louis, Mo.: Telos. Also see Wilson 1985. *Adorned in Dreams*, Ch. 3, 'Explaining It Away'.

23. Miller, D. (ed.) 1995. *Acknowledging Consumption*. London: Routledge.

24. For example Attfield, J. 1999. 'Bringing Modernity Home: Open Plan in the British Domestic Interior', pp. 73–82. In Cieraad, I. (ed.) *At Home: An Anthropology of Domestic Space*. New York: Syracuse University Press.

25. For example Fine. B and Leopold, E. 1993. *The World of Consumption*. London: Routledge; Auslander, L. 1996. *Taste and Power: Furnishing Modern France*. Berkley: University of California Press.

26. Macquarrie, J. 1980. *Existentialism*. Harmondsworth, Middlesex: Penguin; Heidegger, M. [1927] 1998. *Being and Time*. Oxford: Blackwell.

27. Mauss, M. [1950] 1990. *The Gift*. London: Routledge.

28. Lipovetsky, G. 1994. *The Empire of Fashion: Dressing Modern Democracy*. Princeton: Princeton University Press.

29. Polhemus, T. and Proctor, L. 1978. *Fashion and Anti-Fashion*. London: Thames and Hudson.

ephemerality. His theory depends on the so-called postmodern economic system which is flexible enough to adapt and inter-act with the fickle caprices of the individuated consumer thus ensuring a pluralistic democracy.[30] While Polhemus's proposition of fashion as a symbolic representation of time is based on the binary opposition between fashion and 'anti-fashion', the former representing 'change, progress and movement through time'[31] and the latter – continuity and stasis. The intriguing aspect of fashion which lends it the very subtlety that makes it so amenable to manifesting the complexities of modern life is its lack of logic or rationality. Regarding the study of fashion in the form of representations provides it with a false historicity since it depends on immediacy. Once 'past it' the fashion is dead and becomes a different type of artefact – a static historic costume. It is precisely the dynamic quality of fashion's fast-changing forms that make it analogous to time, and such, an appropriate material phenomenon through which to observe the cultural process of fashion practice.

This is not the place to mount a detailed historiographical review of the many theories of fashion which have attempted to explain its strange workings since this has been thoroughly covered elsewhere.[32] The mention is to emphasise the power of intrigue fashion has held for many generations of academics, not to speak of fashion designers, fabricators, media promoters, and dedicated followers of fashion – the consumers themselves. The object of the exercise is to offer material culture as an additional frame of analysis to the semiological method that concentrates on interpretations of the meanings of 'the look'.[33] Here a discursive approach is proposed in order to draw out the particularity of the modern mentality which required a coming to terms with ephemerality – the adaptation to rapid changes occurring within one human lifetime through the medium of fashion – as a means of

30. For a counter argument re. the viability of the concept of the flexible postmodern workforce based on empirical research see Lee, M.J. 1993. *Consumer Culture Reborn: The cultural politics of consumption*. London: Routledge.

31. Ibid., p. 12.

32. For example: Breward, C. 1995. *The Culture of Fashion: A New History of Fashionable Dress*. Manchester: Manchester University Press; Craik, J. 1994. *The Face of Fashion: Cultural Studies in Fashion*. London: Routledge; Roach, M.E. and Bubolz Eicher, J.1965. *Dress, Adornment, and the Social Order*. New York: John Wiley; Wills, G. and Midgley, D. (eds) 1973. *Fashion Marketing: An anthology of viewpoints and perspectives*. London: George Allen & Unwin; Wilson 1985. *Adorned in Dreams*.

33. As in Barthes, R. 1984. *The Fashion System*. New York: Hill & Wang.

attempting to gain some understanding of the way in which the sense of time has been experienced as a modern material phenomenon. Ephemerality suggests more than a fleeting moment – it offers a condition resistant to closure and materialises uncertainty – now you see it, now you don't. Fashion has that special blend of in-your-face brash confidence of unadulterated truth, but it doesn't last long enough to convince. There is always a better version on the way. . .[34]

The conventions that refuse to advance fashion as a serious subject of study propound 'style' as the more value-rich face of visual culture, not subject to the fickle caprices of fashion. The 'classic' is the ultimate materialisation of style as unchanging – the timeless, ever-appropriate, beautiful, fully formed solution that appears to evolve naturally from an inherent teleology of perfection. The classic always looks right, never 'dates' nor loses its appeal. In contradistinction to the ephemeral, fugitive quality of fashion, the classic stands in for eternity. A useful distinction can be pointed out by comparing the classic with the ephemeral in parallel with the difference between modernism as the realisation of the ultimate rational solution based on tapping apparent inherent immutable qualities that are out there and only need be discovered, and modernisation as a dynamic process that, like desire, is driven from within itself by a powerful impulse that disturbs rather than resolves and never quite achieves its ultimate goal. Thus the objectification of these two different conditions produce two quite distinct type-forms.

David Harvey's enquiry into the origins of cultural change is useful in understanding the difference between modernism and modernisation within the context of critical theory, problematised by studies of postmodernity in the last two decades. He describes the suspicion with which the drive towards modernisation in the twentieth century – 'the Enlightenment project' – was greeted by mid-century cultural critics Theodor Adorno and Max Horkheimer. In the context of Hitler's Germany and Stalin's Russia, they saw the danger of Enlightenment rationality turning 'against itself and [transforming] the quest for human emancipation into a system of universal oppression in the name of human liberation'.[35] In their estimation the attempt to

34. Attfield, J. 1989. 'A foot note with some point to it', p. 6. In the *Weekend Guardian,* Saturday-Sunday April 8–9.

35. Harvey, D. 1989. *The condition of Postmodernity: An Enquiry into the Origins of Cultural Change.* Oxford: Blackwell, p. 13.

dominate nature entailed the domination of human beings [. . .]. The revolt to nature, which they posited as the only way out of the impasse, had then to be conceived of as a revolt of human nature against the oppressive power of purely instrumental reason over culture and personality.[36]

In the world of goods rationalisation by means of technological prowess over nature demanded homogenisation and the sacrifice of individuality. In theory the condition lent itself perfectly to the production of the classic that would theoretically suit all persons at all times. But the process of modernisation also demanded constant change, variety and individuality in 'the quest for emancipation'. The beauty of the fashion system is that it not only accommodates both but also creates hybrids that dodge and escape categorisation. It also enables a certain amount of agency even if only at a low-key level, and keeps a continuous dialogue going thus ensuring against early closure. This brings us to the third feature which refers to 'containment' as a way of conceptualising that process.

Containment – the Installation of the Commonplace

Just as authenticity and ephemerality can be said to materialise the relation between time and change in ordinary things like houses and garments, so containment relates to the space both geographical and intellectual, that locates where such changes and continuities 'take place' both as in 'taking place', that is as in happening, as well as in the literal sense of the physical experience having a reality in geographical space. Containment itself is not to be taken to refer to an actual state in the material sense, but as a way of conceptualising, ordering, categorising, defining, redefining, making, remaking and unmaking the material world as a dynamic process; the frame and map on which the everyday world is reflected and through which an understanding is gained. The everyday version of location in the context of this project to consider the material culture of the everyday can be styled 'the commonplace'. In the same way much of the activity described above in relation to fashion as an everyday practice is not profoundly intellectual as in the act of making a casual purchase, window shopping, flicking through a magazine, or just opening the wardrobe and deciding what to wear. As Deborah Fausch wrote of the American architects,

36. Ibid., p. 13.

Robert Venturi and Denise Scott Brown's 'Ugly and Ordinary' project which attempted to incorporate the features of popular buildings in their architectural practice – 'The everyday resists theorizing'.[37] What happens in the commonplace is mainly a matter of common sense. Such activities can be thought of as trivial but they do constitute independent acts and as such represent a significant part of the make-up of the everyday world – the commonplace.

The kind of agency exercised in the commonplace, however is much less deliberate than the self-conscious process of 'design' which is concerned with control over the form of the physical environment and the world of goods. The design process professes to be able to predict and control the product of its invention within specific social contexts. Thus the issue of ethical accountability comes into play in terms of social responsibility in taking account of public demands and the common good as perceived by the particular interest group in control of the design process. At a macro level the politics of design defined at the point at which the public's needs and conditions are generalised into a so-called consensus often clashes with private, more specific, localised demands, and is inevitably tempered by power relations established by public agencies who control design through monitoring of planning and other statutory forms of design regulation. At a more personalised local level, however, the question of how far an individual or small group can have an impact on the physical environment, goods and products that have been 'designed' for them, means entering the private world of personal creations and locating it within the larger social context.

Although on the face of it this would seem to be an improbably chaotic scenario to attempt to analyse, nevertheless, in order to conceptualise the material culture of the everyday it is essential to acknowledge those aspects which defy definition. As mentioned above postmodern critique has undermined the concept of autonomy by deconstructing the paradigms of social order. But at the same time the postmodern mentality has also contradictorily created the conceptual framework for entertaining the possibility of countless interpretations of individuality. The logic, or illogicality if one applies the critique of relativism, of such an analysis, is the acknowledgement of the complexity of cultural diversity – that the principle of freedom decreed by

37. Fausch, D. 1997. 'Ugly and Ordinary: The Representation of the Everyday', pp. 75–106. In Harris, S. and Berke, D. (eds). *Architecture of the Everyday*. New York: Princeton Architectural Press.

modernism stood for but could not realise under the rules of standardi-sation. Conversely and most importantly, design as agency whether at the macro level of city planning or the micro level through manifestation of personal individuality, also underwrites the possibility of the objectification of social change implicated by the modern mentality, that is – design as a practice of modernity.

Studying the Particular

A word is needed here on the case study as a justifiable method to weather the theoretical debates that inevitably arise around the study of the particular in the pursuit of an understanding of the general. A recent reappraisal of the problems of modernity identified 'the turn to micrology' as a common theme in the interpretation of postmodernism.[38] It is only through a micrological approach – a study of the particular – and its application to questions about the incorporation of meaning into peoples' material world as a means of self-creation, that it is possible to encounter some sense of the multifarious nature of the contemporary artefact. The need to defend the study of material culture from the accusation of fetishism has codified the field as a study of 'social relations' which ignores and even denies the specificities of individual identity.[39] While the scientism of cultural studies, sociological analysis and economic history insists on studies of collectivities that by their nature produce typological generalisations. Yet a recent reappraisal of cultural studies[40] which recognises the need to locate the discipline within the contested space of diversity, at the same time refutes the idea of singular identity and refuses to engage with anything that might be construed as 'expressive individualism'. But at the same time resistance to the concept of the autonomous sits alongside the contra-dictory assertion that what is sought is not an 'imagined consensus, which we are all supposed to share'.[41] A 'third way',[42] increasingly seen as an alternative to the dualistic type of thinking which pitches one side against another in favour of a more strategic accommodation of the paradoxes of modernity.

38. Dews, P. 1991. 'Adorno, Poststructuralism and the Critique of Identity' pp. 1–22. In Benjamin 1982. *The Problems of Modernity*, p. 1.

39. Miller, D. 1987. *Material Culture and Mass Consumption*. Oxford: Blackwell, p. 64.

40. McRobbie, A. (ed.) 1997. *Back to Reality? Social Experience and Cultural Studies*. Manchester and New York: Manchester University Press.

41. Murdock, G. 1997. 'Cultural Studies at the Crossroads' pp. 58–73. In Ibid., p. 63.

The self-reflective sense of crisis experienced by academics redefining their own subject areas and practices, nowhere more acute than in cultural studies, has engendered a loss of confidence in tackling any question which might be interpreted as politically incorrect. This is a condition I am deeply aware of in proposing to engage head-on with the issue of expressive individualism embodied in the material culture of everyday life. But it is the evidence encountered in researching case studies that testify to some kind of common-sense personal agency that challenges the theoretical stance against such an approach. This is not to say that there is no common ground for interpretative analysis, but conversely to suggest that it is from the starting point of the dynamics of everyday life that such an analysis should flow. Though it is accepted that ethnography depends on analysis of local knowledge[43] and oral history is contingent upon the bias of the willing interviewee, these pragmatic methods of investigation are only valid insofar as their findings are properly contextualised. This trend runs in parallel with cultural studies' current critical self-analysis, giving primacy to a 'question-driven' practice that does not proceed from theory but rather is engaged in the production of theory.[44]

Although at a certain macro level generalisations are obviously invaluable for the insights they offer in matters regarding group identity, nevertheless they tend to reproduce the self-reflective 'lifestyles' of marketing. Even in the face of crude interpretations and while acknowledging the vital, almost desperate desire for individuality that drives the motor of consumerism, the irreducibility of its miriad faces is unamenable to study according to the rules of typological classification and therefore it is not surprising to find that it has not been a focus of much academic interest.[45] The defiant opposition to the ideological order of universalisation imposed by the imperatives of mass production

42. This is currently a widely used term indicating a pragmatic rather than a dogmatic or censorious approach adopted by many, from politicians – such as the so-called 'New' Labour branch of the Labour Party, to academics – such as the French social anthroplogist, Bruno Latour in *We Have Never Been Modern*. London: Harvester Wheatsheaf, 1991, pp. 29–31.

43. Geertz, C. 1983. *Local Knowledge: Further Essays on Interpretive Anthropology*. New York: Basic Books.

44. Morris, M. 1997. 'A Question of Cultural Studies', pp. 36–57. In McRobbie *Back to Reality?* p. 44.

45. Psychoanalysis has addressed the development of the psyche in the abstract and quotes clinical cases that deal with the abnormal.

and consumption, has emphasised the specificity of individuality as a burning contemporary desire. Yet its main claim to attention by academics has been as a butt for the condemnation of consumerism, accused of manufacturing and selling inauthentic desires to manipulate consumers into buying functionless goods.[46] And at the same time the uses of material culture studies are put towards identifying cultural practices of diversity – generation,[47] nationality,[48] gender and sexuality and so on.[49] Apart from within the discipline of psychoanalysis, the drive towards individuation still seems to be regarded as a no-go area of study to be avoided at all costs because of the dominant meaning individualism inherits from the social sciences that critiques capitalism for the 'reification of the self'.[50] Yet it is at the level of the personal where the individual relates to their social context and the world at large. Where the process of self-creation is played out modernity offers a sense of agency, even if only through the insignificant nuances of personal interpretation through which individuals can make an impact on their personal space and body.

Much of the work which has been done by popular culture theore-ticians has concentrated on transgressional self-knowing oppositional acts of appropriation to reveal fragmentary subcultural and tribal consumption practices but nevertheless as groups, rather than at the level of individual experience. The effect of this type of stereotyping is particularly clearly exemplified in the controversy surrounding the interpretation of 'street style' presented by the Victoria and Albert Museum, which in an exhibition of the same name showed examples as representative of different sub-cultural groups, only to find that individuals who claimed to actually belong to those groups did not necessarily agree with the Museum's interpretations.[51] The art historical method of characterising a typology around a representative example is contrary to real-life practice where the display of individualism is the motivating force. The curators' main object in the Street Style exhibition, however, was to present a case that disproved the 'trickle

46. For example see Haug,W.F. [1971] 1986. *Critique of Commodity Aesthetics: Appearance, Sexuality and Advertising in Capitalist Society.* Oxford: Polity.

47. Willis, P. 1993. *Common Culture.* Milton Keynes: Open University Press.

48. Miller, D. 1994. *Modernity: An Ethnographic Approach.* Oxford: Berg.

49. McRobbie 1997. *Back To Reality?*

50. Miller 1994. *Modernity: An Ethnographic Approach,* p. 142.

51. Polhemus, T. 1994. *Street Style: from sidewalk to catwalk.* London: Thames and Hudson.

down' theory by showing the influence on couture from below. This was demonstrated literally by using a two-tier display system showing the street-style fashions at ground level with the 'bubble-up' derivative exhibited above it. What was not taken into account was the tranformative and therefore neutralising effect of placing sub-cultural 'street' style within the doubly inflected establishment context of high fashion and the premier museum of design.

Studies that have concentrated on diversity within the mainstream have typified difference around static class analysis and ignored the possibility of considering mundane things as a dynamic site of social change. Although the insights revealed by Bourdieu's study of taste in the 1960s as an indicator of social distinction have been invaluable to the analysis of culture,[52] his typification of social classes is antipathetic to the common-sense view that taste is individual and cannot be predicted or determined. The case of reproduction furniture which purports to be 'the real thing' but is very much a modern confection, exemplifies how modernity has given new meaning to old things according to the requirements of contemporary cultural concern for experiencing authenticity.

The analysis of 'instances' in which things constitute the central focus, presented as cases of 'undesign' in Part II give some examples of strategies adopted by different interest groups to make sense of the complexities of modern life. This will centre on the issue of identity illustrated by means of specific examples of how people use things to mediate their sense of being in their own time and place in a social context. The appropriation of meaning happens at the point of production or conversely well beyond the act of consumption. Thus incorporating things into the material culture of everyday life can take place through such banal acts as the disposition of furniture within a domestic interior or the use of dress to 'fit-in', rather than dressing-up to 'stand-out', so to speak. Whereas in some cases an individual may find it alienating to be different and would rather feel part of a group by blending in, others set out to make a spectacle of themselves. Either way it is all too easy to overlook the banal as the site of meaning construction for it is in the ordinariness of the everyday that people interact with their own particular place and time. The circumscribed space in which they find themselves enmeshed is where there is any possibility of agency. And even while conforming, it is conversely the *untypical,* for which people strive in the desire for distinctive personal

---

52. Bourdieu 1984. *Distinction: A social critique of the judgement of taste.*

identity, that is one of the most complex and least likely subjects open to analysis that concerns this study.

A number of methods have been mooted by theoreticians trying to get at the subtle contradictory character of contemporary culture in the interest of taking it out of the theoretical into the reality of the social space where life is lived – such as Miller's theory of 'objectification'[53] and Grossberg's 'articulation'.[54] Miller's localised anthropological analysis of material culture identifies consumption as a form of 'creative appropriation' that enables the preservation of cultural specificity in contradiction to theories of globalisation. While Grossberg envisions how to conduct cultural studies in an international frame proposing 'articulation' as a form of multiple mapping of particular events, practices and apparatuses within specific spacial and temporal contexts as organisations of power in relation to 'the lived milieux of everyday life'.

Conclusion

In the paper that closed the 'Futures' conference[55] at the Tate Gallery in 1990, Dick Hebdige 'recommended salvaging banality in its original sense of the common, open to all – as a democratic virtue for the future' and suggested the metaphor of the journey – 'for the way we move forward through time' – invoking the sense of modernity that dares to imagine a better future. Hebdige's address was given nearly a decade ago, yet his evocative words still have a certain powerful resonance with the aspirations of many of the academics working in this field, although few would dare to express it in such romantic terms. In this, my attempt to 'salvage' the 'banal', by which I take to mean the everyday, however, it seems necessary first to recognise it. There is no naive way of rescuing the banal from the dross. Putting forward a criteria for picking out the 'right' stuff suggests some idea of what might constitute a category of everyday that is more 'pure' than the general. But that is not the intention since it is the very contingency of things in the kind of cultural context which actualises individual and social change that is sought. The process of selection needs to neither reduce and therefore

53. Ibid., p. 81.

54. Grossberg, L. 1997. 'Cultural studies, modern logics and theories of globalisation' pp. 7–35. In McRobbie *Back to reality?* p. 18.

55. Bird, J. et al. (eds) 1993. *Mapping the Futures: Local cultures, global change.* London and New York: Routledge.

restore the ordinary to banalisation, nor to transform it into a romantic interpretation – one of the accusations levelled at Hebdige's seminal work on sub-cultural styles.[56] The measure therefore taken here is to seek out the type of things that provide a space where some degree of what Miller calls 'appropriation' and Grossman, 'mobility', takes place and which I have referred to earlier as the role of artefacts in the process of social change.

56. Hebdige 1979. *Subculture: the Meaning of Style.*

Part II

Themes

Introduction

The chapters in Part II will discuss the characteristics of the themes introduced in the last chapter – authenticity, ephemerality and containment, selected for their special power in mediating issues of identity and social change in the context of the modern world. Authenticity is characterised as a desire for an encounter with a raw sense of reality that has not been contaminated by artificial refinement. As in art, 'authentic' refers to the original, and in design terms it suggests the first version from which copies and serial production derive. Authentic has an ambiguous relationship to time since it means original in the singular sense of never having taken a particular shape before, and the first of a series that follow in varying degrees of exactitude. Its most valued attribute is the sense of being in the presence of the one and only 'real thing', a quality often exploited by marketing which makes the original all the more meaningful. Age gives even more value to an original since it 'proves' its standing in the test of time. The case study of reproduction furniture is used to illustrate need for historicity to validate the authentic in an age of modernity where novelty is not unusual, and the omnipresence of virtual reality which emphasises the quality of materiality all the more.

While authenticity connotes continuity, ephemerality implies disjunction and plugs straight into the vibrant sense of passing time, illustrated in the figurative role of fashion which never stays still enough to become consolidated into a resolved form except in the case of the classic which as it enters that category stops being fashion. Forever on the move it reflects and materialises the contradictory nature of modernity that in the process of seeking resolution creates more complexity. Containment is the figure that provides a means of understanding this complexity reflected in the hybrid nature of contemporary material culture which cleaves to open-ended juxtaposition and metaphor rather than resolution.

Figure 11. Period style dining-room furniture from the 1939 Perrings catalogue.

Continuity: Authenticity and the Paradoxical Nature of Reproduction

if the differences between the genuine and the spurious be so light, why not collect the fake? The answer is why not *providing that one knows the difference between the two* [. . .] Inability to discern the difference between a real pearl and an imitation does not alter the fact that the one is real and the other imitation, it is of some importance that one should not pay pearl-price for the substitute, especially if one comes to sell again.[1]

Many turn-of-the-century books on furniture history such as T.A. Strange's *English Furniture, Decoration, Woodwork and Allied Arts* first published in 1900, were written by furniture designers and used as manuals by furniture makers, 'reproducers and fakers'. It was with this knowledge that Herbert Cescinsky's *The Gentle Art of Faking Furniture* published in 1931 from which the quotation above is taken, ostensibly addressed the collector.

The object of the exercise in this chapter is to consider design as a practice of modernity through an investigation of how meaning is actually inserted at the point of making the literal, material and existential fusion of skill, knowledge and ideals into an everyday type of artefact. Since the characteristic that gives the authentic its value is its inability to be reproduced, the concept of producing a 'reproduction' of an authentic piece is an impossible and contradictory project. By definition a 'reproduction' is a degraded version of that which it is reproducing. It represents the ultimate modern phenomenon, born out

1. Cescinsky, H. [1931] 1967. *The Gentle Art of Faking Furniture.* London: Chapman & Hall, p. vii.

of the tranformative conditions made possible by the processes of industrialisation that enabled the multiplication of the 'original', that has variously been thought to democratise access while at the same time increasing the auratic and exclusive authenticity of the original.[2]

Reproduction period furniture is a genre of objects particularly well suited to represent the characteristic of authenticity valued in contemporary material culture, both at the point of its manufacture and in the transformative activity of 'furnishing' which endows a space with meaning. Authenticity was assumed and therefore unknown as a special feature in traditional furniture production until the advent of modernism which brought in the category of the 'original design' with the establishment of the professional designer. Although among histories of furniture produced since the nineteenth century there are a number of contextualised studies as part of the history of design and material culture which consider social change, technological innovation, business organisation and labour conditions as determining,[3] most histories of furniture based on the conventional art historical model celebrate the unique features of fine examples of craftsmanship associated with particular makers and period styles.[4] The conventions of this approach reflected the hierarchical structure of the traditional furniture trades which discredited the majority of the furniture industry including the large number of reproduction furniture produced in the interwar years. Research by design historians like Pat Kirkham and Julia Porter have gone some way towards revealing the history and culture of mainstream furniture production that acknowledges the popularity of the antique styles.[5] At a more general level of cultural history

2. For example the debates around Walter Benjamin's essay 'The Work of Art in the Age of Mechanical Reproduction' in Arendt, H. (ed.) 1968. *Illuminations: Walter Benjamin Essays and Reflections*. New York: Schocken, pp. 217–51.

3. For example: Ames, K.L. 1992. *Death in the Dining Room and Other Tales of Victorian Culture*. Philadelphia: Temple University Press; Cieraad, I. (ed.) 1999. *At Home: An Anthropology of Domestic Space*. New York: Syracuse University Press; Edwards, C.D. 1993. *Victorian Furniture: Technology and Design*. Manchester: Manchester University Press; Moody, E. 1966. *Modern Furniture*. London: Studio Vista.

4. There are innumerable examples among which the most authoritative in this category are: Macquoid, P. 1904–1908. *History of Furniture in 4 Volumes: The Age of Oak, The Age of Walnut, The Age of Mahogany and The Age of Satinwood*. London: Lawrence & Bullen; Gloag, J. 1934. *English Furniture*. London: Adam & Charles Black; Fastnedge, R. 1955. *English Furniture Styles From 1500–1830*. Harmondsworth, Middlesex: Penguin.

5. Kirkham, P., Porter, J. and Mace, R. 1987. *Furnishing the World: The East London Furniture Trade 1830-1980*. London: Journeyman.

authenticity is recognised as a recent invention acknowledging the sham or false as alienting characteristics of modern culture, as well as the way institutions such as museums hold the power to confer value and authenticity.[6]

Whereas reproductions can be said to be honest copies, fakes are one of the wilder type of things which have much to reveal about the way that authenticity has been valued at different times. There is something both fascinating and dangerous about fakery because it puts us in touch with our relationship to truth, subverts concepts of beauty and falsifies history. But sometimes truth is too dangerous to confront and an illusion of authenticity is more acceptable.[7]

What is a fake today may not always have been considered as such. When the Victoria and Albert Museum's woodwork and furniture collection[8] was brought back to London from its place of safe-keeping after the Second World War, a number of pieces were declared fakes and summarily burned 'like heretics.[9] But since then the interest in authenticity as a relative term rather than a transcendent attribute has encouraged the study of fakes among museum professionals, acknowledging the vulnerability of expert opinion and challenging what Mark Jones, curator of the British Museum exhibition 'Fake? The Art of Deception', identified as the very 'conception of reality itself'.[10] The changing attitude to restoration no longer seeks to return objects to their original state having found that much can be learnt from the various stages in the history of an artefact. According to Jones fakes 'provide a unique portrait of the changing focuses of human desires, they also delineate the evolution of taste with unrivalled precision. Where there are fakes it is clear that there is a booming market in the

6. Phillips, D. 1997. *Exhibiting Authenticity*. Manchester and New York: Manchester University Press.

7. Lowenthal, D. 1990. 'Forging the Past', pp. 16–22. In Jones, M. (ed.) 1990. *Fake? The Art of Deception*. London: British Museum, p. 22.

8. The original collection first acquired by the predecessor of the Victoria and Albert Museum – the South Kensington Museum – was made up of a mixture of antique and contemporary pieces as well as 'forgeries' justified on the grounds of displaying 'fine workmanship' and disregarding the usual requirement of authenticity. (Phillips 1997. *Exhibiting Authenticity*, p. 8.) However, by the mid-twentieth century what had been admired as skilled craftsmanship in the late nineteenth century was considered Victorian bad taste and in an age of modernism 'copy' had become a bad word.

9. Cocks, A.S. 1980. *The Victoria and Albert Museum: The Making of the Collection*. Leicester: Windward, p. 78.

10. Jones 1990. *Fake? The Art of Deception*, p. 11.

things thus imitated'.[11] But while authenticity is sought in the original this does not mean that the desire for it can only be satisfied by the unique. Many consumers prefer 'new reproductions' to real antiques. And as Hillel Shwartz has pointed out 'the culture of the copy is pervasive . . . authenticity can no longer be rooted in singularity'.[12]

The following case study is based on the firm of J. Clarke, a small and unremarkable but typical furniture manufacturing firm operating in the traditional chair-making centre of High Wycombe, Buckinghamshire between 1893–1978.[13] The purpose of presenting this example is as a case through which to investigate the internal workings of the culture particular to the localised furniture trade in the Wycombe area where the advent of 'reproduction' had particular significance in respect of both the value of the tradesmen's skill and the product of its industry.

Originals and Copies

Authenticity is not an inherent feature in the culture of furniture production, it only comes into play when considered in relation to the category of the 'original' (design) which in turn only makes sense when it is predicated in contrast to the 'copy'. The concept of originality is closely associated with modernism, and the recent idea that it is possible for a designer to produce an entirely new design without reference to a traditional model.

In keeping with the conventions of the Wycombe furniture trade the furniture J. Clarke manufactured was not necessarily 'designed' by them. The firm's founder John Ralph Clarke came from a line of builder/cabinetmakers and was trained as a craftsman and maker of traditional furniture. Originating design was a wholly unfamiliar concept to the type of design he practised,[14] although to his son Maurice, who trained part-time at the local technical college, design was accepted as part of the maker's role. But by the third generation, Maurice's son Laurence,

11. Ibid., p. 13.

12. Shwartz, H. 1996. *The Culture of the Copy: Striking Likenesses, Unreasonable Facsimiles.* New York: Zone, p. 17.

13. The case study of J.Clarke derives from part of the research carried out for a doctoral thesis: J. Attfield 1992. 'The role of design in the relationship between furniture manufacture and its retailing 1939–1965: with initial reference to the furniture firm of J. Clarke', University of Brighton.

14. The small firm of J. Clarke was established by John Ralph Clarke (1874-1944) and carried on by his sons Alfred John and Maurice whose son Laurence joined the firm in 1966 and worked with his father until 1986 when the workshop closed down.

who completed his full-time training in furniture design in the mid-1960s, design was part of his vocabulary even though he had little chance to practice it in his father's workshop. While in the case of John Ralph Clarke – Laurence's grandfather – his first experience of working with new designs that departed from the rustic Windsor chair typical of the Wycombe area, was two chairs he made in 1904 that were designed and carved by his brother-in-law, Edmund Hutchinson,[15] in what was then called the 'New Art' style.

In traditional production processes, not only of furniture, but also of textiles, ceramics and other industries, reusing traditional patterns was standard practice and to some extent still remains so today. Trade designers were taught to draw by 'copying'. Whereas the concept of a 'copy' or 'to copy' only has negative connotations in the context of modern attitudes to design which prized originality. This is exemplified by the section on 'Furniture' in a report by the Committee on Industry and Trade (1927), which stated that 'generally speaking historical styles form the basis of all furniture design' and 'with few exceptions, the subservience to the *antique* extends downwards through the trade with a lessening of accuracy and refinement owing to considerations of cost and mass production'.[16] While in the *Furniture Working Party Report* of 1947 the complaint that 'for the past fifty years design in the furniture trade has been tied to imitations and derivations of past styles'[17] illustrates the continuing concern of mid-century advocates of modern design to encourage designers to find forms appropriate to contemporary manufacturing processes and what they considered to be the correct aesthetic in keeping with modern times.[18]

15. According to Maurice Clarke, Edmond Hutchinson, his uncle, was the son of one of the first makers in High Wycombe to introduce fine chair making learnt in London, to an area where until the late nineteenth century, a chair maker meant 'a maker of Windsor chairs', and the main source of business was supplying material for chair making in other areas. Attfield, J. 1992. 'The role of design', p. 89; Mayes, J.L. 1960. *History of Chairmaking in High Wycombe*. London: Routledge & Kegan Paul.

16. *Factors in Industrial and Commercial Efficiency*, HMSO, 1927, pp. 360-1. In the same report the section on Glassware (p. 367) states: 'The designer usually spends only a small proportion of his time creating new designs, the remainder being employed in adapting old designs . . .' On the Registration of Silverware and Electroplate designs the same report commented that 'Two or three of the higher-class firms register their designs, but find that, nevertheless, they are usually copied.'

17. *Furniture Working Party Report*, HMSO, 1947, p. 117.

18. The committee which drew up the *Furniture Working Party Report* included a number of would-be modern design reformers such as Gordon Russell and Jack Pritchard during

Factories like J. Clarke did not use drawing in their method of designing. They depended on producing 'moulds' or templates from which chair legs or other parts were cut, and subsequently conserved for reuse. It was also quite customary for Clarkes and other small makers, not known for branded goods, to copy the designs of better-known firms.[19] Copyright set by patents and registered designs could always be skirted by slight variations from the original.[20] A letter from one of J. Clarke's sales representatives working for them in 1939, demonstrates his attempt at securing a contract order by suggesting one of Clarkes' own 'Criterion Cord' models as an alternative to the well-known branded chairs by Parker-Knoll on which their design was based.

> Send at once your lowest price for 12 chairs in No. 2031 for Hotel contract .... We have recommended Criterion Cord chairs against Parker-Knoll and if we secure the order there will be more to follow.[21]

This instance is an example of how Clarkes operated within the competitive context of the late 1930s when it was not unusual to take orders for copies purposely undercutting the better-known firms' products. Clarkes' copies of Parker-Knoll were also produced in a better quality and sold at a higher price. Sales records in the mid-1960s show that Clarkes were still making 'specials' (non-standard designs) and taking instructions from their sales representatives to copy other well-known branded designs such as 'Fyne Lady', the proprietary name used by Stones of Banbury. This type of copying, typical of a firm which did not set itself up as a market leader, was more to do with their pragmatic response to market trends as interpreted by the retail trade and relayed to them through their intermediaries – the sales representatives. Clarkes' mainstream designs had nothing to do with keeping to traditional forms in any authentic sense, since they treated design as a pragmatic practice rather than prescribing limitations on principles of correctness. Their most highly valued type of work was in 'reproduction', a more exclusive branch of their repertoire of production. It was not 'designed'

a period in which there was a concerted attempt to reform design practice in keeping with modern industrial methods of production. Maguire, P.J. and Woodham, J.M. (eds.) 1997. *Design and Cultural Politics in Postwar Britain*. London: Leicester University Press.

19. Turner, C. 1955. *The Parker Knoll Collection*, Northampton: Vernon.

20. In Worden, S. 1980. *Furniture for the Living Room* [unpublished PhD thesis] Brighton: University of Brighton, the author discusses the development of the Clarke Criterion Cord spring, a copied variation of Parker-Knoll's patented spring, in the 1930s.

in the modern meaning of the word but belonged to another category of copy based on the idea of authenticity.

The Classic and the Reproduction

Reproduction was the category on which Clarkes formed their design criteria, as opposed to their pragmatic practice in which they were not averse to the sort of copying described above. Reproduction was based on a set of classic period styles which informed their design vocabulary and provided the model against which judgements were made. This ideal type was the traditional English furniture of the eighteenth century, in Cuban mahogany if it was 'Chippendale' style, or English walnut if it was 'Queen Anne' or 'William and Mary', and manufactured by means of labour-intensive highly skilled techniques of making, carving and polishing acquired in the traditional way through trade apprenticeship.

Clarkes' practice of producing 'specials', that is designs based on existing models but to the client's own specifications, was often the starting point of a model that later became a 'running line'. Countless subtle variations based on previous models were added to the Clarkes' repertoire over the years, clearly pointing to the influence of changing fashions. But novelty was never achieved by any deliberate break from tradition even though many unlikely hybrid versions were produced, such as the anachronistic Jacobean style 'easy' chair, a type unknown in the seventeenth century and produced for the Dutch export market in the 1960s.[22] The common feature shared by all the variations they produced was their affinity with previous forms evolved over time. Rather than the result of a wholehearted embrace of industrialisation, as in the case of those makers of modern furniture who deliberately set out to reform their method of production in order to be able to use new materials and produce modern designs thought to be more in keeping with modern times,[23] Clarkes relied on traditional workshop processes of manufacture and handcraft, and always worked in wood. Although Clarkes operated in the context of an established hierarchy of types of furniture trade, they moved within different sectors pragmatically picking up work where they could get it, although their

21. Letter from Sydney Trevett to J. Clarke, 27 January 1939. Archive of Art and Design (AAD) 11/4001-1986: Correspondence Reps 1939 and AAD 11/4194-1986 Orders 1939.

22. Attfield 1992. 'The role of design', p. 40.

23. Moody 1966. *Modern Furniture.*

preferred type was in exclusive, skilled, fine chairmaking. However the vast range and number of designs produced over the lifetime of the firm, evident in their written and photographic records,[24] shows a surprising diversity of forms, the large majority of which were not necessarily entirely hand-crafted items, nor could be remotely associated with straight reproductions of fine examples of English antiques. At their most successful Clarkes were producing an innovative type of modern armchair which, though based on the winged Queen Anne, used modern upholstery techniques using innovative spring technology.[25] It was only after the Second World War that they reverted to more traditional forms when they could not keep up with their more up-to-date competitors.

Traditional designs (classics) in the furniture-making culture of the Wycombe trade signified those designs that had acquired that status over time; even though when they first appeared they may have been a departure from tradition, such as the changes resulting from walnut to mahogany in the eighteenth century.[26] The radical changes in furniture design were explained by the availability of different types of imported woods with different properties enabling, for example, more delicate members and finer carving, or expanses of veneer to exploit the decorative qualities of a highly figured grain. Among traditional makers there was never any question of furniture being made from any material other than wood.

'Reproduction' is a very particular category of furniture in the furniture maker's vocabulary, referring directly to the typical repertoire of classical period styles, but by its own announcement a simulation of the real thing. There was clearly a difference between the copy, the reproduction and the 'original design' among traditional makers like Clarkes whose highest aspiration was to produce the most accurate reproduction of the classic models of historic English furniture styles. Maurice Clarke spoke of the long hours he spent in the Victoria and Albert Museum copying fine examples of chairs. Reproduction even in its wildest most inaccurate versions would appear to have had more of an affinity with a sense of authenticity than 'originality', the latter being a modern concept based on the assumption that it is possible to

24. Attfield 1992. 'The role of design'. See Chapter 3: 'Clarkes' Chair Designs and Best Sellers', pp. 61–124.

25. Worden, S. 1989. 'The Development of the Fireside Chair 1928–1940' pp. 5–9. In *Antique Collecting*, Vol. 24, No. 2.

26. Macquoid 1904–1908. *History of Furniture.*

create an entirely novel form never produced before, requiring new methods of manufacturing and non-traditional materials.

Authenticity

In order to point out the historical specificity of the meaning of authenticity in furniture design, an illustrative comparison can be made between the period before and after the First World War. Stefan Muthesius has discussed the revival of interest in 'old' furniture between 1870 and 1910 when he attributed the emergence of reproduction styles to the popularity of revivalism.[27] Muthesius's argument is predicated on the greater value accorded by the arts and crafts movement to the more authentic 'materiality of furniture' over that of its style or 'art' content, seen at that time to be an imposed form of artificiality. This went together with the disapproval of fashion, novelty and the 'absurd love of change', which Muthesius approvingly analysed as an 'anti-consumerist' attitude,[28] amongst the arbiters of good taste such as Pugin, Ruskin and Eastlake. Muthesius observed the solidity of the timber joint, the tradition of oak, and the patina[29] formed by the built-up layers of grime and wear over many years, to be the characteristics most sought after in the search for authenticity in furniture. Indeed, the concern in joints is still apparent in the advice offered by later advocates of good design like John Gloag who in 1934 wrote, advising the inexperienced furniture buyer of post-war 'contemporary' furniture not to take the goods at face value:

> investigate all joints. Ornament applied to the surface of a cabinet or wardrobe or bookcase may hide careless construction. Avoid applied ornament, which often expresses the taste of the furniture manufacturer trying to please the retail buyer and is generally unspeakable. Look all round a piece of furniture, and underneath and on top of it too.[30]

In the case of Clarkes it has been noted that although a small firm, it produced a huge variety of different types of chairs in the course of its

27. Muthesius, S. 1988. 'Why do we buy old furniture? Aspects of the authentic antique in Britain 1870–1910', pp. 231–54. In *Art History*, Vol. 11, No. 2, June.

28. Ibid., p. 235.

29. Patina was reproduced in the form of 'antique finish' in all qualities of reproduction furniture down to the cheapest most inauthentic 'repro'.

30. Gloag [1934] 1973. *English Furniture*, p. 163.

existence. But it was from variations and reproduction of traditional eighteenth-century English chairs, in which Maurice Clarke could exercise his skill as a furniture designer and maker, that he derived the greatest personal satisfaction. His pride came from a sense of being associated with the chair before it became transformed into a commodity, a sentiment expressed as 'making furniture and not money'.[31]

In the 1940s the Utility range of wartime furniture designs were brought in by the government of the day to control distribution of rationed materials, labour and goods. Maurice Clarke refused to recognise the Utility range as 'real' design because it was devised for a deskilled workforce, thus removing the maker's control over the design process and making his craft skill redundant. So although it may at first seem contradictory that 'reproductions' should be valued as more authentic than new designs, it makes sense from the maker's perspective. The process of designing by pragmatic adaptation typical of vernacular design, does not lend itself to the practice of historical dating that links a particular model to a given date. Evolutionary design is much more in keeping with a traditional craft practice based on a more organic series of slow change of form over long periods of time. This is very similar to David Lowenthal's observations of 'authentic early musicians' who

> Until recently [. . .] worked within a lengthy living tradition. They treated the past as a continuous corridor leading to the present'. Nineteenth-century performers altered Bach to retain the currency of his music. Adapting Bach's clavier works for the modern pianoforte enabled them [. . .] more truly to realise Bach's own aims. By contrast those who now perform with conscious fidelity to original forms use early music as a storehouse, fashioning repertoires from relics of other times. They demand historical purity unthinkable when the present was an unbroken extension of the past. The liberties that Liszt took with Bach [. . .] are now condemned as frauds analogous to the restorations for which Ruskin and Morris condemned Victorian restorers like Giles Gilbert Scott.

Generally within the furniture trade hierarchy the upper echelons were occupied by those firms which upheld a traditional image indicating links with a pre-industrial age of authentic fine craftsman-

31. Attfield, J. 1990. 'Then we were making furniture, and not money': A case study of J. Clarke, Wycombe furniture makers', pp. 54–7. In *Oral History.* Vol. 18, No. 2 'The Crafts'.

ship. In furnishing shops, this image was maintained preferably through an inherited[32] or a purchased[33] association with a well-established firm of makers, even long after they had ceased being manufacturers. In these cases the style of furniture they preferred to be associated with was invariably reproduction although alongside the traditional they also stocked modern furniture and kept up with fashionable trends in furnishing styles.

The advocates of 'good design' according to the principles of modernism like the firm of Heal's, despised reproduction and any kind of 'style' in the fashionable sense, valuing authenticity in the form of modern, 'honest' design, which did not pretend to be anything it was not, particularly 'old' if it was new. Their concern with authenticity took a different shape and was referred to in terms of integrity, reason and use rather than age and tradition. While reproduction furniture, so obvious an artificial confection, was also seen by some factions of the furniture trade as authentic. Reproduction furniture is therefore a good medium through which to see how the concept of authenticity takes on different forms. It also illustrates the role of design in the objectification of authenticity raising the contradictory opposition between the 'real' and the artificial. Amongst Maurice Clarke's generation of traditional makers design was subsumed as an integral common-sense aspect of making, rather than considered as a separate intellectual endeavour.

Amongst the furniture trades the terms 'reproduction' or 'repro' conventionally apply to copies of old furniture in styles which are recognisable as belonging to a period and often referred to by maker/designer (Chippendale, Sheraton, etc.), or period in the monarchy (Regency, Queen Anne, etc.). Most references to 'reproduction' in the literature of furniture history[34] discuss it in terms of authenticity, making a distinction between 'an honest reproduction', taken to mean 'an exact copy' of the original, and a 'fake' antique,[35] in which dating, origins and provenance, used to establish the genuine antique would

32. As for example Waring & Gillow.

33. As for example Maples.

34. See Note No. 4 above for some titles among the vast literature on the history of furniture, much of it aimed at the connoisseur giving instruction on how to spot authenticity.

35. Agius, P. 1978. *British Furniture 1880–1915*. London: Antique Collectors Club. See Chapter Seven: 'Exact Copies and Fakes'.

have had to be concealed or falsified.[36] Reproduction might appear to be the obvious opposite to authentic, but it does not pretend to be what it is not and is only made to signify by virtue of the perceived existence of an original model which it purports to reproduce.

Pat Kirkham has suggested that 'reproduction' was used to 'evoke the past'[37] while Muthesius has explained it in historical terms as deriving from the interest in genuine antiques during the nineteenth century, inspired by a desire for the 'materiality' of old furniture. It could be argued that 'materiality' in this context is synonymous with authenticity and could also be related to Bourdieu's analysis of taste as a means of social distinction in which antiques are the preoccupations of the privileged classes as a sign of cultural pedigree.[38] In the hierarchy of furniture there was a range of qualities of reproduction from cheap 'repro' or 'dark' (stained) furniture of indeterminate style at the bottom end and the fine copies of English furniture based on particular examples at the top, with various shades of middle between. Firms like Parker-Knoll made great play of their own collection of antique pieces to show the provenance of their designs as genuinely period.[39]

From Maurice Clarke's accounts of chairmaking[40] it is evident that reproduction may have been the copy of a style, but to a traditional maker like him it represented real labour in terms of skill. Whereas to the type of professional designers who supported the values of the good design movement, and delegated the work of making, reproduction was a copy of an old design and required no originality and therefore represented no work on their part.

The concept of 'real' furniture, however, can also be seen to operate in 'good design' criticism from the perspective of furniture history experts like Gloag who wrote about 'pseudo handwork' and 'furniture substitute' where the reference was not necessarily referring to old pieces. In the furniture trade authenticity adhered not just to traditional style but to a concept of 'quality' of workmanship and materials which was not always visible. An example of the transition from hand to

36. There are of course copies of 'old' modern pieces but these are usually called 'modern classics' and do not apply to the category under discussion.

37. Kirkham, P. 1987 'Furniture History' pp. 58–85. In Conway, H. *Design History: A Students' Handbook*. London: George Allen & Unwin, p. 67.

38. Bourdieu, P. 1984. *Distinction: A Social Critique of the Judgement of Taste*. London: Routledge & Kegan Paul.

39. Turner, C. 1955. *The Parker-Knoll Collection*. Northampton: Vernon.

40. Recorded interviews. For transcribed extracts see Attfield 1992. 'The role of design'.

machine production in furniture trade was the compromise made to adapt to the material economy of the Second World War when the government enforced rationing of materials, labour and goods through the Utility scheme.[41] The most widely used of the Utility designs incorporated the solid timber joint in conjunction with frame and panel construction of the type used in medieval joinery. But while the motifs that Muthesius characterises as redolent of 'materiality' – the joints and patina from the revival of interest in old furniture and romantic notions of the medieval crafts – Gloag had more modern craftsmanship in mind when he referred to plywood as a 'good' material, and warned that 'it must be properly used: not tacked on to the frame'.[42] To determine if plywood was 'properly used' required particular attention, because although Gloag asserted that to be well designed, furniture had to be 'visibly well made', the ply-frame construction of 'sheathed' ply skin depended on being invisibly glued over a hidden frame to achieve the perfect flush streamlined finish. Gloag's modernist yet historicist interpretation of authenticity rejected reproduction in favour of so-called 'real English tradition' referring to a kind of integrity derived from honesty, which according to him had been

> submerged by a wave of faking and imitation: and the real English genius for design was masked by a false 'Olde England' – a shoddy and flimsy form of taste which still persists [in 1973]. Only very slowly is it being realised that; 'ye olde England' is neither old nor English but shallow sham, and the real English tradition in design is [. . .] alive today [. . .] in the wayside shelter of glass and steel [. . .] in the cast iron telephone kiosks [. . .] In such work as the spirit of England resides: exuberant and vivid as ever, different in execution but changeless in character.[43]

With designs such as Chippendale-style chairs which survived the eighteenth century well into the nineteenth and were still being made in the traditional way by chairmakers like John Clarke, it is difficult to draw a distinct line between 'genuine' and 'copy'. There was no sentiment or wish to evoke the past in Maurice Clarke's preference for the traditional English chair. To him it was a living tradition existing in the present as long as the craft continued to be passed on through

---

41. Attfield, J. ed. 1999. *Utility Reassessed: The role of ethics in the practice of design.* Manchester and New York: Manchester University Press.

42. Gloag 1973. *English Furniture*, p. 163.

43. Gloag, J. 1947b, *The English Tradition in Design.* Harmondsworth: Penguin, p. 35.

the apprenticeship system, a cause he actively pursued throughout his career – training apprentices, teaching and campaigning. Among the many initiatives in pursuance of his belief was a letter he wrote to a trade associate in 1945 in which he warned against what he foresaw would be the consequence of rationalisation, a first step put in place by the Utility scheme in anticipation of post-war reforms.

> The craft side has been the foundation of the Industry. If a policy of ruthless efficiency is pursued great harm will ultimately be done to the whole Industry and firms of value to the country will disappear.[44]

The History of Reproduction Furniture

The official recognition of the term 'reproduction' by the British Antique Dealers Association in 1918, marked a distinction between 'genuine' and 'copy'. Regulations were instituted insisting that members mark 'reproductions' as such when displayed alongside originals.[45] This would have meant that a maker could no longer make an 'original' in a classic style; an 'original' could no longer be new. Traditionally 'cabinet makers' in Chippendale's time may also have been what Wills in his treatise on *Craftsmen and Cabinet-makers of Classic English Furniture* [46] called 'lesser men who were solely furniture retailers', selling ready-made and second-hand furniture rather than 'actual working cabinet-makers'. Before furniture specifically sold as 'antiques' there is no way of telling how much of what was sold was new or used. There have always been some furniture retailers who specialised in 'second-hand' for those who could not afford to buy new. But from the 1830s onwards some specialist shops in London were known to have advertised old furniture as luxury items 'unsuitable for persons in moderate circum-stances'.[47] But whether that was because it was valued on account of its quality or its 'antiqueness' is not clear.

Michael Thompson's rubbish theory can be applied to explain the changes in the way in which old furniture has been valued at different times. When dealers transformed 'second-hand junk' into 'antiques',

44. Letter from M.Clarke to M.A.Benson, 29 November 1945. Archive of Art and Design (AAD), National Art Library Special Collections, London. AAD 11/3951-1986.

45. Muthesius 1988, p. 243.

46. Wills, G. 1974. *Craftsmen and Cabinet-makers of Classic English Furniture*. London: John Bartholomew.

47. Ibid.

they conferred it with value more durable than that available from more transient areas of commodification such as that which operates in the ephemeral fashion system.[48] Thompson's example of the transformation of a Georgian terrace from 'rat infested slum' into 'glorious heritage', through the process known in the housing market as 'gentrification', is analogous to the revival of medievalism which prompted the appreciation of the old furniture discussed by Muthesius.

The revival of old styles during the nineteenth century made the difference between the real antique from the new imitating the old (reproduction), much more self conscious. It also brought into prominence the danger of 'fakes', passed off as antiques. The category 'Antique Furniture Makers' listed in the 1880s' London directories shows that the best 'high quality copies' such as those made by Gillows of Lancaster and Edwin Skull of High Wycombe,[49] although sold as reproductions were, nevertheless intended to deceive. One firm assured their clientele that

> in appearance they possess just that old time-worn effect which gives such charm to the old work [...] no pains are spared to collect the materials necessary for this in the nature of old wood for the frames, old velvets and embroideries, etc, for the covering, with a result which has frequently deceived the expert.[50]

The fake in Cescinsky's vocabulary was a copy that could pass as 'genuine', and it was that authenticity which gave it 'its rarity, and, in consequence, its value.[51] A 'faker' he wrote 'is quite a worthy individual ... at the mercy of the dealer ... doing good by stealth, and merely catering for a popular demand'. According to him 'good faking commences ... only where reproduction finishes' while the 'commercial fakers' who worked for 'quasi-antique dealers' and 'so-called lady decorators' did not waste 'good faking' on those who were easily deceived.[52] Here we see again a good example of what Bourdieu described as the 'aristocracy of culture' in which only those educated

48. Thompson, M. 1979. *Rubbish Theory: The Creation and Destruction of Value.* Oxford: Oxford University Press.

49. Agius 1978, p. 145.

50. Hindley and Wilkinson Ltd catalogue between 1900-1912 cited in Agius 1978, p. 146.

51. Ibid., p. 15.

52. Ibid., p. 4.

enough would recognise the subtle difference between a 'good' and a 'poor' fake. But there are other implications for the valuation of the craftsman's skill which Cescinsky refers to vaguely in the fine distinction he made between the 'good' fake and the 'reproduction'. We can guess that he valued the good faker above the maker of the 'reproduction', for although dishonest, a good faker was a skilful expert. Whereas a 'reproduction' according to Cescinsky was only a 'modern copy' reproducing

> everything but the appearance of antiquity . . . no attempt will have been made to produce even the effect of age, other than perhaps, by a vile so-called 'antique shading' of the surface or by a glass-papering which leaves the bare wood exposed through its stain, known in the trade as an 'antique finish'.[53]

He went on to explain in great detail that there was no set formula for the detection of fakes and that an informed collector could only learn through experience and understanding the way a faker worked. In other words it was only a faker who could really spot a fake. By advising that 'good fakes' did not necessarily reproduce existing pieces or follow a set formula to get their antique effect, he explained that the best way to inform the readers on the tricks of the trade was to go through a number of examples and describe how each was achieved. Thus while ostensibly advising the discerning collector, at the same time he was providing the perfect excuse for giving detailed instruction in 'how each piece may be forged'.

Cescinsky's 'true collector [. . .] with a cultured eye' to whom a fake 'is a thing of sham and deceit', would only be satisfied by a 'fine piece'. Merely being 'antique' did not make it necessarily worth collecting. For all his preference for the antique, Cescinsky recognised the benefits of modern machinery and the factory system which rewarded the fine furniture maker with better pay and conditions.[54] This acknowledgement revealed an affinity with attitudes in tune with modernism and the good design ethic in circulation in the 1930s through the legacy of the politics of the arts and crafts movement and the efforts of bodies like the Design and Industries Association. Cescinsky was a dealer in antiques and a professional connoisseur with the knowledge to discrimi-

---

53. Ibid., p. 6.
54. Cescinsky, H. 1925. 'America: Glimpses into Furniture Factories', pp. 386–7. In *Cabinet Maker*, May 23, 1925.

nate and advise on the difference between 'poor' and 'good' taste based on his understanding of the different categories of fakes, antiques, handcraftsmanship and machine-manufactured designs. Of craftsmanship he wrote:

> If mere perfection of workmanship be the criterion, then the maker of the present-day is far better equipped, and can do, without effort, what his eighteenth century fellow achieved only with great labour and skill [. . .] What is then implied by this ignorant laudation of the old makers?[55]

Furnishers like Waring & Gillow and Maples, in an effort to influence the public to buy their fine reproductions in preference to antiques, similarly advised their customers that 'old' did not necessarily mean 'good'. While in answering his own question, Cescinsky revealed his own preference for eighteenth-century styles over those of earlier periods which spawned the popular 'Jaco' (Jacobean style) of the inter-war period, and explained the vogue for heavy oak reproduction as deriving from the nineteenth century:

> when furniture was valued for its weight [. . .] and when such atrocities as Early English and Domestic Gothic were regarded as the last word in taste.[56]

The Authenticity of 'Reasonable' Furniture

Authenticity in the context of the modern ideals objectified in the good design movement just before the Second World War took a different form to that which demanded direct contact with age which could only be provided through what Cescinsky called the 'original patine' of old furniture. Authenticity in modern furniture was to do with rationality, or as the 1939 Heal's catalogue described it – 'Reasonable Furniture'.[57] 'Reasonable', it explained, referred to 'more than the mere colloquial use of the word by which it is made synonymous with "cheap" '. It referred to *real* furniture as opposed to 'what passes for furniture made of faulty materials, put together in the flimsiest way ("blown together", the cabinet maker calls it), its worst blemishes

---

55. Cescinsky 1967. *The Gentle Art of Faking Furniture*, p. 15.

56. Ibid.

57. Heal & Son Ltd. *Reasonable Furniture & Furnishings for Small Houses, Cottages and Flats*, 1939.

concealed by machine-made ornament'. 'Indeed', it declared, 'it may fairly be called *furniture substitute'*. While the 'jerry-built goods taking in vain the names of Chippendale and Sheraton' made furniture to sell, Heal's furniture purported to be

> made to use. The pieces [. . .] are planned first of all for convenience and durability and secondly with an eye to good proportion and pleasant outline, their beauty is of the kind that is an inherent quality and not of the kind that has to be stuck on afterwards to mask intrinsic ugliness [. . .] where the machine makes for economy it has been used frankly and straight-forwardly, with due regard to its possibilities and limitations, and not as a shamefaced accomplice in the turning out of pseudo handwork.

The Clarkes were also concerned with the kind of authenticity they distinguished between 'making furniture' and 'making money'. Much value was placed on 'quality' through features invisible to the retail customer, such as the weight of the frame hidden by the upholstery and the hand-applied finish. It would appear that the bestowal of authenticity provided a means through which artefacts such as furniture could create a sense of eluding or resisting commodification by retaining what Muthesius, referring to authenticity, called their 'materiality'. The medieval style of furniture called attention to the joints and rustic construction, the solidity of the wood, on heaviness and generosity of size. The supposition of the furniture-buying public at that time, in contrast to the affluent post-Second World War period was to buy for a lifetime. The derivative Elizabethan and Jacobean styles adapted for the smaller inter-war house became the 'dark' stained (antique finish) furniture of indeterminate 'repro' style considered a debasement, both by connoisseurs of antiques and advocates of modern design.

The 'realness' of furniture for makers like Clarkes seems to have been in traditional methods of manufacture and real wood as opposed to the reconstituted wood products such as ply and blockboard. While would-be 'good design' reformers like John Gloag and Gordon Russell who never joined the modern movement wholeheartedly, preferring traditional furniture forms derived from the arts and crafts movement and the golden age of classic English furniture, not only because they considered them more 'genuine' than the 'spurious modern antiques', but because they had connections with a traditional Englishness.

The main motifs that appear to have signified authenticity among traditionalists were oldness and the elusive attribute of quality. 'Quality' could signify hand workmanship which was not necessarily 'fine' and would sometimes be interpreted as more genuine when it was roughly finished indicating the imperfections of hand production rather than a perfect machine-like finish. The value of quality, age, handcraftsmanship and tradition could be represented in reproduction-style furniture to denote 'antique'. It did not include the features that gave the genuine antique its special value. The reproduction could not offer the special attribute of scarcity, singularity, uniqueness and rarity which presence and materiality alone could confer – a higher value reflected in the price. This is not meant to infer that antiques avoided commodification, although they may well have connoted a certain distance from the marketplace. While in the context of modernism authenticity applied self-referentially to interpretations of the principles of 'good design' – 'fitness for purpose', 'form follows function', durability, economy and standardisation – qualities that referred to use value, pretending that the form was immaterial and that the look naturally followed on from conforming to the production of the correct solution.

Authenticity, Time and History

Spooner's anthropological analysis of the value placed on authenticity in the Western taste for oriental carpets provides a model which can also usefully be applied to this study. His definition that 'authenticity is a conceptualisation of elusive, inadequately defined, other cultural, socially ordered genuiness' and a 'form of cultural discrimination projected into objects' can be mapped on to the question of taste for authenticity in furniture. 'Genuineness' in this connection refers to a past prior to the modern period. Conversely, Gloag interpreted it to refer to a future ideal in which Englishness, innovation and change would be magically transformed into an appropriate 'contemporary' style for the modern period. The fact that the question of what constituted an 'original' only arose in a period when 'antique' furniture became a category in its own right, is central to this analysis. In defining the antique along strictly temporal lines, the category of the 'reproduction' was brought into existence by default. It highlights the fact that 'originality' only became a concern in modern design when a break from tradition and craft production became an issue. Spooner explains the concern for authenticity as historical, arising

at a particular stage in our evolution – when with the appearance of mechanically produced clone-commodities we began to distinguish between social meaning of handcraft and that of mechanical production, as well as between uniqueness and easy replaceability. [. . .] Authenticity is a form of cultural discrimination projected onto objects. But it does not in fact inhere in the object but derives from our concern with it. In seeking authenticity people are able to use commodities to express themselves and fix points of security and order in an amorphous modern society.[58]

Conclusion

Within the culture of furniture makers like J.Clarke, brought up in the tradition of the dissemination of skills through the apprenticeship system, there was no equivalent to the modern concept of 'design', either as a practice or a product. Specialised modern design education taught second- and third-generation Clarkes to approach design as a problem to be broached from first principles and provided them with the techniques to conceptualise their ideas through drawing. Although equipped with qualifications however, their formal design education did not provide them with entry into the strictly class-based professional design circle, nor did their design expertise command respect within the trade which at best held it as an alien practice and at worst regarded it with contempt. The latter was an attitude shared by Maurice Clarke whose early experience in attempting to gain commissions through joining a professional association met with no success, only served to reinforce his identification with his father's furniture trade rather than as a designer. Therefore it is not surprising to find that their formal education had little impact on either Maurice's or his son Laurence's careers. Far more formative was what they learnt 'at the bench' in the Clarke workshop and from the firm's habit of flexible response to their clients' demands, and not taking risks by producing innovative models. Maurice Clarke's persistent reluctance to modernise was the only, but in the end fatal, failure to compromise and adapt to changing times.

Design in the Clarkes' book was not abstract but material. They did not approach it as a problem that could be solved in an entirely new way through an intellectual process or by means of drawing. The solutions always lay in the pragmatic adaptation of something that had been done well before, a tried and tested form which held no risk

---

58. Spooner, B. 1986. 'Weavers and Dealers: The authenticity of an oriental carpet', pp. 195–235. In Appadurai, A. (ed.) *The Social Life of Things: Commodities in Cultural Perspective*. Cambridge: Cambridge University Press, p. 226.

of failure. To them a 'design' was a model that had no specific date and had more affinity with a timeless craft tradition than a fashion system. There are no records in the Clarke papers of when specific designs were first introduced. There is evidence of some attempt at introducing a few new models at certain times of the year, but these were always variations of models that had previously sold well and was probably instigated by client demand in the first place. Even when they used contemporary styling it would be based on forms like the Queen Anne wing armchair. It is therefore reasonable to conclude that reproduction of traditional forms was the typical form produced by J. Clarke. Once the chairs were transformed from products to commodities and entered distribution channels they joined a fragmented and complex structure of furniture retailing outlets in which they took their place among a massive selection of different furniture types. In the context of the retail trade they objectified a particular set of values to those envisaged by their makers. In much the same way as Spooner observed of the oriental carpet – it was the dealers (furniture retailers) rather than the weavers (furniture makers) who informed the public of 'the lore' of their wares. Clarkes conformed to the traditional hierarchy of the furniture trade, maintaining their craftsmanship until the end. But once their products entered the retail shops, they no longer had control over their meaning. In the furniture hierarchy it was the antique furniture dealers like Strange who informed the public of 'the lore' of antique furniture which indirectly had an impact on the design of reproduction furniture. Thus the authenticity on which the meaning of 'antique' depended was transmitted through the various allusions to the classic repertoire of English period styles. While in contemporary styles it was the professional designers in the good design movement who occupied the top of the hierarchy and informed the public of the lore of modern furniture. And as we have seen even modern furniture needed to be imbued with a sense of authenticity but defined according to an entirely different set of criteria, 'new' rather than 'old', 'simple' rather than 'fancy' and so on. But ultimately it was the realness, the materiality, the authenticity of the piece which gave it a sense of presence in a world increasingly invaded by the ephemerality of constant change, and which seemed to be valued by the generation of designers and consumers troubled by the complexity of modernity.

One of the most significant characteristics of reproduction is the contradictory meaning it holds in the context of modernity, in that a 'reproduction' is by its own announcement a copy yet at the same time it objectifies authenticity even though it is *not,* nor does it pretend to be, that most valuable of commodities in this modern age – the real thing. The other significant feature of the objectification of authenticity in the form of the reproduction is the importance of the historical context in which this phenomenon was made manifest. The specific moment which set the rules of what was to constitute an 'antique' – that only an object which was at least one hundred years old could qualify as such – at the same time redefined traditional furniture renaming it 'reproduction'. That act of nomenclature deprived current traditional craft production as obsolete by pronouncing newly produced furniture within the culture or 'lore' of the furniture trade as not 'the real thing'. But it was within the good design movement that the objectification of authenticity was realised in terms of innovation. The return to first principles in search of the 'original' meaning was intended to produce the model of the prototype for reproduction, not as in a copy or a turning to the past for emulation, but in a standardised model adapted to mass production. During the period in question it was envisaged that such a process would popularise the perfect design, the modern 'classic' turning towards the future as the time-place in which such an enterprise could eventually be effected.

Change: The Ephemeral Materiality of Identity

I had already decided upon some of my mementoes, including a 1940s black velvet coat which my mother bought second-hand from the local bookmaker's wife (who could afford more expensive clothes than any of the other women in the pit village); an object still so powerfully redolent of memories of the gutsy ways in which one woman negotiated enjoying life to the full . . . that my wearing it almost makes her 'real' and almost makes me her.[1]

Pat Kirkham's powerfully resonant reminiscence of the significance of the item she chose for herself from her mother' effects while distributing her possessions after her death, is one example of the way in which objects mediate emotions, relationships and identities. Had the object been a piece of furniture, an ornament or a book she could not have clothed herself in her mother's persona in quite the same way. Clothing and textiles have a particularly intimate quality because they lie next to the skin and inhabit the spaces of private life helping to negotiate the inner self with the outside world.

This chapter will make a case for the place of textiles in the material culture of everyday life as an embodiment of self and group identity, particularly with reference to time in relation to age, generation and stages in the life cycle. D.W. Winnicott's transitional object[2] – the baby's blanket – is postulated as the exemplary metaphor of material culture because of its role in the first developmental stages of an infant's individuation. Drawing from Winnicott's psychoanalytic theory as a

1. Kirkham, P. (ed.) 1996. *The Gendered Object.* Manchester: Manchester University Press, Preface p. XIV.

2. Winnicott, D.W. [1971] 1991. *Playing and Reality.* London and New York: Routledge.

Figure 12. House as commodity. (Sunley Homes)

starting point the analysis is extended to encompass the way in which the particular quality of textiles can be seen to offer the means through which to examine how people use things to transact certain aspects of being-in-the-world at a direct sensory level of experience particularly with reference to time. The use of metaphor as the most appropriate figure of speech to encompass the discussion of entities from different domains is adapted from Christopher Tilley's exposition of its use in the understanding and interpretation of material forms in social archaeology.[3] A case is also made for the particularly unstable quality of identity at the cusp of the new millennium, locating this study within

3. Tilley, C. 1999. *Metaphor and Material Culture*. Oxford: Blackwell.

an historical context that has given particular importance to difference as a constituent of the modern sense of self. Thus it follows that recent concerns in social anthropology have concentrated on the process of objectification that, taken one step further, leads to self-creation. Lipovetsky's theory of fashion as a social system presents the 'modern individualist ethic' particular to Western culture as 'a nodal phenomenon constitutive of modern democratic societies'.[4]

Textile objects in the form of clothes and soft furnishings such as curtains, comfort blankets and carpets, are made of a particular type of material in two senses of the word – the physical and the cultural. This is a generalisation, a truism even, of all artefacts – things made by means of human thought and hand. But it is the specific material properties of textiles as an interpretative tool, represented in the transitional object that differentiates it from other kinds of things. Thus textiles present a particularly apposite object type to illustrate how things are used to mediate the interior mental world of the individual, the body and the exterior objective world beyond the self through which a sense of identity is constructed and transacted within social relations.

Nor is it accidental that the central thing-type object selected as exemplar – the baby's comfort blanket as representative of cloth in general – is an ephemeral material particularly susceptible to the ravages of time. So the experience of time passing is sensed physically and subjectively through fabric as a form of transitional object that acts as a mediating tissue between the body and the external world. Textiles have been considered as just one type of thing among many in studies that group it in with the world of goods in general and do not necessarily differentiate its specific physical properties. As such it has been considered in various studies of material culture, for example in the objectification of social relations, as commodity, fetish and gift.[5]

4. Lipovetsky, G. 1994. *The Empire of Fashion: Dressing Modern Democracy*. Princeton: Princeton University Press, p. 242.

5. See for example Weiner, A.B. & Schneider, J. (eds) 1989. *Cloth and Human Experience*. Washington: Smithsonian Institution Press; Spooner, B. 1986. 'Weavers and Dealers: the authenticity of the oriental carpet', pp. 195–235. In Appadurai, A. (ed.) *The Social Life of Things: Commodities in cultural perspective*. Cambridge: Cambridge University Press; Stallybrass, P. 1998. 'Marx's Coat', pp. 183–207. In Spyer, P. (ed.) *Border Fetishisms: Material objects in unstable spaces*. New York and London: Routledge; Jarman, N. 1998. 'Material of culture, fabric of identity', pp. 121–46. In Miller, D. (ed.) *Material Cultures: Why some things matter*. London: UCL Press.

Here, however, the properties of cloth are considered for the particular physical characteristics that produce certain types of relational effects in its role within social relations. Because clothes make direct contact with the body, and domestic furnishings define the personal spaces inhabited by the body, the material which forms a large part of the stuff from which they are made – cloth – is proposed as one of the most intimate of thing-types that materialises the connection between the body and the outer world.

Cloth and clothes therefore can furnish the kind of examples of object types that demonstrate the materialisation and unfolding of different human life-stages of identity formation within specific historical and cultural contexts. The social construction of subjectivity can be observed objectified via garments in relation to the body, and via interior decor of the immediate intimate domestic environment.[6] The ephemeral characteristics of cloth lend a sense of scale to formative social contexts in terms of space and time through the dynamic act of consumption in which it is used for processes of dressing up, wearing out, using up, transforming, possessing, absorbing, ordering, containing and embodying, that all go towards the constructing of identities.

The 'not-me-object'[7]

The unorthodox use of 'object' in this chapter, extrapolated from three different disciplines, deserves some explanation especially since it is sometimes used interchangeably, and in some cases in several senses of the word at the same time. This is particularly the case where 'object' is used metaphorically, as in the case of Winnicott's transitional object, where the blanket-object (the thing) made from spun fibres into thread, and woven or knitted into a fabric, is used as a means of letting go of

6. This theory is suggested and backed up by findings based on the ongoing Oral History and Ethnography Workshop Project [hereafter to be referred to as the' Oral History Project'] that I have been running since 1994 in conjunction with MA students on the MA Design History and Material Culture and MA History of Textiles and Dress courses at Winchester School of Art, University of Southampton. The unit researches the history of textiles and dress in particular, and design in general based on oral testimony gathered through recorded interviews and centred on a series of group projects. Some of the themes investigated have included: 'Generational and gender differences in attitudes to dress within a family or household unit', 'Attitudes to consumption in a period of austerity', and 'Dressing up in the seventies'.

7. Phillips, A. 1988. *Winnicott*. London: Fontana, pp. 113–26.

the mother-object acknowledging the person beyond the self – the 'other' or what Winnicott calls the 'not-me'. The artefact – the thing fabricated by means of human technology – at the same time also refers to the object in the material-culture sense which defies the duality of Cartesian thought that separates nature from culture and form from content, and therefore the physical thing from the idea that gave it form in the first place, or the meanings that it accrues in the course of its existence. The material culture object, rather than splitting, conflates subject and object as a social relation. These definitions of object derive from psychoanalytic theory of object relations,[8] from consumption theory developed within social archaeology and anthropology[9] used to explain the role of artefacts in exchange strategies to bypass the alienating tendencies of commercialism, and, with the advent of 'virtual society' an initiative within the social sciences to investigate the relationship between sociality and materiality.[10] It has already been noted in Chapter I that within the disciplinary context of design history there has also been an increasing interest in material culture arising out of the growing awareness of the museum as a cultural context where the meaning of artefactual objects are contested. This has meant a move away from the rather literal 'object analysis' which only recognised the actual physical properties of the material, the technologies of its manufacture and the factual conditions of its provenance and distribution gathered from documentary *material* evidence,[11] to a more subtle approach to interpretation that recognises the contingent nature of such a process according to the cultural context within which it is located. Thus the material culture object finds meanings in many different conceptual contexts so that its definition in this chapter needs to be clarified. To this end the Winnicott 'not-me' object is recruited to illustrate the specificity of textiles in negotiating social relations as

8. Greenberg, J.R. and Mitchell, S.A. 1983. *Object Relations in Psychoanalytic Theory.* Cambridge, Massachusetts, and London: Harvard University Press.

9. Miller, D. 1987. *Material Culture and Mass Consumption.* Oxford: Blackwell.

10. For example the 'Sociality/Materiality: The Status of the Object in Social Science' conference in association with the ESRC 'Virtual Society?' project, Brunel University, 9–11 September 1999.

11. Although a bit of a side issue the reference to 'material' as evidence in law is worth mentioning because of the implications it has in terms of truth and reality. This was brought to my attention by the keynote paper given by William Pietz, 'Material Considerations: Towards a Forensic History of Capitalisation' paper at the 'Sociality/Materiality' conference. See note 10 above.

one of the many different types of object inhabiting the material culture of everyday life.

Winnicott's theory of the transitional object was devised during the course of his clinical practice in child psychology during the 1950s in which he observed the incidence of babies' appropriation of a piece of cloth as a means of coping in the absence of the mother's breast. This he surmised to be one of the earliest steps in the maturation of the child adjusting to separation from the mother. Thus the comfort blanket as one of the first 'not-me' possessions can be seen to mediate the process of ontogenesis through which the child first becomes aware of itself as a separate entity and the first step towards the formation of the individual. Daniel Miller has referred at length to Melanie Klein, one of Winnicott's colleagues and mentors in psychoanalytic research, in his theory of modern material culture and mass consumption as a social process of objectification.[12] But neither he nor other writers who refer to psychoanalytic object relations delve further into the particularity of the physical object type.[13] For Jay Greenberg and Stephen Mitchell 'object relations' only refer to 'people's relationship with others'.[14] They discuss Winnicott's transitional object ignoring the significance of the particularity of the blanket, the actual material object that facilitates that first separation of the subject from the object. The contention here is that Winnicott's conceptualisation of the dynamics between inner and outer reality enacted through play is specific in the quality of the phenomenon – the piece of cloth, string or toy used by the child as the means through which the object/subject relation is first experienced. Winnicott's clinical observations led him to interpret transitional phenomena as an unresolved paradox in which the role of the transitional object was to both join *and* separate the subject from the object at one and the same time. And it is to that distinctive and unresolved quality of things that this chapter is dedicated. It is possible to postulate that the transitional object could be anything, that the piece of cloth is incidental. However it hardly needs to be observed that textiles have a particularity which cannot be replaced by say a tractor or a needle.

12. Miller 1987. *Material Culture and Mass Consumption*, pp. 90–3.

13. Steedman, C. 1998. 'What a Rag Rug Means', pp. 259–82. In *Journal of Material Culture*. Vol. 3, No. 3, p. 277; Campbell, C. 1995. 'The Sociology of Consumption' pp. 96–126. In Miller, D. (ed.) 1995. *Acknowledging Consumption*. London and New York: Routledge, p. 116.

14. Greenberg and Mitchell 1983. *Object Relations in Psychoanalytic Theory*.

In *Playing and Reality,* the publication in which Winnicott pro-
pounded his theory of the transitional object beyond the confines of
the psychoanalytic community,[15] he linked the knowing subject with
a sense of shared reality in terms of how people related to each other
(object relations). Unlike Klein who confined her work to the relationship between parents and children and did not concern herself with
the social context within which the socialisation of the child occurred,
Winnicott went on to look at older child and adolescent development
and was particularly interested in the environment in which the
maturation process took place, including the 'abstractions of politics
and economics and philosophy and culture seen as the culmination
of natural growing processes'.[16] And it is because of Winnicott's interest
in the wider social world which he described as 'a superimposition of
a thousand million individual patterns' that his theory regarding the
development of the individual through various stages of maturation is
so apt in positioning the process of individuation in the construction
of identity.[17] Winnicott's perception is not dissimilar to that of Michel
de Certeau who produced a theory of the practice of everyday life.[18]
Working against the grain of most analyses of cultural theory which
seek to categorise commonalities, de Certeau insisted that his project
was the investigation of 'a *science of singularity;* that is to say, a science
of the relationship that links everyday pursuits to particular circumstances [. . .] the characteristically subtle logic of these "ordinary"
activities comes to light only in the details'.[19]

Winnicott recognised the difficulties surrounding his theory of the
transitional object identifying with the 'eternal controversy' over
transubstantiation, similar to the defence material culturists feel bound
to mount against the accusation of fetishism. Yet his theory was
grounded by means of material things – objects and places as well as

15. The theory of the transitional object was first formulated in 1951 and first
published in 1953 in the *International Journal of Psycho-Analysis,* Vol. 34, Part 2; and in
D.W. Winnicott 1958, *Collected Papers: Through Paediatrics to Psycho-Analysis.* London:
Tavistock Publications.

16. Winnicott, 1991. *Playing and Reality.* p. 138.

17. This is not to suggest a model of society based on self-determined individuals
but, rather as I go on to explain more fully below, to acknowledge individuality as an
aspect of society.

18. de Certeau, M. 1988. *The Practice of Everyday Life.* trans. Steven Rendall. Berkley:
University of California Press.

19. Ibid., p. ix.

through the evidence of his clinical observations. This example should not to be misinterpreted as a form of crude essentialism, in that the material objects used as conductors of social acts are for that very reason also cultural objects and as such cannot be reduced to the sum of any amount of 'factual' evidence. But nor does the awareness of cultural and historical contingency rule out the case to be made for the particular characteristic of ephemerality pertaining to textiles that makes it so amenable to Winnicott's transitional object used to mark a particular stage in the life cycle.[20] Furthermore the ephemeral quality of textiles can be seen to materialise changes in the object/subject relation showing the ephemeral and constantly changing aspects of identity formation that characterises the modern mentality.

Winnicott saw the child's use of the transitional object as the first step towards individuation in the maturation process. Winnicott's blanket was not a substitute for the mother, or a step towards a form of 'progressive objectivity' but according to Phillips a form of 'inclusive combination'[21] which rather than splitting the subject from the object, performed a transition from subjectivity to objectivity. Thus the transitional phenomena 'provided a bridge between the inner and outer worlds . . . where previously . . . there seemed to be only mutually exclusive options: either subjectivity or objectivity'.[22] In addition to the usefulness of the transitional object as a material form that combines the object with the subject in dynamic tension, its physicality in the form of cloth is suggestive of the tissue connecting the body to the object world. Thus textile presents the genre of artefacts ideally suited as exemplar, or better still, metaphor, for the study of material culture in general, and in particular, the ephemeral materiality of identity in the context of current material culture.

Metaphor and Textuality, Materiality and Textility

In exemplifying Winnicott's transitional object as the paradigmatic metaphor for material culture my intention is twofold. Firstly to expand on the use of metaphor in theorising design as an aspect of material

---

20. Although the example of the transitional object referred to here is mainly that of a textile used by the infant, I do not mean to imply that a transitional object cannot be of another type of object nor that the device of the transitional object is exclusively used by children.

21. Phillips 1988. *Winnicott*, p. 114.

22. Ibid.

culture and textiles as the paradigmatic 'thing' in that context. Metaphor has been selected rather than any other figure of speech specifically because it does not operate at the level of literal descriptive explanation, refusing any form of essentialism or crude realism that attempts to reduce all things to provable categories of set universal properties. Metaphor allows things to exist in their own thing-like terms merely framing them in language for discursive purposes without lapsing into solipsism.

And secondly metaphor is useful in reflecting on the theoretical impossibility of abstracting things into language by employing a trope which does not rely on translating a thing into a word, but conversely enables a like-for-like definition openly substituting one thing for another. Thus metaphor is posited as an appropriate form of textuality to reflect on how things can exist in language but not be reduced to language and thus disintegrate and dematerialise in the process.

Textuality is thus not to be mistaken for textility, and is only referred to here in order to make that point clear and highlight the materiality of textiles. Metaphor provides a conceptual framework that can cope with how people interrelate with things within the field of cultural production where the process is experienced through the material world rather than through language. And the way Winnicott's transitional object works is, in microcosm, analogous to the objectification that takes place within the context of material culture. The metaphor is recruited here as a compact and vivid method of conveying the complex configuration of culturally specific effects which may be found embodied in such objects as textiles; and because it supplies the 'proof, ' if such were needed, that expunges any possibility of a literal translation of material culture into linguistic terms. Tilley's persuasive essay on metaphor actually uses textile terms (thread, weave) as metaphors of metaphor when he writes:

> Metaphor provides an interpretative thread by means of which we can weave together into a fresh constellation the brute 'literal' facts of the world. In an empiricist or objectivist account of the world a body is a body and a pot is a pot. Metaphor provides a powerful means of overcoming this fragmented view of the world and examining systematic linkages between different cultural and material domains. Metaphor provides a way of mediating between concrete and abstract thoughts.[23]

23. Tilley, C. 1999. *Metaphor and Material Culture*. Oxford: Blackwell, p. 8.

Thus textiles lends itself as the artefact par excellence to render the object/subject relation in material form.

The Textility of the Transitional Object

So in moving from textuality back to textility and to the case of Winnicott's transitional object in particular – the child's comfort blanket as the paradigmatic cultural object – it is necessary to consider the specific features which categorise textiles and compare them to the characteristics of material culture in general. Winnicott's description of the physical features of the transitional object with which the child starts to relate to the outside world as a separate entity, specified that it usually incorporates: mobility, texture and warmth,[24] all features which are present in textiles. It is entirely appropriate therefore that the comfort blanket in particular and materials like cloth in general, which display those tactile features, should be used here as an exemplar of the material culture object par excellence. As P.K. Lunt and S.M. Livingstone have observed, [25] certain objects lend themselves more readily to certain meanings, for example photographs to memory. Here textiles are cited because they clearly lend themselves to the role of transitional object, incorporating the fluidity, warmth and texture of Winnicott's definition, to which could be added ephemerality as the feature which best incorporates the transitory nature of the transitional object. Furthermore Winnicott instances specific textile objects as transitional phenomena – 'part of sheet or blanket, napkin, handkerchief' – and uses textile analogies to describe 'the tendency on the part of the infant to weave other-than-me objects into the personal pattern'[26] of its development.

There is nothing inherently particular about the pieces of cloth that are taken up by infants for use as transitional objects in their first experiencing of not-me-ness. But what starts out as a random, temporal adoption of a napkin or cot cover develops into a process of cathexis which transforms it into a personal possession. Cathexis is a form of emotional investment transferred into an object to form a link between a person and the outside world, so that a simple object like a mug or a sweater becomes a mediator and is experienced as a reinforcement to the sense of self. The transformation that makes a transitional object

24. Winnicott, 1991. *Playing and Reality.* p. 5.
25. Lunt, P.K. and Livingstone, S.M. 1992. *Mass consumption and Personal Identity.* Buckingham and Philadelphia: Open University Press, p. 67.
26. Winnicott, 1991. *Playing and Reality.* p. 3.

out of the satin binding on the corner of a blanket is an active participatory act of making on the part of the child, for example, the case of Sarah[27] who transformed a hand-knitted blanket into her 'abu' every time she picked it up, carefully selecting a section of it for softness. Then bunching it in one hand she proceeded to pluck at it with the other until it unravelled into a soft fluffy mass of yarns with which she patted her mouth. As a result of being subjected to continuous unravelling, over time the blanket dwindled down to a small matted rag. But the disintegration of the transitional object seemed to coincide with the child relinquishing her dependence on it. One day after impulsively deciding to throw it away she retrieved it from the rubbish bin. The dramatic gesture weakened the abu's power and asserted her independence. But the retraction soon after prevented the entire dissipation of its potency so that a certain amount of residual meaning was retained. The act also transformed it once again, but this time into a reliquary that was put away and eventually forgotten.

This example is similar to those cited by Winnicott except that he did not necessarily follow the biographies of the artefacts used as transitional phenomena through to trace the circumstances of their demise. His account speaks generally and figuratively of the ephemerality of the transitional object stating that

> Its fate is to be gradually allowed to be decathected, so that in the course of years it becomes not so much forgotten as relegated to limbo ... It loses meaning and this is because the transitional phenomena have become diffused, have become spread out over the whole intermediate territory between 'inner psychic reality' and 'the external world as perceived by two persons in common', that is to say, over the whole cultural field.[28]

Winnicott went on to explore the role of transitional phenomena in the creative act of play, an activity he saw as the enactment of the search for the self, a further stage of individuation in the course of the life cycle. This is a rich area of psychological and psychoanalytic theory[29] which though not pursued in any detail here, is introduced as a stepping stone towards the consideration of the relationship

27. Personal observation.
28. Winnicott, 1991. *Playing and Reality.* p. 5.
29. For example see Piaget, J. 1962. *Play, Dreams and Imitation in Childhood.* London: Routledge and Kegan Paul.

between the material world and the development of the self in the temporal context of the life cycle.

While textiles can be described as tentative and provisional in character because of their ephemeral properties and consequently the temporal meanings that have been attributed to them, they are not physically brittle in the sense that they do not break if dropped. In fact they are remarkably resilient, and under favourable conditions early fragments dating as far back as the second century have been known to survive to the present.[30] Textiles can be both ephemeral and durable, withstanding years of wear, laundering and change of use from coat to clip rug and from curtain to patchwork quilt. The history of textiles and dress reveals the high value placed upon cloth at all stages from new to rag through various stages of disintegration and reconstitution into shoddy woollen cloth for the making of cheap clothes or paper from cotton waste.[31] Textiles' ability to withstand and adapt to changing conditions, and still manage to retain vestiges of their original form, is not unlike the resiliency of contemporary identity. Yet their ephemerality is also a feature which figures importantly in the particularly adaptable character that makes textiles analogous to the provisional nature of the contemporary sense of self-identity.

Textiles have an infinite potential for change of appearance that can be achieved through the use of different fibres, techniques, structures and applied decorations. Dress and textile terms such as mask and veil are often used in a metaphorical sense to refer to the subtle interface between the interior self and the outside world.[32] Without wishing to be too literal or overwork the analogy it is presented as one which is worth testing in the interests of discovering what kind of insights a focus on textile might yield in the search for an understanding of how individuality is embedded into the material culture of everyday life. In order to do this it is first necessary to explain in what way individuality is different from identity and to suggest that a consumption framework is not the best context for such an investigation.

30. Volbach, W.F. 1969. *Early Decorative Textiles*. London, New York, Sydney and Toronto: Paul Hamlyn.

31. Wilson, E. and Taylor, L. 1989. *Through the Looking Glass: A History of Dress from 1860 to the Present Day*. London: BBC Books, p. 41.

32. Warwick, A. and Cavallaro, D. 1998. *Fashioning the Frame: Boundaries, Dress and the Body*. Oxford and New York: Berg, see Chapter 4: Surface/Depth – 'Dress and the Mask'.

The Sociality of Individuality

So in returning to individuality, the question at the heart of this study of the role of things in the material culture of everyday life, the first step is to specify the place of individuality within the context of identity formation as a social process. One of the main reasons for the introduction of textiles has been in order to wrest the definition of individuality from too abstract an interpretation so as to be able to discuss their particular pertinence in the objectification of individuality at a *material* level.

The commentary that follows is purposely contextualised within the controversy which inevitably assails any reference to individuality and makes it almost impossible to pursue it as a social phenomenon since as such it would appear to set up an insoluble contradiction. How can individuality be conceived of as social when its existence depends on uniqueness? Although there are studies that define individuality as a social phenomenon,[33] psychoanalysis would seem to be one of the few disciplines which accepts it as a legitimate area of enquiry since it is based on the concept that 'each individual has his own idiosyncratic experience of life'.[34] An important exception is Michel de Certeau whose work 'defies definition' because of his specific interest in the status of the individual not as an atomistic element to which all groups are supposed to be reducible, but as a means of being able to discuss how individuals who are otherwise assumed to be passive and manipulated, 'operate'.[35] But generally the social sciences have difficulty accommodating the issue of identity at the level of the individual – how people resolve a sense of themselves as unique in a world full of different unique persons when its main concern is that of society. Although both disciplines recognise that the individual lives in a social world their different agendas give particular weight to their own concerns. However the paradox of Winnicott's transitional object would appear to offer an accommodation to the concept of the individual within a social context, since it both unites and separates the self from others, so that individuality can only be experienced in its relation to others.

33. Morris, B. 1991. *Western Conceptions of the Individual.* Oxford and New York: Berg.

34. Greenberg, J.R. and Mitchel, S.A. 1983. *Object Relations in Psychoanalytic Theory.* Cambridge, Massachusetts and London: Harvard University Press, p. 400–3.

35. de Certeau, M. 1988. *The Practice of Everyday Life.* trans. Steven Rendall. Berkley: University of California Press, p. xi.

The aim in promoting 'individuality' as a valid concept in the context of material culture is because of its centrality to an understanding of how people relate to the world through things in the process of individual identity formation. It will be argued that individuality is not transferable to a commodity that can be bought, but on the contrary is a trait that is experienced as emanating from a sense of interiority which grounds people in the everyday world. The necessity to have a strong sense of self is recognised and exploited by marketing as evident in the way that advertising tries to suggest that it is possible to acquire individuality through the act of consumption, a sophisticated marketing technique called 'lifestyling'.[36] But as Miller so perspicaciously observes, 'desire is at the least discriminatory and often unpredicted by commerce'.[37] Because consumption is a field of studies which has largely concerned itself with issues of identity it presents an obvious context and explains why it has developed alongside the growth of material culture studies. Nevertheless, as I argue below, consumption theory does not lend itself readily to exploring the autonomy or agency that pertains to a sense of individuality. Individuality cannot really be distilled into a general category although consumption does purport to attend to an entity called the 'active consumer' who has a mind of their own but who can nevertheless only be envisaged as a series of sub-groups (categories). So if individuality as a facet of subjectivity is to be discussed through active engagement in material culture practices such as appropriation and objectification it needs a framework which will allow its exploration in experiential terms which theories of consumption do not necessarily accommodate.

The type of individuality to which I refer here, which has a psychological inflection, is not allowed in cultural studies where it has come to be characterised as synonymous with a range of artificial stereotypes that presuppose a contaminating effect from materiality – that consumers 'buy' prefabricated individualities by matching up with packaged lifestyles in the form of consumer goods. What I am trying to argue however is that a more provisional definition is needed in order to locate the space where the relationship between things and individuality is transacted. Even when consumption is qualified as an open and negotiable relationship, according to Peter Jackson and Nigel Thrift's definition as 'a process that extends well beyond the point of

36. Williamson, J. 1978. *Decoding Advertisements: Ideology and Meaning in Advertising.* London: Marion Boyars.

37. Miller, D. 1998. *A Theory of Shopping.* Oxford: Polity, p. 139.

sale [. . .] fluid and dynamic [in] nature rather than assuming identities to be in any way fixed or singular',[38] the discussion remains at a dematerialised non-specific level. Nor is Russell Belk alone among researchers on consumer behaviour in recognising that 'certain goods may come to be seen as extensions of the self'.[39] But that type of observation does not extend our knowledge of individuality in the context of the dynamics of identity formation. So how can changes of individual identity in the course of a lifetime be accounted for? What part, if any, does consumption play in these kind of negotiations and if so how can a focus on how people relate to things help to explain how they create themselves through the object world? If it is accepted that identity formation is an active cultural practice mediated through the material world of things it is possible to imagine how it could be objectified in the form of textiles so that the ephemeral nature of identity can be experienced through the materiality of cloth.

There are those who do not believe the study of individuality to be a legitimate or valuable line of enquiry because it is not seen as socially significant. Studies of consumption from within the social sciences, a discipline which by definition refuses to conceive of such an entity as 'the individual', can only deal with it as a social 'construction', removing any agency that might otherwise pertain to individuals. In spite of feminists' assertion that the personal is political and therefore of social concern,[40] nevertheless sociological studies that turn to the investigation of anything to do with the personal still feel obliged to justify themselves. For example Giddens's study of the role of sexuality in modern culture, which he interprets as a transformation of intimacy, starts by stating that 'sexuality [. . .] might seem a public irrelevance – an absorbing, but essentially private, concern'.[41] He does, however go on to explain why it 'now continually features in the public domain'

38. Jackson, P. and Thrift, N. 1995. 'Geographies of Consumption' pp. 204–37. In Miller 1995, *Acknowledging Consumption*, p. 227.

39. Belk, R.W. 1995. 'Studies in the New Consumer Behaviour' pp. 58–95. In Miller 1995. *Acknowledging Consumption*, p. 72.

40. Sichtermann, B. 1986. *Femininity: the Politics of the Personal*. Oxford: Polity, cited in Attfield, J. 'FORM/female FOLLOWS FUNCTION/male: Feminist Critiques of Design', pp. 199–225. In Walker, J.A. 1989. *Design History and the History of Design*. London: Pluto, p.220. For a much more recent reference to the same perspective in a history of design text see Auslander, L. 1996. *Taste and Power: Furnishing Modern France*. Berkeley, Los Angeles, London: California University Press, p. 4.

41. Giddens, A. 1992. *The Transformation of Intimacy*. Cambridge: Polity, p. 2.

and demonstrates the way in which it 'represents a potential realm of freedom', in other words that freedom can be gained via personal life. A sense of individuality is undoubtedly one of the locations for self-realisation which can begin to be understood through the study of material culture.

The particularity of understanding individuality must start from the ground in the context of everyday world as a social place, through individual accounts of subjective experiences and the observation of how people appropriate things to construct a sense of individuality. It is therefore very feasible to envisage how textiles can make the ephemerality of individuality material. In appointing the material object as the focus in the investigation of individuality, the role of textile things in the process of identity formation, it is suggested that consumption can only provide a part of the greater story of object relations.

Beyond Consumption and the Denial of Individuality

Consumption has been used as a form of shorthand for a field of academic enquiry to lift it out of the production/consumption dyad and concede that there is such an entity as an 'active consumer' with competencies to engage in the process of consumption and to exert some measure of influence on production, rather than just as a passive audience that receives what it is given. Thus consumption has occupied a place of central importance in material culture studies which have looked at the social meaning of things[42] and developed convincing and sophisticated theories that appreciate its role as a means of self-definition. Nevertheless consumption as a context still falls short at ground level when it comes to explaining the specific singularity of autonomous identity – how different things have different meanings to different individuals at different times, in different places. It is even less capable of furnishing a context for observing how the material world accommodates to the contemporary nature of individuality which, while shifting and restless, is at the same resistant to change. Most of the cultural studies literature directed to this study has concentrated on the fantasies created to sell goods rather than the actual experience of consuming them. The fear is that to attend to such concerns negatively labelled as 'expressive individualism' is somehow

---

42. Appadurai, A. (ed.) 1986. *The Social Life of Things: Commodities in Cultural Perspective.* Cambridge: Cambridge University Press.

to regress into some kind of self-indulgent 'relativism in which anything goes'.[43]

Just to focus on mass consumption has its limitations in explaining individuality; therefore a switch of focal point to specific material things such as textiles may prove more productive, in that specific physical properties lend themselves more readily than others to the construction of sociality. This is not meant to suggest that individuality is proposed as a trait that can be bought in the form of a commodity. It cannot be defined in terms of a provision missing from the store cupboard that is available out there in the shops. But nor can individuality be considered a pure sense untouched by the things of the material world, nor totally detached from the rest of humanity or ethical principles. So far theories of consumption have failed to deal with the sense of individuality that consumers derive from the process of living in a material world.

In this respect I part company with C. Campbell's analysis of the consumption of clothing in which he makes a separation between 'the meaning of objects and the meaning of actions'. This distinction is based on an assumption that the meaning of things is derived from 'putative socially shared and commercially manipulated symbolism'.[44] This would suggest that the meanings that consumers deduce from the goods they choose to buy are somehow illegitimate and that it is only once the goods have been cleansed of their commercial association by being personalised that they can graduate into the higher realms of culture. Such an assumption – that authentic meanings can only be constructed and expressed through actions – depends on things that in themselves cannot be attributed with 'real' meanings because in so doing one would be reifing a human propensity by rendering it into a mere material object.

But in Campbell's assertion that the meaning in garments that refers to 'an individual's sense of self [...] derives from the actions that individuals engage in, actions that cannot be deduced from a knowledge of the products with which they may be associated',[45] ignores the way in which the knowledge of products is produced within a material world in the first place. It may be that the separation can be made notionally

43. McRobbie, A. (ed.) 1997. *Back to Reality? Social experience and cultural studies.* Manchester University Press, pp. 62–3.

44. Campbell, C. 1996. 'The meaning of objects and the meaning of actions' pp. 93–106. In *Journal of Material Culture*, Vol. 1, No. 1, p. 103.

45. Campbell, 1996. 'The meaning of objects', p. 103.

for the purpose of abstract analysis, but on the ground where people encounter and interact with things no such clear-cut separation can be made. The relationship between things and people (material culture) cannot be neatly encapsulated into such convenient compartments, since it is the dynamics of the combination of culture and materiality, object/subject, which produces meaning.

The kind of critique of consumerism that equated mass consumption with degraded useless goods, dumbing down and stereotypical identikit lifestyle products has been tempered by recent research and writings on consumption and material culture that have viewed it more positively. Yet one still gets a whiff of moralising in the tone of studies like Lunt and Livingstone's enquiry into the relationship between mass consumption and 'personal identity' which only referred to the individual in social terms and warned that though consumption 'affords possibilities for personal development [. . .] increased freedoms go hand in hand with increased responsibilities'.[46] Social psychology also gets round the difficulty of 'the individual' by explaining it as a contract of shared understanding between consenting subjects whereas H. Dittmar's rather literal interpretation of the acquisition of identity through personal possessions asserts 'To have is to be'.[47] These are obviously over-generalised characterisations of research which has nevertheless been usefully applied in trying to understand how consumption helps people to make sense of the world in which they live through the purchases they make and the possessions they amass. There is also an obvious correlation between ability to choose what to buy through access and financial status with varying degrees of autonomy and strengths of identity definition acquired thereby.

But there is a limit as to how far the composite term 'consumption' can be applied in the study of the material culture of everyday life with reference to the formation of individuality. Therefore, before going on to discuss how textiles' ephemeral features exemplify the character of contemporary forms of individuality, the next task is look at the historiography of consumption since it is the only field which has started to deal with the problem of how people form their identities through a dynamic interrelationship with the material world. Paul Glennie attributes the marginal significance given until recently to the historical study of consumption, to the view on the part of some

46. Lunt and Livingstone, 1992. *Mass Consumption and Personal Identity*, p. 24.

47. Dittmar, H. 1992. *The Social Psychology of Material Possessions: To Have Is To Be*. Hemel Hempstead, Hertfordshire: Harvester Wheatsheaf.

historians that until the second half of the twentieth century only a relatively small sector of the population was able to participate in the acquisition of goods.[48]

The changing definition of consumption represented in Miller however,[49] shows how consumption studies have grown to form a new interdisciplinary field attracting interest from subject areas in both humanities and social sciences. It is no longer confined to an outcome of the advent of the so-called modern 'consumer society', a phenomenon that has consistently confounded definition in historical period terms. The problem is illustrated in Carolyn Steedman's historical account of the meaning of the rag rug in which she defines it as a nostalgic symbol of the past and reflects on the relationship between historical specificity and nostalgic reconstruction. Her interpretation prioritises production rather than consumption as determining and points out the reality of the pre-twentieth century English economy

> in which such a tiny number of things circulated again and again, among so many people. Where scarcity and technological underdevelopment created a shortage not of the poor, but of the traditional symbols of the poor, their rags; and where even a handful of tattered clothing was worth a trip to the rag merchant, reckoned as it was until the late 19th century, as half a loaf of bread, in contrast with the present.[50]

Steedman's implied criticism of making too much of consumption studies in a period when consumption was not an activity which many people could afford to indulge in, illustrates the type of historical studies which assumes a relation to the actual amount of disposable income and goods in circulation in different places and times. But her account also gives importance to considering the object (rags) as a carrier of meanings both for those who possessed it in the eighteenth century and historians who interpret it in the twentieth century.

While Glennie's summary of approaches to consumption studies offers an alternative point of view held by some social historians who do not consider the inability to make cash purchases to be a bar to participating in consumption practices. Consumption thus becomes a

48. Glennie, P. 1995. 'Consumption within Historical Studies' pp. 164–203. In Miller 1995. *Acknowledging Consumption*.

49. Miller, D. (ed.) *Acknowledging Consumption*. London and New York: Routledge.

50. Steedman, C. 1998. 'What a Rag Rug Means' pp. 259–82. In *Journal of Material Culture*. Vol. 3, No. 3, p. 277.

much more indeterminate range of cultural activities through which subjects form their identity. Therefore it is useful to make a distinction by defining consumption as more than the exchange of commodities within the larger frame of object relations where there exist other forms of object/subject interactions (economies). Seen in that way, the Steedman example serves to illustrate a different kind of material culture to that which pertains where there is an abundance of things.

But the question here is how does consumption help to explain how people form their identities as singular individuals. This is where it helps to make a distinction between consumption as a very general and rather amorphous cultural activity and the development of individuality as a process of object/subject relations as two quite separate approaches. Object/subject relations, a term extrapolated from psychoanalysis as described above in referring to Winnicott's transitional object, helps to clarify some of the roles allotted to thing-type objects in the social context of the material culture of everyday life. What needs clarifying before going any further is the difference between the type of 'object' as the self-aware person referred to in psychoanalysis who has attained a level of individuation, the 'object' as a thing within the world of goods, and finally the more abstract 'object' in the object/ subject (material culture) social relation sense which provides the means through which to effect the objectification that transforms an idea into a reality in the world beyond the self.

In *A Theory of Shopping* Miller cites the category of 'treat' shopping as one with particular satisfactions because it 'helps to define [. . .] the experience of individuality'.[51] This would suggest that a way of getting at a more detailed understanding of the particularity of the sense of individuality than can be gained from the process of acquisition is by starting with the object that mediates it. However, Miller's theory of shopping downplays the connection between consumption and individuality by schematising it as a form of sacrifice to the loved one – the object of devotion, although he does allow the loved one sometimes to be the self. But consumption, I would contend, only deals with one aspect of the material culture of everyday life. If shopping is considered as a ritual practice it is quite plausible to ally it with a form of devotion in which there are certain established forms of practice that need to be carried out in order for it to make sense in a socially meaningful way. In spite of allowing a certain amount of self-gratification Miller's interpretation of shopping denies that it has anything to do with

51. Miller, D. 1998. *A Theory of Shopping*. Oxford: Polity, p. 100.

identity,[52] escaping the difficulty of dealing with the tricky issue of individuality by not following the product beyond the check-out and consigning the interpretation of personal meanings attached to goods consumed to the work of novelists, citing among others R. Sennet's references to Balzac[53] not unlike W. Benjamin[54] before him.

In defence of my pursuit of the specificity of individuality as a central concern in the study of the relationship between identity and the world at large – of things and people – it is necessary to assert that individuality and sociality are not mutually exclusive. The misconception still abounds that to attend to the 'individualistic' is somehow to neglect, abandon or reject any form of sociality. To have a strong sense of self does not preclude also having a sense of social responsibility and being in the world as a place inhabited by other individuals. The paradox of individuality is that it can only be constructed within a social framework.

It is clearly a contradiction in terms to attempt to model up a schema with a frame of analysis that could deal with an infinite variety of individualities. Therefore the material forms that best express the nuances of individuality present a more realistic starting point. As already suggested above, textiles is one such thing-type that might manage to accommodate the contradictory combination of consistent *and* provisional forms that provide the means of expressing individuality. The inbuilt provision that must accompany such a project is that the meaning of textiles are seen in relation to the subject who acquires, dresses, furnishes, gives them away, discards them and the countless other purposes for which they are used. Although textiles obviously have a physical trajectory that can be traced without necessarily linking them with their human connections this is not what concerns this study. It is their role in the object/subject relation mediating the experience of the space between the interior mental world of individuals with the exterior physical world in which they find themselves that is the focus of this project.

Personal Effects

The next step towards an understanding of the role of things in the search for individuality is to consider how the process of objectification

---

52. Ibid., p. 140.
53. Sennet, R. 1977. *The Fall of Public Man*. Cambridge: Cambridge University Press.
54. Benjamin, W. 1985. *Charles Baudelaire: A Lyric Poet in the Era of High Capitalism*. London: Verso.

is transacted through the active use of textile possessions, in particular through clothes and furnishings because of their immediacy in relation to the body. This presupposes that identity is constructed as a social process and experienced as personal acts of self-creation, but challenges the stereotypical characterisation as discussed, for example, within certain ideological discourses of femininity in which clothes are said to constitute part of a form of masquerade. Efrat Tsëelon's study of how women reveal their identity through their appearance, noted the mismatch between the ideological stereotypes of femininity which define female identity as 'non-identity' to include both the misogynist essentialist view of femininity and the deconstructionist view which, while liberating, at the same time destabilises it.[55] In both models she observes the double bind that femininity can only be expressed through its denial – that the masquerade is what announces femininity, or that such an artificial appearance must be renounced in order to recuperate any sense of feminine authenticity. However her findings based on ethnographic study suggests a sense of self which is expressed in different forms or 'sartorial faces' without any sense of loss of authenticity. This would indicate the reflective ability to be self-aware enough to know at once that a particular style of individuality is purposely adopted, but at the same time is not felt as any less 'real' for being purposely created.

Similar issues are broached in Christopher Breward's recent historical study of masculinity and consumption that investigates the inter-relationship between gender identity and fashion practices in the urban context from the mid-nineteenth century to the period just prior to the First World War. His analysis suggests that the use of the stereotype is only helpful when recognised as a fictive starting point.

> Seen in this light, the English gentleman's sartorial image becomes not so much a badge of unchanging social stability but rather a contested site for the playing out of struggles for pre-eminence between waning and rising social groups and outlooks.[56]

The examples that follow are intended to illustrate some changing perspectives on dress and textile history with a material culture focus and how this development within various disciplines has uncovered

55. Tsëelon, E. 1995. *The Masque of Femininity,* London: Sage.
56. Breward, C. 1999. *The Hidden Consumer: Masculinities, fashion and city life 1860–1914.* Manchester: Manchester University Press, p. 59.

the way in which the meanings of objects get transformed from commodities to personal 'effects'. Effects here refers to both the material personal property *and* the subjective result of actions so that it is possible to conceptualise the objects and actions in a unitary way as 'objectification' according to Miller rather than according to Campbell's formulation. Thus the process of transformation an object undergoes in becoming a personal effect in the practice of everyday life, superimposes one layer of experience over another so that the original public shared meaning becomes obscured by the personal meaning a garment takes on in objectifying individuality. This is not an aspect of dress practice which takes place at the point of consumption if consumption is defined as the point when the exchange takes place and money changes hands; but at the point of appropriation where the owner takes possession of the item which may be long after it has actually been bought, as in the case of the leather jacket referred to below.

It is significant that at the 'Cracks in the Pavements'[57] conference on gender, fashion and architecture held at the Design Museum in 1991, Janice Winship's contribution for which she was asked to talk about fashion in magazines turned instead to an ethnographic study because she wanted to engage with 'the *practice* of fashion' (my emphasis) in the context of everyday life and at a local level, rather than its representation in the media. She located her study in two areas based on a group of students who were friends in each location. The focus was on their complete wardrobes so that the investigation would include garments which were acquired but not worn, as well as favourite items. The 'bad buys' were not because their owners didn't like the material, cut or look of their respective garments but because they couldn't bring themselves to wear them, exposing a gap between their aspired image and their perceived inability to carry it off. The most striking case of this phenomenon that Winship characterised, after Hebdige,[58] as 'the impossible object', was that of the leather jacket acquired by one of her interviewees with the conscious purpose of changing her image. It took her a long time to decide on what style of leather jacket to buy because of the implications she was fully aware it would have in changing her identity. It was only once she embraced the subculture it represented that she finally found the courage to wear

57. *Cracks in the pavements: gender/fashion/architecture. Papers from a Study Day at the Design Museum.* 1992. Compiled by Lynne Walker. London: Sorella Press.

58. Hebdige, D. 1987. 'The Impossible Object: Towards a sociology of the sublime', pp. 47–76. In *New Formations*, Vol. 1, No. 1, Spring.

it. The act of changing image involved daring and courage because it represented more than a mere change of clothing but a change of identity requiring a strong sense of individualism. There are very clear gender implications in discussing how identity is defined, experienced and manipulated as implied from the account of the leather jacket story in which the subject carefully made her choice after considering a range of alternatives including a heavy metal style and a softer more fashionable, feminine version.[59]

The example above is characteristic of a specific period and generation. In findings from the Oral History Project[60] it is evident from the responses elicited from different generations, even from among members of the same family, that such a self-conscious awareness of the possibility of reinventing one's identity is not a given condition, but historically specific, a distinctly recent phenomenon since the 1970s. In a study of three generations of the same family it was found that while Hester, the grandmother of the Martin family was always mainly concerned to appear 'neat and tidy, respectable', her daughter Betty had only since becoming a mature student started to take more of an interest in expressing her individuality through her choice of dress. The third generation of the family, Betty's two daughters Shelly and Gudrun displayed much more confidence in creating their own looks, distinguishing themselves not only from their mother's generation but also from each other. The same symptoms were observed across various different families and genders so that it would be feasible to speculate that there is more of an affinity across the same generation than between members of the same family. Although more difficult to spot, it was also clear that certain less conscious, 'force of habit' traits do get passed down from one generation to the other.

It could be argued that the process of transforming objects from commodities into personal possessions is part of the consumption process; indeed Winship states as much in asserting that 'to be truly embraced [. . .] the garment must be consumed, made into something other than commodity, by being worn and to a degree shared with others'.[61] However the post-commodity phase is usually ignored as irrelevant to the process of consumption which is usually taken to imply

59. Winship, J. 'Dress Sense' 1992, pp. 1–18. In *Cracks in the pavements: gender/fashion/ architecture. Papers from a Study Day at the Design Museum.* Compiled by Lynne Walker. London: Sorella Press, p. 12.

60. See Note 6 above.

61. Winship, 1992, p. 14.

a form of teleological using-up which may well be the case with some types of 'consumable' commodities. Therefore in defining the acquisition of a commodity as the process of consumption and distinguishing that from a further post-commodity phase that goes on to look at how the object is assimilated into everyday life, opens up a different dimension of the history of things. The post-commodity phase refers to an object once it has been personalised and thus transformed to mediate certain social transactions related to identity formation which do not necessarily have anything to do with the acquisition process, thus acknowledging that objects change meaning with the passing of time as a result of being incorporated into the life of an individual world together with all the changes that take place in the life cycle. And the changing meaning of things like clothes does not only apply to what people wear. Research shows that people keep certain clothing items long after they serve any practical purpose.[62] This can be for a number of different reasons. Among the older generation it was found that clothes could only be discarded if they were given away to someone who would wear them, mended if parts of the cloth were worn out or by saving the 'good' material for reuse.[63] But many items were just kept because their owners were not in the habit of throwing anything of that sort away. To redeem them from the unacceptable category of waste was to keep them in case they might come in handy. But often when you actually got down to it the reasons were not functional.

The material culture of memory has been the focus of some attention by historians and anthropologists acknowledging the importance of the meaning of things in relation to time.[64] Among the findings of the Oral History Project it was also discovered that many garments were kept long after they went out of fashion or no longer fitted, not out of a moral sense of thrift but because their owners could not bear to part with them. They were kept as souvenirs, imbued with memories

62. Much of the material evidence discovered by participants in the Oral History Project depended on interviewees preserved garments, often kept as treasured possessions even though they had not been worn for many years.

63. This was particularly evident among the generation who lived through the Second World War in which the government's intervention through 'make-do-and-mend' propaganda only served to reinforce a practice of thrift which was already common. Burman, B (ed.) 1999. *The Culture of Sewing: Gender, Consumption and Home Dressmaking*. Oxford: Berg.

64. Kwint, M, Breward, C and Aynsley, J. (eds) 1999. *Material Memories: Design and Evocation*. Oxford: Berg.

of youth, of significant persons, occasions and rites of passage. These kind of objects can be termed a form of transitional object helping people to come to terms with the passing of time – the separation from their own youth, or from the loss of a loved one, a parent, child or partner.

The dress historian Juliet Ash, in her meditation on her husband's ties occasioned by his sudden death, reflected:

> Clothes relate to our feeling more than perhaps any other designed artefacts, and thus require 'subjective' as well as 'objective' analysis [. . .] clothes, their smell and texture, remind the spectator of the past presence of the person to whom they belonged, their inhabiting them, a moment when they wore them – or a moment in which they removed the item of clothing. The garment becomes imbued with the essence of the person[65]

The particular poignancy of clothing in memorialisation so aptly illustrated in the example above has no place in the process of consumption when it stops at the point of sale and therefore can so easily be overlooked.

Similarly Mary Schoeser's account of the way she came across an old suit belonging to her father long after his death has nothing to do with consumption. In her case it was not a melancholy experience.[66] Rather it put her in touch with a neglected part of her life – the search for happiness. She describes the way in which the actual sensory encounter with the cloth of the suit awakened memories of her relationship to her father and helped her to reassess her values at a time in her life when she felt there were decisions to be made. She found the suit a good fit and wearing it intensified the relationship to her own history providing an insight into the formative aspects of her background that explained the trajectory of her life so far. She was reminded of her father's advice to seek happiness rather than achievement. The intensely personal experience described in the details of finding the suit and her response to it was very much to do with what I refer to above as 'textility', a material quality which is particular to textiles.

65. Ash, J. 1996. 'Memory and objects' 219–24. in Kirkham, P. (ed.) *The Gendered Object.* Manchester : Manchester University Press, p. 219.

66. *Talking Through Their Hats.* A radio talk given by Mary Schoeser (Part 2 of four programmes), produced by Hannah Andrassy. BBC Radio 4, broadcast on 15 January 2000, 7.45–8.00 p.m.

In his essay on the penury of the Marx household that drove the family to resort to the pawnbroker, Peter Stallybrass uses the example of Marx's coat to illustrate the way in which the commodity system insists on the stripping away of any 'sentimental' value attached to an object in order to turn it back into an empty fetishised commodity.

> The pawnbroker did not pay for personal or family memories. To the contrary. In the language of nineteenth century clothes-makers and repairers, the wrinkles in the elbows of a jacket or a sleeve were called "memories". Those wrinkles recorded the body that had inhabited the garment. They memorialised the interaction, the mutual constitution, of person and thing. But from the perspective of commercial exchange, every wrinkle or "memory" was a devaluation of the commodity.[67]

It is precisely when the 'feel' (subjectivity) is ignored in the study of objects that the dynamic process of the object/subject relation is reduced to generalised static symbolism. The latter can be produced by traditional stereotypes or by marketing's fictional narratives or lifestyles. Sentiment comes attached with the purchase of a wedding dress but would be transformed by the lived experience of a divorce. Leora Auslander's historical study of French furniture gives a lucid account of the importance of considering the nuances of the personal experiences of the everyday and how they are mediated through different senses and different types of things

> All experiences must pass through some kind of classificatory, meaning-generating process in order to lodge in memory. Such processes are not necessarily linguistic – the "language" of the ears, eyes, tongue, and skin, including music, painting, sculpture, food, and fabric are neither the same nor reducible to natural language.[68]

Commenting on the camisole worn by Nicole Kidman in Stanley Kubrick's film *Eyes Wide Shut* on the Women's page of the *Guardian*, Louise Young reported 'product placement has never had it so good' attributing the commercial success derived to its manufacturers to the 'emotional charge' invested by Kidman's character in the film who

67. Stallybrass, P. 1998. 'Marx's Coat', pp. 183-207. In Spyer, P. (ed.) *Border Fetishisms: Material Objects in Unstable Places*. New York and London: Routledge, p. 196.

68. Auslander, L. 1996. *Taste and Power: Furnishing Modern France*. Berkeley, Los Angeles, London: California University Press.

happens to be wearing it while confessing her sexual fantasies to her husband.[69] Musing on the idea of an emotionally charged garment Young moves away from marketing to recount some personal experiences illustrating the way in which '[u]nderwear more than any other garment, can be horribly significant'. She recounts the experience of one of her friends who associated a certain bra with a particular sexual encounter in which the man in question had asked 'Were you thinking of me when you put that on?' so that thereafter it always reminded her of him. So much so that when she fell in love with someone else she had to discard it because 'it brought the first man back into her bedroom whenever she wore it'. Thus the personal experiences associated with garments infiltrates the fabric, not to transform the garment but to change the user's practice, so that what was once worn had to be discarded.

It is the nature of the material that makes cloth so receptive to the nuances of meaning associated with the materialisation of identity. Its accessibility, adaptability, fluidity and the infinite possibilities of variation that renders it so amenable to matters of individuality, also make it easily disposed of, whether by folding it away and allowing it to lie forgotten in the attic, turning it to another use, passing it on or throwing it out. Because textiles lose their bloom, fade and rot more quickly than other materials, meanings dependent on longevity cannot rely on textiles to keep them fresh. The ephemerality that makes textiles susceptible to the ravages of time is what gives it the particular physical characteristics that materialise the impermanence of modern identity.

There is nothing more telling of social change than the rotting swags of faded curtain drapery left crumbling away to dust at the windows of some grand old country house where the National Trust has not been invited to take over, transform it into Heritage and open it to the public; but where an impoverished aristocratic family struggles on in draughty unheated halls with leaking walls and curling wallpaper because to sell the house would mean to relinquish the inheritance that defines their social identity.

69. Young, L. 1999. 'A slip of thing', pp. 8–9. In the *Guardian*, 30 September.

Containment: The Ecology of Personal Possessions

Introduction

One of the most moving scenes of Mike Leigh's 1995 movie *Secrets and Lies* takes place between the estranged made-good brother and his single sister when he visits her in the old family house where she still lives with her grown-up daughter. As he looks around the house, a typical unmodernised nineteenth century London terrace with outside lavatory, he is shocked by the squalid conditions many years of neglect have wreaked on the house. His sister takes him up the stairs to show him the damp patches and they go into the main bedroom which has obviously been left untouched since the death of their parents. He looks around at the clutter of a lifetime of accumulated clothes, furniture and bits and pieces, and as he lifts a hair brush from the dressing table, still loaded with the hair of his dead mother, he asks 'Why don't you get rid of all this old stuff?' She doesn't answer. And we know that the roomful of their parents' belongings represents her past, full of bitterness and disappointments from which she has not been able to break free and dares not confront yet.

It was the hair on the brush that gave me that frisson of recognition of how personal remains, while standing-in for the presence of the deceased also remind you of their irreplaceability. I'm not even sure if my reconstruction of the scene is entirely accurate but it chimed with Kirkham's recollection of her mother's coat and my own recent experience of coping with my father's death when, as the only daughter, the duty fell to me of having to go through his clothes and decide how to dispose of them. The shoes under the bed were the most difficult. I've kept his most loved cardigan. He had simple, almost monastic tastes. He hated clothes, especially new ones. He only got to love the cardigan as it grew old and threadbare so I darned the holes and mended the ragged cuffs so it would last a little longer. He died soon after. The cardigan lies in my jumper drawer rather like a transitional object in reverse, reminding me of his permanent absence. My account of the scene from the Mike Leigh film is referred to here to illustrate the particular poignancy of the accumulation of a lifetime of personal possessions left behind by an individual after their death.

Museums use the *mise-en-scène* of the artist's studio or the writer's study to create a sense of presence through the insignificant minutia of their everyday life strewn around as if they had just left the room for a few minutes. The peculiar combination of particular things left in apparent disarray offers an intimate slice of life view that the process of organising and displaying objects in museum categories transforms into a depersonalised catalogue.

Getting Real – Containment and Clutter

In February 1996 Jane Graves and Steve Baker ran an interdisciplinary symposium under the title of *Clutter: Disorder in the Spaces of Design, the Text and Imagination* in the Art Workers Guild in Queen Square, London.[1] It was an attempt to address material objects in the context of the everyday world where things do not conform to the orderliness of a recognisable, much less an approved aesthetic; an area not normally broached by design theory except to castigate any unruly maverick which might be found straying from the rationality imposed by the modernism pack. Steve Baker's circulated paper on clutter as the wild dimension of the object that is never alluded to in conventional writings on design, set the scene for the exploration of the question of whether 'the unruly disorder of clutter is *conducive* to invention'. But his somewhat pessimistic conclusion observed that in the end we are always defeated by the stubbornness of objects, cautioning that to try to explain clutter is 'a form of sublimation'.[2] The concern with clutter

1. Published versions of papers given at the conference: Baker, S. 1995. '"To go about noisily": Clutter, writing and design'. In *Emigre*, No. 35; Baker, S. 1995. 'Thinking things differently', pp. 70–7. In *Things*, No. 3; Graves, J. 1998. 'Clutter'. In *Issues in Art, Architecture and Design*, Vol. 5, No. 2; Leslie, E. 1996. 'The exotic of the everyday: Critical theory in the parlour', pp. 83–101. In *Things*, No. 4.
2. Baker, S. 1996. 'Clutter, disorder and excess: The obstinacy of objects'. Unpublished paper circulated to delegates of the *Clutter* symposium.

Figure 13. Dressing table from *Interior Decoration Today,* 1938. (Hayes Marshall)

in spite of there being no obvious place for it in the discourses of aesthetics or design where order and control are paramount, appeared at a moment in 1996 of growing alarm over a combination of issues – the unrestrained growth stimulated by the market-led economic policy under the Thatcher regime and the fracturing of experience brought on by the postmodern mentality and critical deconstructionism. The more positive interpretations of clutter as a life-giving form of rescue from the death wish of over-orderliness came from the papers at the symposium that dealt with psychoanalysis. In particular the child psychotherapist Adam Phillips' characterisation of clutter as the sensation experienced by other people's mess, in his clinical paper 'The disorder of use', highlighted the way things are used to play out different stages of the life cycle. He illustrated his case by contrasting the difference between the 'good mess' of the adolescent's disorganised bedroom, representing the confused feelings of awakening sexuality, with his parents' concern over untidiness.[3] But the symposium never quite grappled with the problem of materiality itself; the actual physicality of objects seemed to remain overlooked in the urge to redeem modernism from the corrupting clutches of things out of control, in spite of the dangers recognised to be inherent in idealism.

This chapter will explore the figure of 'containment' as the embodiment of both order *and* clutter, contextualised in the place and space of the home – one of the most ubiquitous physical manifestations of sociality and one of the few geographical areas over which individuals have some measure of control, however circumscribed. It is also relevant in this context that in psychoanalysis the house represents the self. The term 'containment' first introduced in Chapter 3 is intended to define a particular kind of eccentric order – the objectification of the contradictory nature of modernity, the impulse to reintegrate the increasingly fragmentary tangled texture of contemporary postmodern culture. This section will also relate back to themes discussed in the previous two chapters – authenticity and ephemerality, by suggesting how the traditional is found to exist alongside the temporal and innovative, and how these world views are contained ecologically within the most intimate unit of the built environment – the home.[4] Thus the ecology of personal possessions as contained within the household offers a site for the study of one of the means through which people attempt to achieve integration and the recasting of authenticity and ephemerality in a type of paradoxical identity formation characteristic of the modern sensibility. This is not to suggest that the character

3. Swa'les, V. 1996. 'Clutter: disorder in the spaces of design, the text and the imagination' (review) p. 5. In *Design History Society NewsLetter*, No. 70.

4. Ecology in this context refers to the study of patterns of order according to the logic of specific systems, e.g. biological, or institutional particularly in relation to its effect on the human environment. For the term 'the ecology of the household' see Csikszentmihalyi, M. and Rochberg-Halton. E. 1981. *The Meaning of Things: Domestic Symbols and the Self.* Cambridge: Cambridge University Press, pp. 11–12.

of containment is necessarily mediatory in reconciling the complexity of modern life. It may hide and subjugate disorder, fail to reconcile contradictory wild elements introduced because they refuse to kowtow to the prevailing normative sense of order, or just contain and maintain a state of clutter. As Miller observes

> material culture promotes framing, which provides for the maintenance of diversity, while keeping contradictory forces operating without coming into conflict [. . .] Consistency of self or object is not a noticeable feature of the modern age [. . .] the modern personality appears as a kind of counter-factual self, which keeps afloat several possible characters, aided by a range of goods which externalise these into different forms, this may be a possible response to a necessarily contradictory world.[5]

The dwelling place and its periphery anchors the individual and acts as a sort of lodestone in providing a point of departure and a point of return. Its physical form and contents offers one of the richest sources for the study of material culture as a mediating agency – the means through which individuals relate to each other within a household and beyond it to the world at large. Dwelling furnishes the most fundamental spatial experience in the orientation of individuals in relation to the external world through the everyday mundane practices of managing and ordering domestic life and the special rituals which mark particular moments of change in the life cycle. While the furnishings and physical contents of the dwelling represent the material manifestation of its inhabitants' sense of the world in microcosm. As Mihaly Csikszentmihalyi and Eugene Rochberg-Halton observed

> one can argue that the home contains the most special objects: those that were selected by the person to attend to regularly and have close at hand, that create permanence in the intimate life of a person, and therefore that are most involved in making up his or her identity [. . .] Although one has little control over the things encountered outside the home, household objects are chosen and could be freely discarded if they produced too much conflict within the self.[6]

As the last sentence of the quotation indicates, Csikszentmihalyi and Rochberg-Halton's analysis depended on an idealised sense of agency

5. Miller, D. 1987. *Material Culture and Mass Consumption*. Oxford: Blackwell, p. 208.
6. Csikszentmihalyi and Rochberg-Halton 1981. *The Meaning of Things*, p. 17.

in contrast to more recent studies which have analysed material possessions in terms of the dynamic interplay between alienation and appropriation, rather than static forms of symbolism.[7] Nevertheless Csikszentmihalyi and Rochberg-Halton's *The Meaning of Things*, derived from a realisation of the neglect accorded to questions relating to how people use actual material objects to define themselves, remains a seminal study of the social significance of artefacts within the domestic context, and has provided a model for detailed case studies.

Tracking Identity across the Threshold

Although there is now more attention focused on objects as a result of the interest in the social significance of material culture, for example in the household as a social unit in systems of provision in consumption studies,[8] and historical and critical studies in architecture, [9] furniture and the decorative arts within the disciplines of art and design history and cultural studies,[10] there is still much to be gained from considering the dwelling as the materialisation of space and part of a network of associated practices in terms of material effects.[11] In locating containment through the case study of the private abode as a personal space it is possible to consider the material contextualisation of the individual within the home as the repository or objectification of social relations. What is meant by objectification here, based on Miller's definition,[12] is the material resolution – the making of the idea into a reality, whether of the temporal kind as in ephemeral, the seemingly eternal type as in authentic, or more often than not a combination of both in which

7. For example Attfield, J. 'Pram Town' [1989] 1995, pp. 215–38. In Attfield, J. and Kirkham, P. (eds) *A View From the Interior. Women and Design.* London: The Women's Press; Miller, D. 1990. 'Appropriating the State on the Council Estate' pp. 43-55. In Putnam, T. and Newton, C. *Household Choices.* London: Futures; Cieraad, I. (ed.) 1999. *At Home: An Anthropology of Domestic Space.* New York: Syracuse University Press.

8. Fine, B. and Leopold, E. 1993. *The World of Consumption.* London and New York: Routledge.

9. For example Friedman, A.T. 1998. *Woman and the Making of the Modern House: A Social and Architectural History.* New York: Harry N. Abrams.

10. Colomina, B. 1994. *Privacy and Publicity: Modern Architecture as Mass Media.* Cambridge, Massachusetts and London: MIT Press.

11. For example Bachelard, G. [1958] 1964. *The Poetics of Space.* Boston: Beacon; Lefebvre, H. 1996. *The Production of Space.* Trans. Donald Nicholson-Smith. Oxford: Blackwell; Rapoport, A. 1969. *House, Form and Culture.* Englewood Cliffs, NJ: Prentice Hall.

12. Miller 1987. *Material Culture and Mass Consumption.*

some sort of mediation takes place at the point of materialisation and forms an internal logic of sorts characterised here as an ecology of personal possessions.

The inconsistencies between designers' utopian plans and the realities of living in human spaces are often revealed through the boundaries that separate public from private domains. Thus transitional boundaries between personal and common spaces such as the threshold, the door and the window can be seen as areas of containment or places of negotiation. Most analyses derived from architectural theory emphasise the designer's gaze as the dominant sense of perception through which this relation is meant to be experienced. Whereas the actual experience of inhabiting a particular space may be quite different to that intended by the designer or analysed by the critic. For example, even where Beatriz Colomina's analysis of the domestic interior refers to Benjamin's 'traces' as the materiality of domestic life – the impression of the occupants' presence – she nevertheless explains the construction of the sense of interior, using Loos as a case study, through the control of visuality – the design devices used to force the gaze away from the windows and into the centre of the interior.[13]

Less apparent and less researched, but even more revelatory because hidden, is the way in which interpersonal relations are materialised within the spatial organisation of the home interior through furnishing arrangements and specific articles. Particular items of seemingly inconsequential furniture such as the dressing table, and small personal effects collectively termed ornaments, offer comparative examples of the material specificity pertaining to different types of things and their role in defining, performing, rehearsing and mediating aspects of subjectivity.

The concept of 'separate spheres' based on nineteenth-century ideology that set up a binary opposition between male/female and private/public, used to formulate studies such as those on domesticity, consumption and women's studies, has tended to divide aspects of culture in terms of polarities.[14] Although this has been an invaluable aid in highlighting perspectival views from groups not previously given much space or attention, the focus which emphasised the previously disregarded has also tended to stereotype and airbrush out the nuances of the process of self-creation. Thus the stereotype of the home as

13. Colomina 1994. *Privacy and Publicity,* pp. 233–81.

14. Davidoff, L. and Hall, C. 1987. *Family Fortunes: Men and Women of the English Middle Class 1780–1850.* London: Hutchinson.

wholly feminine is an exaggeration, a representation for the sake of argument, and an analytical device without a real-life equivalent, it is nevertheless not an out-of-the-blue imaginary construction and has ideological effects which are very real indeed.[15] However the main thrust of this study is the ecology of personal possessions, the role of domestic things in the materiality of the construction of self-identity in the context of the home.[16] A referent can always be traced back to the everyday world of lived experience where the domestic world has largely been a woman's domain and from which the stereotype draws its power and its meaning in the first place. But as Breward discerned in his study of masculine consumption, because it is an area stereotyped as feminine so 'masculine consumption habits have been effectively obscured by an uncritical explanation of the separate-spheres ideology as a social fact rather than a pervasive mythology'.[17] What needs to be acknowledged is the pervasive effect of that ideology built into the material environment that outlives the social changes that make it out of date.

The same separate spheres ideology that draws a conceptual boundary between the public and the private – the collective and the personal, the male and the female, if taken too literally – makes it impossible to venture beyond the boundaries that define the geographical parameters of the home. The consumption of information and communication technologies within the household provided a link through the use of media by individual members of households with the world beyond their front door. This 'doubly articulated public and private culture' has managed to some extent to transcend the limitations set by the physical boundaries of the material object originally instigated by the ideology of separate spheres.[18] If the making of self-identities is to be investigated through the transformative power of material objects and their meanings, the power of the mediating vehicles need to be tracked

15. Reed, C. (ed.) 1996. *Not At Home: The Suppression of Domesticity in Modern Art and Architecture*. London: Thames and Hudson.

16. Although the term 'home' is not universal it is used generically here to indicate the transformation of the house into a cultural entity. As for example Birdwell-Pheasant, D. and Lawrence-Zúñiga, D. (eds) 1999. *House Life: Space, Place and Family in Europe*. Oxford and New York: Berg.

17. Breward, C. 1999. *The Hidden Consumer: Masculinities, fashion and city life 1860–1914*. Manchester: Manchester University Press, pp. 10–11.

18. Silverstone, R. and Hirsch, E. (eds) 1992. *Consuming Technologies: Media and information in domestic spaces*. London: Routledge, p. 15.

in their trajectory across the threshold from private to public domains, so that

> Objects and meanings, technologies and media [...] cross the diffuse and shifting boundary between the public sphere where they are produced and distributed, and the private sphere where they are appropriated into a personal economy of meaning.[19]

The example of household things such as the dressing table and their associated furnishing practices that follow, have been selected for their role in the process of self-creation. Therefore, although contextualised within the household where as objects they abide as more or less permanent fixtures or take their place as part of the furnishing arrangements, effects also take place beyond the physical container that can only be perceived by contextualising the household within the broader canvass of the cultural field that encompasses public as well as private life. In his study of social production of space, referring to the dwelling, Henri Lefebvre has acknowledged that 'Private space is distinct from, but always connected with, public space. In the best circumstances, the outside space of the community is dominated, while the indoor space of family life is appropriated.'[20] He elaborates this private 'indoor' life as 'a spatial practice which, though still immediate, is close, in concrete terms to the work of art' referring to the creativity of the practice of homemaking and notes that 'appropriation is not effected by an immobile group, be it a family, a village or a town' acknowledging that 'time plays a part in the process, and [...] cannot be understood apart from the rhythms of time and life.'[21]

In detailing the materiality of the dwelling as context and process with effects beyond the geographical boundaries, the notion of identity is also conceptualised beyond the sociological groups which tend to stereotype gender, class, age and ethnicity. When the ecology of personal possessions is embodied by the household as both a social unit and a material accumulation of things contained in time and space, a feasible framework is formed to investigate how people form their identities through things.

19. Silverstone and Hirsch, 1992. *Consuming Technologies*, pp. 18–19.
20. Lefebvre 1996. *The Production of Space*, p. 166.
21. Ibid.

The Dressing Table

> The small tables with drawers which [in the seventeenth century] were probably the type most favoured as toilet table in bed or dressing rooms were made in walnut and oak and, according to contemporary inventories, were covered with a carpet or a cloth, sometimes referred to as a 'toilet'. They vary considerably in style [. . .] Two or three drawers were usual; these contained the numerous cosmetics used by men and women alike. Painting, rouging and patching were fashionable and elaborate sets for the dressing table, comprising boxes for the combs and brushes, powder and perfumes, etc., were to be encountered in silver plate, or in Japan work.[22]

In Chapter 5 we saw how the ephemeral quality of textiles lends itself to the materialisation of changing identities. This is not only because of its adaptability to the fast rate of change required by the fashion system which works to a time-scale commensurate with the human life span. It is also because of its propensity to establish an intimate relationship to the body in the case of clothing, and its ubiquitous presence in the daily routines of everyday life in the home in the form of household linens and furnishings. The dressing table is therefore posited here as a contrasting type of object even though it does have a certain indirect affinity with textiles in as much as it provides a representative aspect of the intimate spatial setting where dressing practices take place.

According to Auslander the dressing table was invented by women in the French court of the eighteenth century and directly associated with two of Louis XV's mistresses – Pompadour and du Barry.[23] The introduction of the 'boudoir' in the eighteenth century marked the feminisation of the dressing room which until then had been just as standard a feature of the gentleman's apartment[24] as exemplified in the description of its centrepiece, the dressing table, in the quotation above. Amongst the leisured classes in the eighteenth century dressing was a social activity performed in the company of friends and servants.

22. Fastnedge, R. 1955. *English Furniture Styles From 1500-1830*. Harmondsworth: Penguin, pp. 42–3.

23. Auslander, L. 1996. *Taste and Power: Furnishing Modern France*. Berkeley, Los Angeles and London: University of California Press.

24. Marshner, J. 'Boudoirs and Dressing Rooms' pp. 166–8. In Banham, J. (ed.) 1997. *Encyclopedia of Interior Design*. London and Chicago: Fitzroy Dearborn.

But with the privatisation of domestic space the dressing table was rendered a consummately feminine accoutrement that became a conventional part of the bedroom. The addition of elaborately decorated swags of drapery, bows and tassels, that marked a lady's dressing table, was a style that remained unchanged well into the mid-twentieth century, serving to show the resistance to change in furniture in contrast to the ephemeral nature of fashionable dress and in spite of radical social changes in the life of women that occurred throughout that period.

Although the modern movement did attempt to reform the design of domestic furniture to adapt it from crafted woodworking processes to a functional aesthetic, standardised industrial production and non-traditional materials such as tubular metal, glass and plastic, such innovations remained a minority taste in domestic furnishing. The more acceptable version of modern furniture was stripped of carved enrichment but continued to be manufactured in traditional forms and materials.[25] The persistent rejection of innovation in domestic furniture design is instanced in the account given in Chapter 4 of the invention of the reproduction as a way of underwriting authenticity. Thus the dressing table like most domestic furniture is quite traditional in its form even while providing a prop to the emergence of the modern woman and accordingly the changing identities represented in cosmetic and dressing practices.

The dressing table and its accoutrements is an intriguing item of domestic furniture because although at one time unisex and positioned within the dressing room as an informal space for receiving guests, it is now one of the only purely feminine pieces of furniture still to be found in the modern home located in the bedroom, the most private inner sanctum of the house and the room conventionally characterised as the woman's domain. It is the site for 'making up', part of the ritual associated with getting ready in private to go out in public, still referred today by some women as 'putting my face on'.

25. Attfield, J. 1992. 'The role of design in the relationship between furniture manufacture and its retailing 1939–1965 with initial reference to the furniture firm of J. Clarke' (unpublished doctoral thesis) Brighton: University of Brighton; Attfield, J. 1996. '"Give 'em something dark and heavy": the Role of Design in the Material Culture of Popular British Furniture 1939–1965', pp. 185–201. *Journal of Design History,* Vol. 9, No. 3; Attfield, J. 1999 'Freedom of Design', pp. 203–20. In Attfield, J. (ed.) *Utility Reassessed: The role of ethics in the practice of design.* Manchester: Manchester University Press.

Vulgarity

WE CANNOT RESIST wanting to go beyond the example of ornament inappropriately applied and to give an example of a crude shape poorly decorated. Following our principle that words alone may confuse, the example is reinforced with a visual contrast which defines the meaning of vulgarity. By vulgarity in people we mean just this kind of coarseness of body, cheapness of ornament, and insensitive application of make-up. The parallel in the case of the pottery is exact, in its florid shape and crude cosmetic decoration.

Figure 14. Woman in heavy make-up pictured in front of a mirror, used to illustrate the 'vulgarity' of 'crude cosmetic decoration' as a lesson in good design, in *The Things We See: Indoors and Out* by Alan Jarvis, 1946. (Penguin Books. Photo 'Portrait study' by John Deakin)

Kathy Peiss's study of the cosmetics industry in the United States makes the case for considering the specificity of cosmetics in 'a period of highly unstable and contested gender definitions'.[26] The same claim can be made for the dressing table because of its obvious link to the use of cosmetics in self-identity formation and therefore its historical association with issues of gender and morality. A brief review of the way the dressing table has been treated in the context of the history of furniture and design as an aspect of modernism soon reveals the uncertain status it held because of its gendered associations.

26. Peiss, K. 1996. 'Making Up, Making Over: Cosmetics, Consumer Culture, and Women's Identity', pp. 311–36. In de Grazia, V. (ed.) 1996. *The Sex of Things: Gender and Consumption in Historical Perspective.* Berkeley and Los Angeles: University of California Press.

The specialist literature on the history of furniture suggests that there may be some coincidence between the receding attention given to the dressing table and its feminisation from the nineteenth century onwards, so that few accounts of the modern history of furniture even bother to mention it at all although it continues to form part of standard domestic bedroom furnishing.[27] Its neglect in the context of modernist interpretations of the history of design that classify it as trivial can be explained by the automatic link its association with the feminine makes with the private, the frivolous, the decorative and with popular taste.

John Gloag's 'social history' account of the eighteenth-century 'highly specialised and elaborate' toilet table written in 1966, desists from denigrating it openly but betrays his modernist bias against the decorative (feminine), in his pointed observation of 'the ingenuity lavished on them', compared with the meagre dimensions of washing appliances from the same period.[28] His disapproval of 'the inattention to cleanliness' in comparison with 'the enormous importance given to the artifice of the toilet' was a long-standing moral attitude adopted by modern design reformers allying obviously made-up women with immorality, 'crude' ornament, bad taste and 'vulgarity'. Gloag's assertion of the superiority of English furniture attributed to its restrained use of ornament in comparison with 'French furniture, dominated by decorative considerations [. . .] designed for customers whose lives were dedicated to the modes of a dissolute court',[29] exemplifies the correlation made between bad design and disreputable behaviour. So that even the Rudd 'reflecting dressing table' from Hepplewhite's 1788 catalogue with its ingeniously designed compartmentalised drawers, swing mirrors and simple lines, which visually would have conformed to Gloag's aesthetic sense, could not escape the smear of ill repute accorded to it by its provenance from 'the original model [which] may have been made for Margaret Caroline Rudd, a notorious courtesan'.[30]

---

27. The fullest but by no means comprehensive historical account is given by Ralph Fastnedge in *English Furniture Styles From 1500–1830* first published in 1955, mentioned above. For other examples see Harling, R. 1973. *Dictionary of Design and Decoration*. London and Glasgow: has a small entry, Banham, J. ed. 1997. *Encyclopedia of Interior Design (2 Vols)*. London and Chicago: Fitzroy Dearborn has no entry at all.

28. Gloag, J. 1966. *A social history of furniture design from B.C.1300 to A.D. 1960*. New York: Bonanza Books.

29. Ibid., p. 141.

30. Gloag 1966. *A social history of furniture design*, p. 140.

It follows from the moral indignation, hinted at by Gloag, representative of Victorian disapproval to such a seemingly demure object of feminine furniture, that attitudes to the processes and objects used in dressing and making-up associated with the dressing table should be seen as forming part and parcel of the ecology of domestic furnishings. The disappearance of the dressing table from standard Utility furniture made available during the Second World War testifies to its categorisation as a redundant object of luxury and frivolity in a period of austerity-driven functional design. While its reintroduction after the war announced a period of social change in which there was an acknowledgement of the necessity to cater to popular tastes for the excesses of glamour disseminated via Hollywood films.[31]

Dressing Practices

The anxiety over women's use of cosmetics that arose in the nineteenth century was derived from the belief that the application of make-up constituted a form of deception and that true beauty emanated from within, reflecting the inherent goodness and purity of the character through the appearance.[32] By the turn of the century visible signs of cosmetics could be interpreted in a number of different ways, indicating the independent female consumer or the dangerous traffic of female sexuality. A parallel can be drawn between how the dressing table was regarded in mid-twentieth-century Britain according to Gloag's conservative reaction, and Victorian uneasiness over the line between chastity and sexuality[33] indicated in the etiquette of appropriate well-groomed feminine presentation to appear not too obviously made-up. Peiss's analysis of the use of cosmetics as a symptom of social change to emerge in twentieth-century urban America is employed to describe the state of femininity at that particular geo-historical conjuncture when 'the performance of identity – constituting the self through appearance and gesture – was fundamentally at odds with the notions of fixed personal and social identity'. The American cosmetics industry spread to Europe and other parts of the world legitimating the use of visible make-up until its application was no longer regarded as a disreputable practice and became accepted as a necessary element of

---

31. Attfield, J. 1999. 'Fascinating Fitness: the dangers of Good Design' pp. 233–44. In Attfield 1999. *Utility Reassessed*, p. 237.
32. Peiss, 1996. 'Making Up, Making Over', pp. 314–16.
33. Tsëelon, E. 1995. *The Masque of Femininity*. London: Sage, p. 32.

conventional feminine public dress even among the most conservative members of society.[34]

Although it is beyond the scope of this study to go into detailed descriptions of fashions in cosmetics, it should be noted that during the period that saw the popular take up of cosmetics, there were cultural differences involved in the etiquette of applying make-up between, for example, American, French and English practices. This should however alert us that the type of assertion made by Peiss regarding the widespread emergence of the practice of 'constituting the self through appearance' needs to be treated with caution. The other side of that notion about the intractability of a fixed identity also needs to be considered. And it is through the figure of containment that includes the fixed and intransigent as well as the more fluid innovative objects and practices that people use to articulate their identity that it is possible to get beyond the either/or concept of modernisation or tradition.

Tag Gronberg's study of Paris in the 1920s provides an alternative interpretation to that of international modernism, exploring contesting gendered and engendering representations of Parisienne urban modernity. The feminine aspect of Paris is disclosed as the context for the performative role of elegant dressing and the 'toilette' that constructed the identity of the fashionable modern urban woman. The 'necessaire' or vanity case is cited as 'the consummate feminine modern appurtenance'.[35] Women could now appropriate space in the street where, with the aid of a small fashion accessory – a miniaturised mobile form of 'dressing table' – that which was formerly a private practice could be transferred to the public domain. Making up in public coincided with the increasing social acceptability of women drinking and smoking, signalling women's new-found visibility and freedom to assume a presence in their own right in what had been considered until then a man's world.[36] Such a bold assertion must of course be

34. Wykes-Joyce, M. 1961. *Cosmetics and Adornment.* London: Peter Owen; Wilson, E. and Taylor, L. 1989. *Through the Looking Glass: A History of Dress from 1860 to the Present Day.* London: BBC Books, p. 82; Craik, J. 1994. *The Face of Fashion: Cultural Studies in Fashion.* London: Routledge, pp. 153–64; Anderson, B.S. and Zinsser, J.P. 1988. *A History of their Own: Women in Europe from Prehistory to the Present,* Vol. II. London: Penguin Books, pp. 202–3.

35. Gronberg, T. 1998. *Design on Modernity: Exhibiting the City in 1920s Paris.* Manchester: Manchester University Press, p. 24.

36. Attfield, J. 1997. 'Cocktail Cabinets', pp. 291–2. In Banham, J. ed. *Encyclopedia of Interior Design,* Vol 1. London and Chicago: Fitzroy Dearborn.

accompanied by the proviso that in spite of radical social changes after the First World War, the conservative section of society, usually stereotyped by historians and sociologists as the bourgeois middle class, continued to uphold traditional values and would have rejected such marks of female emancipation as unacceptably 'common'. Jennifer Craik notes that in England even once 'make-up became tolerated . . . there were still exhortations not to apply it in public'.[37] Cosmetics, like fashionable dress and style, was one of the means through which women could transcend their inherited class position.

Appearance was also a very important actualising element in the visible emergence of a number of youth subcultures based on individualised self-realisation in the post Second World War period. Centred around student insurrections in 1968 and developed by a spate of popular protest movements all over the world,[38] the younger generation assumed particular looks to indicate their affiliation to various political and social groups. Hobsbawm attributes youth culture with being

> the matrix of the cultural revolution in the wider sense of a revolution in manners and customs, in ways of spending leisure and in the commercial arts, which increasingly formed the atmosphere that urban men and women breathed [. . .]. It was both demotic and antinomian, especially in matters of personal conduct. Everyone was to 'do their own thing' with minimal outside restraint, although in practice peer pressure and fashion actually imposed as much uniformity as before.[39]

The youth sub-cultures' style of dress was distinguished by informal non-conformity defying the rules of 'good dress', including the refusal of cosmetics or neat hairdressing. The more theatrical sub-cultures used spectacular dress and make-up to play transgressional games with the rules of normative appearance as a self-conscious act of identity reinvention. The popular music and fashion industries exploited subcultural street styles and reprocessed them for mainstream consumption so that to remain in opposition, new and more extreme looks had to be invented.

37. Craik 1994. *The Face of Fashion*, p. 161.

38. Harvey, D. 1989. *The Condition of Postmodernity: An Enquiry into the Origins of Cultural Change*. Oxford: Blackwell, p. 38.

39. Hobsbawm, E. 1994. *Age of Extremes: The Short Twentieth Century 1914–1991*. London: Michael Joseph, pp. 329–30.

40. Wilson, E. 1985. *Adorned in Dreams: Fashion and Modernity*. London: Virago.

Elizabeth Wilson's significant analysis of fashion as a form of performance art[40] and one of the 'new components of the spectacle' manifested a celebration of pluralism, pleasure and the demotic.[41] Her contextualisation of fashion within the postmodern mentality pointed out the acute awareness of the contingency of social identity that challenged conventional definitions of gender and sexuality, although from a very positioned, sophisticated, urban and alternative point of view. Many social historians[42] have chronicled the popularisation of subcultural style in the post Second World War period so that it can be accepted as a further symptom of cultural destabilisation, heightening the importance of constructing self-identity that challenged stereo-typical gender roles. Sociologists have also had something to say about recent social changes instigated by or resulting from genetic engineering which has made it possible to appropriate the body, so that, according to Anthony Giddens

> Genetic transmission can be humanly determined [. . .] thus breaking the final tie connecting the life of the species to biological evolution. In this process of the disappearance of nature, emergent fields of decision-making affect not just the direct process of reproduction, but the physical constitution of the body and the manifestations of sexuality. Such fields of action thus relate back to questions of gender and gender identity, as well as to other processes of identity formation.[43]

The year 1999 saw the marriage of the first British transsexual couple. Janeen Newham born a boy and David Willis born a girl, had to go to Denmark for their wedding to have 'a proper ceremony', a right not accorded them in this country under their newly assumed genders. Their account of the years of struggle to alter 'nature's terrible mistake' offers an example of the physical reconstitution of the body referred to by Giddens. David's experience of being a man trapped in a woman's body made him wish he 'didn't have a body at all'.[44] While Janeen

41. Wilson, E. 1990. 'These New Components of the Spectacle: Fashion and Post-modernism', pp. 209–36. In Boyne, R. and Rattansi, A. (eds) 1990. *Postmodernism and Society*. London: Macmillan.

42. For example Hobsbawm, 1994. *Age of Extremes;* Samuel, R. 1994 & 1998. *Theatres of Memory*, Vols. I and II. London and New York: Verso.

43. Giddens, A. 1991. *Modernity and Self-Identity: Self and Society in the Late Modern Age*. Cambridge: Polity, p. 219.

44. Neustatter, A. 1999. 'Happy ever after' pp. 4–5. *Guardian,* 22 October.

Figure 15. Mrs Winter's 'non-Utility' dressing table in French-polished walnut, part of a bedroom suite bought in 1951, photographed in 1986. (photo: Eva Londos)

conjectured that 'maybe one day there won't be men and women, just people'.[45]

Such an occurrence or such musings by people alleging to live 'ordinary' lives indicate seismic social changes that have occurred over a relatively short space of time, in the way that individual identity is perceived and valued. The overriding importance given to the realisation of the self would seem to enable the transcendence of the 'fact' of the physical body. Yet there are aspects of material culture which are much easier to change but which resist alteration for hundreds of years with stubborn persistence seemingly oblivous to the changing world around them. To go back to the dressing table, why has it not changed to keep up with the deep changes in women's lives that have resulted from modernising social reforms reflected in the fast changes of fashion in clothing the body and making up the face? A detailed look at some

45. 'An Ordinary Marriage', An *Everyman* documentary film screened on BBC 1, Sunday, 24 October 1999.

specific examples helps to explain the way some type of objects act to contain and reconcile the contradictory elements of change and stasis in material form.

Mrs Winter's Dressing Table

If we look at a particular example – the French-polished walnut dressing table acquired by Mrs Winter as part of a bedroom suite in 1951 and still owned by her more than thirty years later,[46] its form is not all that different to an eighteenth-century version. In addition to the dressing table Mrs Winter's suite consisted of two wardrobes and a chest of drawers, and constituted a luxury in 1951. Her savings from high earnings during the War, working the night shift in the Lebus factory manufacturing gliders, enabled her to afford the 'non-Utility' grade of furniture which included in its retail price of £50 the cost of a $33^1/3\%$ Purchase Tax. The 'kidney'-shaped top with drawer below, scalloped mirror and small drawer pedestals either side referred vestigially to the custom of sitting at the dressing table. But the minimally sized rooms of the new town post-war house she moved into in 1952 prohibited the conventional locating of the dressing table in front of the window and certainly did not allow the space for seating in front of it. The wartime Utility furniture scheme had omitted the dressing table altogether, bringing it back after the War in an attempt to counteract the sense of deprivation felt by the population after a period of austerity and shortages.[47] To Mrs Winter it was a source of great satisfaction and pride to have been able to afford to buy the more expensive non-Utility furniture. But her sense of personal social progression, that the move in 1952 from North London to a new house in Harlow shortly after marrying undoubtedly signified, did not extend to remaining financially independent. She was typical of the generation of young wives who moved into what was to become known as Pram Town. Her intention when she took the job in the local typewriter factory was to save up 'to start a family' and give up working. To put Mrs Winter's

46. The photograph was taken as part of study of domestic interiors in a new town. Other material relating to the study is based on recorded interviews housed at the Essex County Council Sound Archives. Interviewees' names have been changed to preserve their anonymity. Also see Attfield 1995. 'Inside Pram Town'.

47. See illustrations of post-war Utility dressing tables in Denney, M. 1999. 'Utility Furniture and the Myth of Utility 1943–1948', pp. 110–24. In Attfield, *Utility Reassessed*, p. 119.

dressing table in context it needs to be considered against the back-ground of a furniture industry which in spite of having been coerced to undergo a form of concentration by state intervention during war, in peacetime soon settled back into its former traditional hierarchical structure.[48] Some technological innovations did have a certain amount of impact on the way furniture was manufactured after the Second World War, but generally both the products and their methods of production did not change as radically as reformers in favour of modernisation and mass production had hoped.

One of the best-known modern designers of the post-war period involved in the movement to reform furniture design for mass produc-tion, Ernest Race, commented regretfully in 1953 that 'furniture is still today largely a hand product, and there is no fundamental difference in conception between a power-operated saw or planer and their hand equivalents [. . .] [T]he strong convention in the furniture industry, largely founded on misunderstandings and a false sense of tradition, have retarded [the] natural development of common-sense design.'[49] His view, representative of the advocates of 'good design', was that furniture should not be subject to fashion trends like dress design but at the same time supported the need for reform because what was offered in 'most of the furniture [. . .] shops up and down the country [. . . was] the same old stuff, bulky, ostentatious, over ornamented, and apparently polished by the process used for making toffee-apples'. His argument was based on the logic of functionalism and the belief that well-designed furniture should be timeless but at the same time appropriate to the modern age in its materials, method of manufacture and looks. To illustrate the illogicality of 'anachronistic' style he ridiculed the idea of a 'Reproduction' or 'Antique' car or aeroplane, and puzzled over why only certain innovations had been readily assimilated in the modern household, while

> there is still many a meal cooked by gas, and washed up in a modern
> sink unit, that is served on a factory made 'Jacobean Type' dining table.
> The lighting throughout being provided by electricity, diffused from a
> modern fitting in the kitchen and from something trying to look like a
> candelabra, complete with plastic candle drips, in the dining room.

48. Attfield, J. 1999. 'Freedom of Design', pp. 203–20. In Attfield, J. (ed.) 1999. *Utility Reassessed*, p. 218.

49. Race, E. 1953. 'Design in Modern Furniture', pp. 62–5. In Lake, F. (ed.) *Daily Mail Ideal Home Book 1952–53*. London: Daily Mail Ideal Home, p. 64.

> Given the choice of a kitchen sink what woman would ask for a copy
> of her old one in preference to a new stainless steel model; or on buying
> a gas cooker demand that it should look like grandma's kitchen range?[50]

And no doubt he would have been astounded to learn that had he posed his rhetorical question today, he may well have had a positive response, given the fashionable return of the Victorian butler's sink and the popularity of the Aga.

There is little doubt that Mrs Winter's dressing table was an anachronism if judged by Race's functional criteria. It would seem unlikely that it had ever been used for sitting at to make up. Thirty-five years after buying it Mrs Winter confessed that she had considered selling it, but changed her mind when a friend admired it and observed that 'they don't make them like that anymore' indicating a change of status from old-fashioned to 'antique'. The carefully arranged still-life adorning the top of Mrs Winter's dressing table – the cut-glass tray tidy with matching covered bowl for face powder and puff and the symmetrically placed candle sticks, each underlined with its own starched embroidered doily – showed no sign of everyday use but indicated the symbolic meaning attached to traditional home furnishing. The 1999 'Christmas Gifts' *Home Shopping Direct* catalogue shows decorative dressing-table accessories of the same ilk still available today – 'the traditional three-piece, silver-plated dressing-table set' comprising of brush, comb and mirror, the musical jewellery box in the shape of a miniature piano 'with cherub lid that opens to reveal a dancing couple', and 'the beautifully crafted porcelain musical Spanish doll' are among the items offered.

The stubborn persistence of traditional furnishings in the face of the far-reaching technological innovations and social changes that revolutionised women's lives in particular, seemed incomprehensible to modernists like Ernest Race in the early 1950s when Mrs Winter's dressing table was new. He would have been even more astounded to witness the value accrued to it by the upgrading to 'antique' in the mid-1980s. There it stood still unused as if frozen in time like a sentinel guarding traditional home values and an out-dated culture of feminine beauty.

There are no neat parallels that can be drawn between theories that challenge the concept of female identity and the reality of people's lives. Recent feminist critique has gone as far as to question the very

50. Race 1953. 'Design in Modern Furniture', p. 63.

category of identity itself as a stable notion because it depends on belief in the concepts of the natural, the original and the inevitable. Judith Butler asserts that 'because "female" no longer appears to be a stable notion, its meaning is as troubled and unfixed as "woman"'.[51] The theory that defines femininity as a self-conscious act of construction through the use of appearance as a means of assuming a false self, remains a theory when tested against real-life cases as that of Jannine and David cited above who show the opposite to be true for them. It is only through the use of the theory of false consciousness, discredited for not acknowledging that there is something to learn from the groups one is studying, that such a view can be taken.[52] Their solution to being 'born into the wrong bodies' was to alter their physical bodies in keeping with their true gender. They were not asserting 'the disappearance of nature' à la Giddens, but on the contrary finding a way of transcending its 'terrible mistake' through human intervention to bring out their true selves. Concerning the relationship between appearance and authenticity, Tsëelon's research reached the conclusion that 'the continuity that can be traced between old misogynies and new psychological and sociological theories regarding the Eve-woman is disrupted when it comes to women's own experience'.[53] This is not to be interpreted as a crude refutation of feminist critique of the questioning of the concept of 'identity', but to point out the complex interrelation between the uses of theory and the experience of the material culture of everyday life.

Part of the Furniture

So to return to the larger question concerning the figure of containment represented by household furnishing arrangements, it is possible to see the way it operates as an ecological system that manages to hold

51. Butler, J. 1990. *Gender Trouble: Feminism and the Subversion of Identity.* London and New York: Routledge, p. viii.

52. As D. Miller's critique of cultural theories that invalidate popular taste so aptly points out in *Material Culture and Mass Consumption* (1978) 'The argument that there is a thing called capitalist society which renders its population entirely pathological and dehumanised, with the exception of certain theorists who, although inevitably living their private lives in accordance with the tenets of this delusion, are able in their abstracted social theory to rise above, criticise and provide the only alternative model for society, is somewhat suspicious.' (p. 167)

53. Tsëelon, 1995. *The Masque of Femininity*, p. 34.

together opposing and contradictory symbolic orders of, for example, to maintain order and clutter, modernity and tradition, authenticity and ephemerality, practicality and fantasy. This has little do with the coherence lent by the kind of unified design scheme governed by the principles of modernism of the type which would have met with the approval of followers of Le Corbusier's theory of urbanism like Alison and Peter Smithson[54] who chose the following quotation to open a book describing their own 'programme' for the regeneration of a new type of city.

> he was dazzled, as soon as he entered, by the brightness of the flat, with its white walls, its gaily coloured curtains and its furniture which was so clean that it looked as if it had come straight from the shop [. . .] Lognon reflected that he would have liked a flat as light as this one, without a single object lying around, without a single speck of dust, a flat which, in fact, made him think of a luxury clinic.[55]

The strictures imposed by Modernism have a certain affinity with totalising social theories that attempt to fit all cultural forms into a particular pattern, mould or trajectory. Containment – the management of personal space, discussed in this chapter in relation to the home – could also be applied as a framing device to other types of appropriated (personal) space, is a hybrid pragmatic practice that has much more to do with a strategy for the survival of individuality than any concern for the rules of aesthetic order. It is the variety and ingenuity of arrangements to which people subject their surroundings that enable them to

54. Alison (1928–1993) and Peter (1923–) Smithson were among the more uncompromising group of young reforming post-war modernist architects, best known as prime movers of 'The New Brutalism' movement. Admirers of Le Cobusier and Mies van der Rohe but with a more hard edged ruthlessly honest approach that integrated the structure, services and materials into the design of the building and gave priority to function producing a particularly austere style that did not prove popular. Best known for the Hunstanton School in Norfolk, considered to be the first Brutalist building, and the Economist building in London, they were also involved in the debates concerning urban planning. Although a particularly English interpretation of Modernism, the Smithsons' version earnt international acclaim and their work and ideas have recently enjoyed a revival of interest among American students of architecture.

55. Simenon, G. 1938. *The Mouse*, Harmondsworth: Penguin, pp. 7–8 cited in Smithson A. & P. 1970. *Ordinariness and Light: Urban theories 1952–1960 and their application in a building project 1963–1970*. London: Faber and Faber.

appropriate their environment, or conversely the intractability of their surroundings which alienates them. The introduction of wild elements placed purposely to stand out conspicuously for maximum impact may coexist in the same household where other items like the dressing table, conform unquestioningly to furnishing traditions and silently take a stand against modernity. It is not for nothing that being 'part of the furniture' assumes the invisibility *beyond* the familiarity that breeds contempt.

Part III

Contexts

Introduction

> It is in the everyday world that politics and polity, economics and the economy, aesthetics and beauty, are concretized, experienced, and perhaps transformed – in short, lived. The everyday is historical and contextual, its boundaries shifting with the changing landscape. The everyday is sensual, bodily, emotional, and intellectual. There is no escape from the everyday, no position outside it, for either the subjects of history or its writers.[1]

And the everyday is also material, its changing landscape is made up of the places, things and selves through which those social processes are performed and negotiated in the context of space, time and the body. It is also the place outside academic discourse where things are not necessarily conveniently ordered to prevent inconceivable encounters. And it is amidst the clutter and stuff of the everyday where those inconvenient juxtapositions found in real life, with such unlikely bedfellows like new towns and old-fashioned dressing tables, can coexist. It is in the familiar and the unlikely, the hidden wild side of material culture where it is possible to see how people use things to come to terms with the apparently relentless change imposed by modernisation – the condition that constantly threatens and works against the grain of individuality, but at the same time the context

---

1. Auslander, L. 1996. *Taste and Power: Furnishing Modern France*. Berkeley, Los Angeles, London: California University Press, p. 3.

within which individuals form their self-identity. The material culture of the everyday is largely unexplored territory because it lies too close at hand to intrigue, there is nothing tantalisingly exotic about the quotidian. As Toby Miller and Alex McHoul observe: 'The everyday is invisible but ever present. It is full of contradiction, and it can be transcended, passed over, and gone beyond, as when the drudgery of the workday is transformed via popular forms and flings'.[2] Once the glamorous or the 'new!' has been absorbed into the everyday it loses its gloss. Design, fashion and things with attitude in general have that propensity to provoke but once they lose the power to demand attention they quickly fade and recede into the background.

So far the book has concentrated on defining the sociality of things: clothes, cloths, furniture, houses – the stuff that makes up the material culture of everyday life. This last part will shift the centre point of the investigation from things and their meanings to bring their context into sharper focus. 'Context' for the purposes of this analysis will be considered in terms of space, time and the body. Context is not a visible entity and although it can be conceptualised as background it only exists to position its subject and therefore has the same characteristic tendency to recede from view. Even analytically, context cannot be torn away from that which it is contextualising – its raison d'être depends on its relational status. Therefore in order to get a grip on the social life of things it is essential to include the contingent realities of their contexts that assign them their grounded existence as meaningful parts of people's lives.

There is no attempt here to review or revise the many theories that have been devised to explain the abstract ordering notions of time and space in relation to human action but at the same time it is those academic frameworks which define what lies outside the frame. David Harvey's analysis of the changing perceptions that direct spatial and temporal practices[3] provides an insightful cultural analysis of some of the structuring theories[4] which have gone furthest towards explaining

---

2. Miller, T. and McHoul, A. 1998. *Popular Culture and Everyday Life*. London and Thousand Oaks, California: Sage, p. 9.

3. Harvey, D. 1989. *The Condition of Postmodernity: An Enquiry into the Origins of Cultural Change*. Oxford: Blackwell.

4. Bourdieu, P. [1972] 1982. *Outline of a theory of practice*. Cambridge: Cambridge University Press; de Certeau, M. 1988. *The Practice of Everyday Life*. trans. Steven Rendall. Berkeley: University of California Press; Lefebvre, H. 1996. *The Production of Space*. Trans. Donald Nicholson-Smith. Oxford: Blackwell.

the particularity of the postmodern experience in the wider context of contemporary culture. The project here is more to do with his acknowledgement that 'The material practices from which our concepts of space and time flow are as varied as the range of individual and collective experiences,' than his overarching schema 'to put some overall interpretative frame around them that will bridge the gap between cultural change and the dynamics of political economy'.[5] The object of the exercise in taking space, time and body as archetypal contexts of modern life is not to dislocate them from each other but to highlight one at a time in order to look at some of the particular ways in which specific places, times and physical individualities have produced and embodied certain types of material culture, set against the broader context of the everyday lives that encompasses them.

The concept of context is a key issue in the practice of design and one which will also be addressed in the three chapters that follow, alongside less self-conscious types of design practices. Some designers have purposely set out to work with that much more elusive realm of the ordinary where design is not conceptualised as things in themselves or the expression of an individual, but in an attempt to provide a background for living, a framework for everyday life or a survival kit for the twenty-first century.

5. Harvey 1989. *The Condition of Postmodernity*, p. 211.

Figure 16. A 1930s London Underground poster depicting a typical suburban commuter at work and at home. (London Transport Museum)

Space: Where Things Take Place

In Chapter 6 we saw how at the same time that Ernest Race was decrying the perversity of mixing anachronistic reproduction furnishing with up-to-date functional design in the same household, Mrs Winter was moving from 'rooms' in war-torn London into her brand new Harlow New Town house with her French-polished mahogany luxury bedroom suite, unaware that she was contravening 'good design' principles. And in the same year, 1952, the Smithsons were mounting a fierce attack on the lack of a radical planning policy for post-war large-scale rebuilding of British cities, criticising new towns like Harlow as 'wishy-washy bands of housing trailing over the countryside – no doubt to a Morris dance'.[1] Their vision of 'the house of today' inspired by Le Corbusier, demanded a total break from the past and although respected, was generally regarded as an extreme view and had no actual impact on post-war planning and housing in Britain. It did however form part of the climate of debate which informed the architects, planners and designers of the post-war period who participated in the realisation of the post-war built environment.[2]

This chapter will look at the way space has been conceptualised as a prime contextualising factor in the material culture of the built environment, by considering urbanisation and the design of housing in particular. The politics of separate spheres touched on in Chapter 6 will be revisited to take a more detailed look at the form and status of

1. Smithson A. & P. 1970. *Ordinariness and Light: Urban theories 1952–1960 and their application in a building project 1963–1970*. London: Faber and Faber, p. 25.

2. Frampton, K. 1980. *Modern Architecture: A critical history*. London: Thames & Hudson, Chapter 2: New Brutalism and the architecture of the Welfare State: England 1949–59, pp. 262–8.

the public and the private domains in terms of property and social status. These differences are exemplified in certain conventional dwelling types in the context of particular urban forms, such as the suburb and street which do not necessarily correlate with the changing landscape of the social map. The dwelling can be conceptualised as a physical reference point from where people relate to their inner and outer lives, their pasts, presents and futures. It is also used as a space for the transaction of individuality, a starting point and return from the external world. The apparently unassailable permanence of buildings and urban forms is explored in relation to its vulnerability or resistance to change. Boundaries are not as impermeable as they might first appear. Just as important are the transitional points – the thresholds, windows, doors, entrances and exits, walls, and façades used to transact, allow, bar or control access to change. The transitional significance of the home also provides a way of examining how such permanent social structures as the family, as objectified in the dwelling, can adapt to different life stages and the changing experience of intimacy and interiority that characterises modern life, and forms a relationship to the exterior world beyond.

Most texts on architectural theory, discuss the experience of space through visuality and in particular through the gaze of the architect; that is to say through the interpretation of the intentionality implanted into the design.[3] Even in the writings of practising architects as, in the case of Robert Venturi and Denise Scott Brown,[4] who set out to 'learn' from popular iconology, the discourse is predominantly visual. The postmodern regime of aesthetics that emerged from a re-found visual sensibility that responded sympathetically to popular culture, such as Venturi and Scott Brown's 'ugly and ordinary' was labelled by Charles Jencks as a 'multivalent architecture' that allowed a more inclusive design language of mixed metaphors and ambiguous meanings.[5] But in spite of such efforts to integrate a postmodern sensibility to the popular, the wilder and more exuberant bad taste manifestations found for example in the aesthetics of popular suburban façades, these have in the main been regarded as 'dangerous' reactionary suburban

3. See the reference to Beatriz Colomina's study of the Loos interiors in Chapter 6, p. 4, Note No. 10.

4. Venturi, R., Scott Brown, D. and Izenour, I. [1972] 1982. *Learning from Las Vegas: The forgotten symbolism of architectural form.* Cambridge, Massachusetts: MIT.

5. Jencks, C. 1977. *The language of post-modern architecture.* London: Academy.

conformity. Roger Silverstone, for example controversially suggests television 'has serious implications for suburban politics and for what can
be called the suburbanization of the public sphere'.[6] But although
cultural critics have used the design of cities as a vehicle for discussing
postmodernism, any engagement with its materiality is rare. David
Harvey for example asserts that place is a social construct and '[t]he
only interesting question that can be asked is: by what social process(es)
is place constructed?'[7] Space and place are both conceptual *and* material,
they are also nowadays conceived of in virtual mode. Designers and
planners working on real projects have to tussle with the materiality,
as well as the economics, the politics and the aesthetics of space as
well as its social meaning. And it is to the processes of designing and
living in the spaces and places that theoreticians discuss that this study
is mainly dedicated. As a means of getting in touch with the materiality
of space both in terms of place and orientation, the chapter will include
examples of the aesthetics of privatisation in house façades and a case
study of moving house. The rationale for the study of moving was
based on an investigation of the way people use change of domicile,
the process of selection of location, dwelling type, furnishing and
household arrangement, to transact and negotiate the passage from
one life stage to the next.

The Public and the Private

The concept of 'separate spheres' is a useful analytic device for the
interpretation of class and gender cultures and has been extensively
applied in social history to highlight the division of labour resulting
from capitalism and industrialisation. And by the same token it shows
up the difference between male and female roles within the domestic
economy.[8] Although, as has been pointed out in Chapter Six, the
concept of separate spheres inevitably leads to a certain amount of
stereotyping which is not always helpful, and as long as the historical

6. Silverstone, R. (ed.) 1997. *Visions of Suburbia*. London: Routledge, p. 11.

7. Harvey, D. 'From space to place and back again: Reflections on the condition of
postmodernity' pp. 3–29. In Bird, J., Curtis, B., Putnam, T., Robertson, G. and Tickner,
L. (eds) 1993. *Mapping the Futures: Local cultures, global change*. London and New York:
Routledge, p. 5.

8. As for example in Davidoff, L. and Hall, C. 1987. *Family Fortunes: Men and Women
of the English Middle Class 1780–1850*. London: Hutchinson.

differences that have blurred the sharp definition implied by it are taken into consideration,[9] it does nevertheless work well in comparing the private and the public domains in political, social and spatial terms. The dynamic relationship between the private and the public also has direct relevance in contextualising individuality in the material culture of everyday life since it literally makes a place for its cultivation while also considering its social relations beyond the personal.

As Giddens points out

> it would be wrong to interpret the growth of privacy (and the need for intimacy) in terms of the erosion of a public sphere which used to exist in more traditional communities . . . privacy as 'the other side' of the penetration of the state, and privacy as what may not be revealed – the private is a creation of the public and vice versa; each forms part of newly emergent systems of internal referentiality. These changes form a fundamental part of the general framework of the transformation of intimacy.[10]

The terms 'public' and 'private' qualify in very class- and politically-specific ways, when appended to property – as in private property, meaning the right of possessing any 'thing' in general, and land in particular. The latter historically belongs to the landowning classes who acquired their social position by inheritance, and, with the rise of the middle class, through self-interested hard work backed by the law and a politics of free market economy. While the former prioritised the rights of all individuals to have a fair share of the 'common' wealth and has been guarded through varying degrees of state intervention in different historical periods.[11] For example in Britain the 1947 Town and Country Planning Act actually took over the control of development through planning regulation. The socialist faction of reformers who favoured the imposition of social control through state intervention assumed this to be the first move in the nationalisation of land that would result from the withering away of the private property

9. For example see Bryden, I. & Floyd, J. (eds) 1999. *Domestic Space: Reading the nineteenth-century interior.* Manchester: Manchester University Press.

10. Giddens, A. 1991. *Modernity and Self-Identity: Self and Society in the late Modern Age.* Cambridge: Polity, pp. 151 and 153.

11. For general definition of 'property' in the context of economics see Ryan, A. 1989. 'Property' pp. 227–31. In Eatwell et al. *The New Palgrave: The Invisible Hand.* London and New York: W. W. Norton.

market and eventualise in an automatic right to be housed by the state.[12]

A similarly suggestive effect is obtained from conjoining 'private' and 'public' to 'life'. Thus 'private life', when defined in spatial terms, is that which occurs within the inner-directed confines of the home and only relates to the family unit. It also stands for a political position that is totally against the socialist principle that acknowledges a public realm, illustrated in Margaret Thatcher's assertion that 'there is no such thing as society, only families and individuals'. Therefore 'public life' does not just refer literally to that which goes on beyond the threshold of the domestic front door on common ground where everyone has right of way, but to a more diffuse outer-directed awareness that individuals are also citizens with a civic sense of responsibility beyond their own immediate private interests and property.

Nowhere are the politics of private versus public more apparent than in urban design. The theory of 'defensible space' first mooted in 1972[13] was used to devise a strategy for designing spaces that would deter crime and disorder by making people feel responsible for public areas through a sense of ownership. Since its inception it has continually been criticised on ideological grounds for discouraging citizenship and encouraging privatisation. A recent row over the effectivity of the cul-de-sac layout in crime deterrence that ensued between the police and Space Syntax, a research project headed by Bill Hillier at the Bartlett School of Architecture in the University of London, shows the debate still to be current. The police challenged Hillier's research that disproved the defensible space theory by finding that houses in culs-de-sac suffered up to five times more burglaries than houses in linear layouts. While police officials involved in crime deterrence claimed the opposite, asserting that 'Consistently, closed culs-de-sac showed substantially less crime.'[14] Hillier's concerned reaction to the attack was to speculate that

12. Ravetz, A. 1986. *The Government of Space: Town Planning in Modern Society.* London and Boston: Faber and Faber, p. 33; Cowley, J. 1979. *Housing for People or for Profit?* London: Stage 1; Alderson, S. 1962. *Britain in the Sixties: Housing.* Harmondsworth, Middlesex: Penguin, p. 140.

13. Newman, O. 1972. *Defensible Space: People and Design in the Violent City.* London: Architectural Press; Coleman, A. with the Design Disadvantaged Team of Land Use Research Team 1985. *Utopia on Trial: Vision and Reality in Planned Housing,* London: King's College London.

14. Fairs, M. 1999. 'Cops in cul-de-sac scrap'. In *Building Design,* No. 1418, Nov 12, p. 1.

'If they go on like this the public realm will go to pot.' But in spite of the police's attempt to weaken his position by accusing him of a biased political agenda that made him 'ideologically opposed to culs-de-sac', Hillier's work has fed into the latest edition of the influential *Secured by Design* guide, officially backed by the DETR (Department of the Environment, Transport and Regions) and other official bodies, which now omits previous mention of culs-de-sac and recommends instead layouts with routes that are 'clear, direct, busy and will be well used'.[15] There are many variable factors left out of this crude type of argument, relating to the relationship between the type of layout and its geographical, socio-economic context which must have some bearing on security. It is also fair to conclude that the particular perspectives of both parties involved in assessing the effectivity of defensible space must have had some bearing on their conclusions. It is therefore important to ask what kind of bearing do the politics of private and public space in design have in relation to the everyday experience of urban life and furthermore how might that be researched and usefully applied. Designers work on the assumption that social uses of space can be built in and are still surprised when their intentionality is not transferred into users' responses.[16]

Design does not necessarily make spaces social, people do that. Amos Rapoport's analytical typology of 'public space' first published in 1977,[17] although based on universal definitions that ignored cultural or historical specificity, discussed some of the ways in which people make space. His project as an anthropologist and an architect was to provide a method for the production of urban design based on the relationship between people (but still using 'man' as the generic term for people) and their environment. The 'territorial model' he proposed was based on 'a spatial-temporal frame of reference'. Taking the individual's perspective of life in a city he described it as an experience of

15. Ibid.
16. For an example of the different perspectives between design decision makers and 'everyday experiences of women' with reference to post-war public housing see for example Boys, J. 1995. 'From Alcatraz to the OK Corral' pp. 39–54. In Attfield, J. and Kirkham, P. (eds) *A View From the Interior. Women and Design.* London: The Women's Press.
17. Rapoport, A. 1977. *Human Aspects of Urban Form: Towards a Man-Environment Approach to Urban Form and Design.* Oxford and New York: Pergamon Press, pp. 288–9.

an extremely complex set of spatial units – personal space, individual territory, territories of various groups, complex sets of core areas, jurisdictions and overlapping home ranges . . .

Considering all scales of spatial domains from the country to the room, Rapoport synthesised three characteristics which he affirmed are always present – 'a sense of spatial identity, a sense of exclusiveness and the control of communication in space and time' – which produced divisions by means of 'boundary creating devices' between us and them defining private and the public space. He acknowledged that 'territory' in an urban context is more than 'the ownership of private property' but rather that it is dependent on the shared understanding of rules and exclusions of occupancy. But his ahistorical and politically neutral definition of privacy as 'the avoidance of unwanted interaction with other people' is far too limited in its negative assumptions. Rapaport's explanation for example does not refer to the different degrees of control that groups may or may not have over the areas they are allowed to inhabit or are forced to move away from according to their gender, class, ethnicity or disability. His typology is more useful in the cultural analysis of those physical features that form the built environment over which designers have some measure of control, as for example in accounting for 'the nature, placement and permeability of barriers' that govern spatial separation. For example the veranda[18] has been cited as a transitional device that gives space for the negotiation of passing through from the public outside space into the privacy offered within the dwelling.

A number of theoreticians have attempted to deal with the way that private and public types of space are experienced in terms of the everyday.[19] Written in the mid-1970s, Richard Sennett's observations on the contemporary lack of any sense of public life[20] in comparison with the eighteenth century, was interpreted as symptomatic of the

18. For a case study of the veranda as an aspect of the domestic material culture of the eighteenth-century American South see Crowley, J.E. 1997. 'Inventing Comfort: The Piazza', pp. 277–315. In Smart Martin, Ann and Ritchie Garrison, J. (eds) 1997. *American Material Culture: The Shape of the Field*. Winterthur, Delaware: Henry Francis du Pont Winterthur Museum.

19. de Certeau, M. 1988. *The Practice of Everyday Life*. Berkeley: University of California Pres; Lefebvre, H. 1996. *The Production of Space*. Trans. Donald Nicholson-Smith. Oxford: Blackwell.

20. See Sennett, R. 1977. *The Fall of Public Man. Cambridge: Cambridge University Press*.

nihilistic degeneration of social ideals diagnosed as part of the post-modern condition.[21] Yet his critique would appear to have coincided with the very perspective he purported to be decrying. He attributed the decline and loss of the eighteenth-century sense of sociality between strangers, to the modern prioritisation given to the narcissistic cultivation of individual identity. In defining the public life of the city purely in terms of the 'opportunities for group life' and 'behaving with strangers in an emotionally satisfying way' he seemed more interested in discussing the stylised formalities that enabled individuals to partake of public life in an uninvolved manner rather than with any altruistic concern developed from a sense of civic responsibility. What appeared as a nostalgic longing for some sense of social conviviality could be interpreted as part of the American 'mid-sixties open-space' ideology that Galen Cranz has characterised as 'premised on a new version of the old idea of public man' but interpreted on the principle of providing aesthetic 'pleasure ground' park sites.[22] Sennett's pessimistic view of the loss of a sense of public space seems symptomatic of the postmodern anxiety, expressed at the time he was writing, by cultural critics who noted a shift from a unitary centre to a confusing fragmentation of labyrinthine complexity in the design of metropolitan architecture and diagnosed as a symptom of late capitalism.[23] Sennett's analysis did not take into account the fact that being able to partake of the so-called public life of the eighteenth century entailed the right to vote and therefore excluded women; nor did it acknowledge any of the public manifestations of altruism and solidarity expressed for example by popular demonstrations. These entailed protest vigils and marches against the Vietnam war in the United States, a whole number of manifestations of the peace movement against nuclear armament attributed with being one of the motivating forces in terminating the cold war that finally materialised in the breaking down of the Berlin Wall. Nor could it have been foreseen twenty-five years ago that public awareness of social inequality would produce popular public manifesta-

21. See also A. Giddens' critique of Sennett (1991) in *Modernity and Self-Identity*, pp. 151–2.

22. Cranz, G. 1989. *The Politics of Park Design: A History of Urban Parks in America*. Cambridge, Massachusetts: MIT, p. 214.

23. As for example Jameson, F. 1984. 'Postmodernism, or the cultural logic of late capitalism', pp. 53–92. In *New Left Review* 146; Wilson, E. 1991. *The Sphinx in the City: Urban Life, the Control of Disorder and Women*. London: Virago.

tions like the Rock Against Racism and Band Aid concerts, the latter to raise aid for the victims of famine in Ethiopia which drew interest all over the world. Other examples like the worldwide student movement that demonstrated peacefully against political oppression and demanded freedom of speech and human rights in protests like the tragic demonstration in Tiananmen Square in Beijing, or the Argentine mother's 'desaparecidos' protest vigil in Plaza de Mayo in Buenos Aires.

The media has in many ways replaced the city forum or the public park as the site for discussing and recording issues of public concern. Recently added to the list of human rights issues is the increasing public awareness of a growing concern in the ethics affecting the most basic aspects of daily life, from food production to human reproduction evidenced in their appearance in the media on a daily basis in some form or another. The logic that underlies these concerns is the deprioritisation of the profit motive that inevitably must take place in favour of longer-term values, in the health and welfare of consumers and producers, in safe and ethically produced goods, the avoidance of needless waste, the conservation of finite resources, the good management for sustainable economies and a fairer distribution of wealth with all its attendant knock-on effects on the natural and social future ecology of the planet. This indicates a very lively awareness of public matters of responsibility beyond small local concerns to encompass global matters. Thus the public arena has grown from the civic dimension, objectified in the city square, to the global so that it is no longer necessary to be in Hyde Park in London or wherever, because interactive technology can bring the event into the domestic private space of any home that has access to a television monitor. Theorists disagree about the existence, nature and quality of the public sphere; some like Sennett and Jürgen Habermas[24] nostalgically regret the loss of the authentic experience that according to their type of vision can only take place in the locality of the event, for political engagement to take place. Others like Roger Silverstone et al. see it as equally real although differently constituted through contemporary media.

A central tenet of the critical history of the capitalist economy is to discredit the notion that it can deliver some kind of democratic utopia through what Victoria de Grazia characterises as 'individual acquisitiveness over collective entitlement [that] defined the measure of the good society as private well-being achieved through consumer spending".[25] But as social historians like de Grazia remind us – whether championing privatisation or collectivism, even under régimes which support free market economy – it is the state which exerts the power through intervention and control via the public sphere. And as Silverstone's and de Grazia's research highlight, an increased awareness of the moral economy of consumption located in the spaces of the feminine and the domestic, because conventionally considered the private domain and therefore entirely determined by production, has until fairly recently been considered as secondary if not totally ignored.

Sennett's type of idealised characterisation of public life, objectified in the public spaces of the eighteenth-century city was not concerned with the work of socially minded designers working on the ground. For example the architects and planners designing the built environment of new urban spaces like the new towns of post-war Britain,[26] were enabled by state intervention in the nationalisation of land through the 1947 Town and Country Planning Act as mentioned earlier. While the Smithsons' major contribution was their vision of an architecture of 'ordinariness' which did not prioritise aesthetics and advocated a much more strategic plan than was ever carried out in Britain.[27] Whatever criticisms may be levelled against planning as a misconceived form of social control, in its more recent form of urban design policy it no longer automatically means 'clean sweep' rebuilding. The urban task force formed by John Prescott in 1999[28] to formulate an integrated urban planning policy depends on working with the existing urban fabric rather than razing great swathes of it to the ground and starting from scratch or encroaching unnecessarily on green-field sites. This means that in theory due regard needs to be paid to the public role of spaces so that the interests of the private sector are not allowed to take control, an ideal which so far has failed to materialise as the many empty units in shopping malls all over the country testify.

25. de Grazia, V. (ed.) 1996. *The Sex of Things: Gender and Consumption in Historical Perspective*. Berkeley: University of California Press, p. 9.

26. Such as Alex McGowan, an unknown architect who worked in Harlow all his life, see Attfield, J. 'Inside Pram Town: A Case Study of Harlow House Interiors' 1995, pp. 215–38. In Attfield and Kirkham (eds) *A View From the Interior*, p. 222.

27. Smithson 1970. *Ordinariness and Light*.

28. Urban Task Force 1999 *Towards an Urban Renaissance: Final Report of the Urban Task Force*. London: Department of the Environment, Transport and Regions.

But going back to the politics of property in relation to the separate spheres debate, home ownership in particular has been a subject of some interest in the study of material culture, considering the way in which house occupiers appropriate their own spaces in the face of the social control imposed by state governance over housing.[29] There are class and gender implications that can be characterised in terms of dichotomies that conveniently map on to the theory of separate spheres and are objectified in the design of housing, the most stereotypical of which is the interior and the suburb typified as female and private.[30] Apart from historically and geographically-specific differences when particular individual everyday experiences are investigated, however, a much more complex web of social relations is revealed. Until the recent interest in the anthropology and politics of domestic space[31] the main studies that prevailed concerned the social history of the middle class, social housing and gender-specific issues related to design and occupancy. But there is a shortage, if not a complete dearth of research in the more intimate relations between members of individual households enacted through domestic arrangements of maintenance and décor. A recent exemplary study that looked at the laundry arrangements within French households revealed how individuals manage to keep their separate identities while working out a modus vivendi as a couple, is one of an increasing number of studies of this subject using an ethnographic approach.[32] While a study of open plan detailed elsewhere[33] considers the significance of the elimination of internal walls within the post-war house as a way of investigating to what extent the democratising intentions of the designers who devised it as a modern innovation were actually realised.

29. See for example Attfield 1995 'Inside Pram Town'; Miller, D. 'Appropriating the State on the Council Estate' in Putnam, T. and Newton, C. (eds) 1990. *Household Choices*. London: Futures.

30. Kleinberg, S.J. 1999. 'Gendered space: housing privacy and domesticity in the nineteenth-century United States' pp. 142-161. In Bryden & Floyd 1999, *Domestic Space*.

31. For example Cieraad, I. (ed.) *At Home: An Anthropology of Domestic* Space. New York: Syracuse University Press; Birdwell-Pheasant, D. and Lawrence-Zúñiga, D. (eds) 1999. *House Life: Space, Place and Family in Europe*. Oxford and New York: Berg; Jackson, S. and Moores, S. (eds) 1995. *The Politics of Domestic Consumption: Critical Readings*. London and New York: Harvester Wheatsheaf.

32. Kaufmann, J-C. 1998. *Dirty Linen: couples and their laundry*. London: Middlesex University Press.

33. Attfield, J. 1999. 'Bringing Modernity Home: Open Plan in the British Domestic Interior', pp. 73–82. In Cieraad, I. (ed.) 1999. *At Home*.

Contrary to the implications that open plan embodied progressive social change objectified in modern design, it became a standard feature of the private property developer's 'universal product' offering an easily adaptable frame for the ephemeral interior decor of occupiers who frequently changed their address as well as their décor. The buoyancy of the property market during the 1980s made it possible for property owners to make several moves to match different life stages from the 'first-time buyer's' property, to a larger family house, to sheltered accommodation in retirement. Privatisation paralleled the loss of faith in the social concept of planning and the political change of policy which did away with the building of public housing as a responsibility of the state, creating an underclass reliant on the severely depleted publicly owned housing stock and inadequate 'not for profit' housing associations assisted by the state through the Housing Corporation quango.[34] The home thus became a commodity rather than a right, leaving the stage open for market forces to rule, to the detriment of the living conditions of those unable to afford to buy into their own home.[35] However the strategies of appropriation that become clearer by delving further into the processes of physical transformation made through DIY decoration and alterations, enabled the kind of transformation that made it possible for both the public and private house occupier to change the dwelling into a home and thus gain some measure of self-actualisation. This refers to the 'appropriation' invoked by Lefebvre mentioned above.[36]

Suburbanisation and the Construction of Middle-Class Identity

If the city is posited as the stereotypical institutionalisation of the public sphere and modern life in an industrialised society, although 'country' is its obvious antonym, the transitional space between the two – the suburb – can be said to represent the space where the middle class constructed its identity. As Raymond Williams has recorded, the history of the country referring to the enclosures in the eighteenth and nineteenth centuries, represents 'a long process of conquest and seizure, the land gained by killing, by repression, by political bargains' and

34. Hetherington, P. 'Council houses unloved, unlettable', 10 November 1998, The Guardian, p. 9; Walker, D. 'Poverty politics'. 17 November 1999. The Guardian, p. 21.

35. Cowley, J. 1979. Housing for People or for Profit? London: Stage 1.

36. See Chapter 6, Note No. 20.

'general changes in property relations which were all flowing in the same direction: an extension of cultivated land but also a concentration of ownership into the hands of a minority'.[37] The suburb occupied the gap between city and the country, the wasteland of the landed gentry and the wealthy industrialist with a seat in the country. The suburb was a transitional space for the socially mobile middle class, a staging post, if only in theory, on the way to acquiring a country residence.

The suburb presents a particularly apt example of the embodiment of the privatisation of space in the form of mass-produced commercial development housing for a rising middle-class. The suburban dwelling form illustrates how typical features incorporated middle-class values of privacy as individuality, and property ownership as independence. The suburb originally derived from the impetus to separate the dwelling from the workplace, locating it in healthy surroundings, with a garden and plenty of fresh air but with easy access to the city by means of modern transport networks.[38]

The suburb has been reviled by critics – both for its perceived aspirant pretensions as well as for its tame middle-of-the-road populism. The suburb became the metaphor of the private sphere of bourgeois home values idealised in feminine domesticity that came to its peak in the nineteenth century and continued to gather momentum in the twentieth century.[39] The neglect of the private sphere in conventional accounts by political economists and historians to some extent can be explained by the lack of recognition given to the home as a site of production and the secondary importance given to consumption and therefore to women's contribution to the economy.[40] This is the main reason why until recently there has been so little interest in bourgeois houses, furnishings and objects in general on the part of art and design historians.[41] Their disinterest can also be attributed to a perceived lack of quality ('poor taste') ascribed to the suburban aesthetic within the

37. Williams, R. 1973. *The Country and the City*. St Albans, Hertfordshire: Paladin, p. 122.

38. Burnett, J. 1978. *A Social History of Housing 1815–1970*. Cambridge: Cambridge University Press; Jackson, A. 1973. *Semi-Detached London*. London: Allen and Unwin; Oliver, P, Davis, I. and Bentley, I. 1981. *Dunroamin: The Suburban Semi and its Enemies*. London: Barrie & Jenkins.

39. Lewis, R. and Maude, A. 1949. *The English Middle Classes*. London: Phoenix House.

40. Mackintosh, M.M. 1979. 'Domestic Labour and the Household', pp. 173–91. In Burman, S. (ed.) *Fit Work For Women*. London: Croom Helm.

context of visual culture, often disparagingly referred to as 'kitsch'. It has been feminist social historians who in the first instance, have done most to uncover the 'inside' history of middle-class women's lives and their contribution to the moral economy of the household.[42] And although some design historians who have looked at the social history of mass design have referred to suburbia, this interest has mainly been directed to its position within the good design movement insofar as it conformed to modernism – the metal windows, electrical appliances and Underground transport posters that embraced a modern aesthetic. There is little mention of the tiled fireplaces, the patterned linoleum or the reproduction hand-carved oak dining sets reminiscent of Olde England that would have been found in the typical suburban semi of the 1930s, except as a pedagogical tool to point out examples of poor design and all the better to demonstrate the virtues of modern mass production exemplified by bent plywood and tubular metal furniture.

The idea of the suburb embodied the romantic notion of the picturesque as a tamed countryside that Nikolaus Pevsner recognised as characteristic of English taste in his 1955 Reith Lectures, *The Englishness of English Art*.[43] There was a contradiction between the intention and the reality of the suburb – that to build it contained its own destruction. If the attraction of the suburb was to go and live in the country, to get away from the city, its noise and smells, in accommodation which offered exclusivity, privacy and status accorded by just the right proximity to the 'select' areas marked by the country house of long-established families of 'quality', those conditions were negated once roads were built where there had once been fields and the 'ideal' house was reproduced in thousands of replicas. But ambiguity rather than uniformity was the attribute that made the suburb so popular,[44] a quality which enabled it to accommodate traditional home values with innovation combined in a hybrid mixture of modern 'all mod cons' with historic styles – Tudor half-timbered gables outside and streamlined tiled bathrooms within.

41. This has been confirmed by historians who *have* taken an interest in that very subject, e.g. Auslander, L. 1996. 'The Gendering of Consumer Practices in Nineteenth-Century France', pp. 79–112. In de Grazia 1996. *The Sex of Things*.

42. For example Davidoff, L. and Hall, C. 1987. *Family Fortunes: Men and Women of the English Middle Class 1780–1850*. London: Hutchinson; de Grazia 1996. *The Sex of Things*.

43. Pevsner, N. 1956. *The Englishness of English Art*. London: Architectural Press.

44. Oliver et al. 1981. *Dunroamin: The Suburban Semi and its Enemies*, p.78.

The suburb also provided a way of buying into the rights that accompany property ownership which confers a certain amount of political power in that it defines the physical meeting point between public and private domains and thereby gives rights of physical exclusion and inclusion in terms of territoriality. The appropriation of space however is not unique to property owners as has been discussed elsewhere[45] and will be elaborated below in connection with the adoption of the suburban aesthetic in public housing estates. The suburb can be described as a particular type of sub-urban geographical entity – neither city nor country – but it is also increasingly referred to as an attitude or structure of feeling to do with a sense of individuality that is translated in particular forms of privatised environmental planning removed from state interference. Recent recognition of the suburb as more than a socio-geographical configuration of space or a minor aspect of architectural history,[46] has suggested that

> Suburbia is no longer to be found simply in the landscapes of tract housing or ribbon development, among Victorian villas or in garden cities. It is to be found also, and perhaps increasingly, in the suburban imaginary, a virtual space no longer visible either on the planner's drawing board or on the margins of cities. Suburbia is a state of mind. It is constructed in imagination and in desire, in the everyday lives of those who struggle to maintain hearth and family and in the words of those who still are brave (or mad) enough to define and defend bourgeois values.[47]

The last sentence quoted above from Silverstone's *Visions of Suburbia* betrays a self-conscious awareness of broaching an awkward subject. Suburbia has connotations with the private, the feminine and the middle class, all areas eschewed until recently as frivolous or tame fields of academic study. The revision of the politics behind the so-called 'great masculine renunciation' which rationalised the interest

45. Attfield 1995. 'Inside Pram Town'.

46. This is not to suggest that historical accounts of suburban development do not exist, (see below); but a generalisation to explain why, according to the now dated convention of architectural history that revolved around biographical accounts of particular architects, it does not include suburban estate developments which were rarely if ever designed by architects, much less well-known ones.

47. Silverstone 1997. *Visions of Suburbia*, p. 13.

in fashion and consumption practices[48] in class and gender identity terms, has extended the 'hidden from history' agenda first mooted by feminist historians.[49] It is now more generally accepted that the personal is as political as the public and therefore that one of the interests in studying the suburb is as a space through which the kind of social transformation was enabled that made a new type of modern self-identity possible.

From Village to Suburb – from Serf to Citizen

My case study of the suburbanisation of Cockfosters[50] showed it to be typical of the inter-war developments that offered semi-detached houses to a new class of prospective owner-occupier. It is used here to illustrate the way a village was transformed into a suburb with the arrival of the London Underground and the development of affordable houses for middle-class commuters. Modern transportation and widespread speculative development encouraged by government grants fomented the demand for suburban owner-occupier housing in the 1930s.[51] A wider selection of the population than ever before could now afford to aspire to higher standards of home comfort. These demands plus wider availability of such technological advances as electricity, caused sweeping changes in large-scale planning of suburbs and towns as well as in the designs of house plans, building components, furniture and household appliances.

The extension of the Piccadilly line ending in Cockfosters on 31 July 1933 marked its transformation from village to suburb.[52] The fast, efficient and cheap method of transport (fares were tailed off towards the extremities to encourage custom) encouraged the middle-class white-collar worker to move out to the suburbs. The attraction of being

48. For example Breward, C. 1999. *The Hidden Consumer: Masculinities, fashion and city life 1860-1914*. Manchester: Manchester University Press; Kuchta, D. 1996. 'The Making of the Self-Made Man', pp. 54–78. In de Grazia 1996. *The Sex of Things*.

49. Rowbotham, S. 1973. *Hidden From History*. London: Pluto.

50. This study of Cockfosters is based on previously unpublished research carried out in 1982 based on a series of interviews with residents of the area, a photographic survey of house façades, and local history documentary sources including Council meeting minutes, period maps, back issues of the *Palmers Green and Southgate Gazette*, old photographs and documents lent to me by interviewees.

51. Burnett 1978. *A Social History of Housing*, p. 221.

52. Howson, H.F. 1979. *London's Underground*. London: Ian Allan, p. 126.

Figure 17. Aerial view over Cockfosters in 1939 showing the newly built terminus to the Piccadilly Line London Underground.

able to buy a new modern house with a mortgage from building societies which, from 1932, introduced various measures to help home purchasers, offered the new residents amenities many had not enjoyed before – the benefits of fresh air and open spaces that came with proximity to the country, electricity, separate bathroom with running hot water, inside WC, kitchens with built-in fitments, and the insulation of brick cavity construction.

'[The gentry] were the benefactors and we were the village people. There wasn't the money there is today. All the people lived off the crumbs from Sir Philip's table.' There was no nostalgia in Mrs Langdale's account of her childhood in Cockfosters during the 1920s before it became a suburb. Then it was still a pre-industrial village with a farm, fields, cottages, and spinneys, centred around an inn and one shop, a small school house and the church built by Robert Bevan in 1839 so that his farm workers would not have to walk all the way to Enfield to go to church. The Langdales were still living in Cockfosters when I interviewed them in 1982. Their semi-detached house was on the

Westpole Estate developed between 1936 and 1938 on the sold-off triangle of land left over from the Piccadilly underground railway line extension crossing the Sassoon Estate from Oakwood to terminate in Cockfosters, and sold by Sir Philip Sassoon in 1935 as a 75-acre plot.

Among the 'benefactors' mentioned above that figured prominently in Cockfosters were the Liptons of tea fame, Sir Francis Walker of Hanbury and Walker, and Sir Philip Sassoon, a millionaire who bought Trent Park from the Bevan family in 1908. The 1777 Act of Parliament divided Enfield Chase hunting grounds to accelerate agricultural cultivation attracting wealthy patrons who built country houses and brought employment for farm workers and servants to the district in the eighteenth century. In 1926 Sassoon restyled the nineteenth-century Trent Park mansion with eighteenth-century facing bricks from Devonshire House in Piccadilly, the last of William Kent's surviving London palaces. In 1982 there were still survivors who recalled the Sassoons' liveried servants, their parties for the Prince of Wales, and visits from other members of the royal family. Mr Langdale, born in Cockfosters in 1911, lived with his great-grandmother in a cottage on the Sassoon estate where his great-grandfather had been a woodman when the estate still belonged to the Bevan family. His childhood reminiscences in 1982 were as from another age – he recalled the oil lamps and his Saturday chores of scrubbing the scullery flagstone floor, of having to fetch water from the well and chopping the firewood, the servants ball 'up at the big house' and sneaking into Hadley Wood with his friends to go bird nesting.

For original inhabitants born into the almost feudal conditions of a pre-war village dependent on the munificence of the gentry, it was the post-war 'Utility' houses such as those built from 1946 in Cockfosters by the firm of Pilgrim under government licence and sold at a maximum price of £1,300, that enabled young couples like the Langdales to gain their first foothold into the middle class, eventually buying a house in the Westpole Estate. The transformation from an almost serf-like existence to middle-class house ownership was not unusual among the generation of Cockfosters inhabitants who lived through its suburbanisation.

Cockfosters was a relatively latecomer to suburbanisation in comparison with nearby Southgate, only mushrooming suddenly between 1934 and 1938 once the tube station was opened. As a contemporary guide book on Middlesex remarked, describing the transformation wrought by modernisation to the area

The charm of Southgate Green persisted, hardly impaired so recently as three or four years ago. But now one side of the Green is lined with modern houses of creditable design, another with still more modern flats, and part of the third with shops where face powder and gramophone records, and other essentials to present day happiness may be obtained. However, it is at the junction of the old High Street with Chase Side that most startling change has occurred, all within a year. Here is a really splendid example of the very latest cosmopolitan design in the new Underground station and its surrounding crescent of shops and flats. The old smithy was demolished in July 1933 and now the buses circle round a traffic circus in an endless procession. All this is inevitable, but, as the lady said in the story, 'so sudden'. Yet, even now, the hamlet of Cockfosters remains as beautiful and as undisturbed as ever, save for the admirably designed station, the terminus of the new railway.[53]

The identification of modern commodities like 'face powder' and 'gramophone records' as 'essential to modern life' contrasted incongruously with the nearby country hamlet which was already on its way into history. Yet inter-war suburban development managed to integrate tradition and modernity in such a way as to reconcile the old and the new and at the same time effect a social transformation that liberated people like the Langdales who in their childhood remembered being beholden to the gentry, to take on a degree of independence unknown to their parents. Another indication of their move into the middle class was their response when asked what they did in their leisure time before the War – 'we didn't have any then'.

Spec Builder's Vernacular – the Style with no Name

The case study of Cockfosters carried out in 1982, which paralleled the findings of the *Dunroamin*[54] study published the year before, showed an almost infinite number of small variations on the traditional Tudorbethan or streamlined 'sun-trap' modern styles of the standard two-storey, three-bedroom-plan, semi-detached house type. The Cockfosters suburban houses contained the same 'repertoire of alternative major features and fixtures' characterised by Ian Bentley[55] and the

53. Briggs, M.S. 1934. *Middlesex Old and New*. London: Allen and Unwin.
54. Oliver et al. 1981. *Dunroamin: The Suburban Semi and its Enemies*.
55. Bentley, I. 1981. 'The Owner Makes His Mark: Choice and Adaptation', pp. 136–53. In Oliver et al. 1981. *Dunroamin*, p. 139.

Figure 18. No.7 Hays Gardens with half-timbered gable and double-glazing.

Figure 19. Suburban inter-war semi-detached house with modern suntrap metal windows.

co-authors of *Dunroamin* as the vital element of individuality providing the consumer with a wide choice of types of windows, doors, gables, porches, stained-glass designs, fireplace surrounds, bathroom suites, and so on. The *Dunroamin* study was instigated by architectural educators in the early 1980s to express their concern in 'Modern Architecture's apparent *lack* of interest in the individual' [56] ending the book with a chapter entitled 'Learning From Dunroamin: Values and the Houses We Live In', in similar vein to the Scott Brown and Venturi's *Learning From Las Vegas* exercise.

The spirit of individualism, interpreted by Oliver et al. to have been the secret of suburbia's popularity, can be said not only to have suited the established middle class ethos; but with the smaller more affordable semi, also helped to created a new middle class among those who in the inter-war period for the first time, could afford to emigrate there from rented rooms. Apart from the change of status, ownership gave the freedom from tenancy agreements which enabled the owners to adapt the house and garden to their individual tastes.

The *Dunroamin* project in the early 1980s that set out to rescue suburbia from its good design movement 'enemies', was historically concurrent with the revival of interest in the rehabilitation of earlier house types as an alternative way of upgrading the housing stock to new building. The revival of interest applied to the 'metroland' type of inter-war semi-detached suburban house found in Cockfosters,[57] as well as to inner-city Victorian terraced town housing considered by an earlier generation of planners as only fit for slum clearance giving rise to the trend in 'gentrification'.[58] By the 1960s taking on an 'older' property in need of repair became a more realistic proposition than buying new, particularly if the house owner took on the renovations.

From its inception inter-war suburbia had continued to be the object of contempt on the part of modernist architects and planners who criticised it for its mock village greens and references to past styles creating pseudo cottages and miniaturised debased country houses.[59]

---

56. Ibid., p.136.

57. Turner, M. (ed.) 1983. *The Decoration of the Suburban Villa 1990-1940*, Middlesex: Middlesex Polytechnic (exhibition catalogue).

58. Thompson, M. 1979. *Rubbish Theory: The destruction and creation of value*. London; OUP.

59. There was one lone voice in favour of the suburbs among the champions of modern architecture in the post-war period – J.M. Richards who wrote *The Castles On the Ground: The Anatomy of Suburbia* in 1946 (London: Architectural Press).

It also attracted criticism from a group not unlike today's 'nimbys'[60] who objected to suburbia's invasion of the countryside. One of its most vociferous objectors was Clough Williams-Ellis, an architect who became known for building Portmeiron, a small pseudo Italian village near Portmadoc in North Wales, a mini forerunner of today's theme parks. In 1929 he wrote a stinging polemic likening London suburbs to an octopus that would eventually strangle 'old England' with its encroaching tentacles.[61] But its many critics were not just eccentric historicists or specialist groups promoting good design. The generally held view among planners and guardians of good design, thinking ahead about reconstruction planning after the War, was how to avoid the uncontrolled growth of suburban ribbon development together with what at the time was seen as unsightly urban excrescences. In 1940 Geoffrey Boumphrey listed some of these as 'advertisement signs and hoardings, untidy garages and petrol pumps, tea shops and all that range of enterprises which deface the very charms they rely on to attract customers.'[62]

What the study of house façades in Cockfosters in 1982 revealed, despite the criticism from design professionals, was the resilient power of suburbia to survive as a desirable place to live and go on attracting successive generations of house owners who went on adapting and remodelling their houses to keep up-to-date with the changing image of modernity, and latterly, postmodernity. Not that the term 'post-modern'[63] has ever been part of the vocabulary of either the speculative builders of suburban houses or their buyers – suburbia's most avid champions who were unmoved by, if not unaware of, the complaints of its small group of detractors. Although the scale of suburban development was vast, the minute space allocated to it in accounts of the history of design can only be attributed to a selective blindness

---

60. 'Nimby' is an acronym for 'not in my back yard' referring to objectors to building developments on sites in the proximity of their own residential locality, often on the pretext of protecting the surrounding countryside.

61. Williams-Ellis, C. 1929. *England and the Octopus*. London: Geoffrey Bles. The book was reproduced in facsimile in 1996 by the CPRE (Council for the Protection of Rural England).

62. Boumphrey, G. 1940. *Town and Country Tomorrow*. London: Thomas Nelson and Son, p. 29.

63. The term 'Postmodern' was used by architectural commentators and historians to describe non-contemporary styles referring back to anything from recent, but by the 1970s outdated 'modern' style, to earlier classical styles of architecture.

that censored anything that didn't conform to modernism.[64] The semi-detached house does not figure in art history because it cannot be attributed to a particular architect, although in most cases the firm of builders responsible can be traced. Nor has its typical style been graced with a name, thus remaining largely unacknowledged as a form worthy of mention.[65] Nor is it found in studies of popular culture which has tended to concentrate on urban youth. It only comes into its own in social history accounts that refer to the middle class, particularly with the advent of gender studies that have taken an interest in domestic spaces. So even though once a new if not an innovative house form, the typical hybrid style that has continued to be popular and is what makes the suburban semi instantly recognisable as part of the visual vocabulary of everyday life, is a style with no name. Because it has been absorbed into ordinary house-building practice, and in the absence of any other claimants other than facetious references of ridicule,[66] it is fair to call the style 'spec-builders' vernacular'.

The loss of confidence in modern building design that made designers turn to earlier conventional building types, techniques and materials, has been identified with the notorious case of the collapse of the Ronan Point high-rise London block of flats in 1968.[67] But it was not only the high-density high-rise type of public housing which suffered attack from the public as well as from professionals. Some responsibility for the well-founded criticism of much of the poor quality post-war public

64. For example see the *Thirties* catalogue of an exhibition of 'British art and design before the war' held at the Hayward Gallery between October 1979 and January 1980 (Arts Council of Great Britain) in which there was no mention of the spectacular scale of suburban house design or its furnishings. The only hint that such a phenomenon actually existed was exhibits of two photographs of semi-detached houses (p. 184) in the Architecture section, one of a house in Edgware and the other of a pair of 'superior semi-detached homes, Becontree Estate', obviously selected because they included modern metal windows.

65. Ordinary inter-war housing was the object of study of two of the early design history units on the *History of architecture and design 1890–1930* Open University Third Level Arts Course. See *British Design Units 19 and 20,* Open University Press, 1975.

66. The style terms like 'by-pass variegated' created by satirists like Sir Osbert Lancaster for the facetious caricatures of suburban semi types in *Homes Sweet Homes* (John Murray, 1938) illustrate the contempt in which builder's vernacular was held. See Oliver et al. 1981. *Dunroamin,* pp. 46–7.

67. Campbell, K. 1976. *Home Sweet Home: Housing designed by the London County Council and Greater London Council Authority 1888–1975.* London: Academy, p. 82.

housing must be attributed to insufficiently tested new materials and factory building techniques resulting in unsafe and unhealthy living conditions caused by such problems as severe dampness from condensation. Sociologists have noted the cross-class shift towards the privatisation of the home.[68] This is not the place to digress into a review of public housing nor to offer an explanation for the very poor image from which it has continued to suffer ever since. And credit must be given for the care and attention given by planners and architects to the design of public housing which has undergone many and varied permutations of design in an attempt to meet the needs of the 'housing problem' since the nineteenth century.[69] It is however fair to conclude that the same critique, put mildly by Oliver (cited above) as the 'lack of interest in the individual', was the ideology behind the application of standardisation in the design of public housing, and has also been applied by recent revisions of the good design movement. It has been observed by several critics that the culture of design that has favoured state intervention in the design of housing, and promoted good design initiatives through such institutions as the Council of Industrial Design,[70] was driven by the class, gender and race bias, and therefore taste, of an established middle-class group of designers. However there were maybe as many, if not more, anonymous designers like Alex McCowan[71] who from his own experience of designing public sector housing, realised that the best solution was to provide 'a basic framework in which people can do their own thing, because they're going to do it anyway'.

The acceptance of the reality that popular taste differed from that of architects makes sense in the context of what has since been stereotyped as postmodern, a pastiche style disliked by designers who did not agree with the 'Learning from Las Vegas' approach that gave 'a humbler role for architects than the Modern movement has wanted to accept'. But Scott Brown and Venturi's celebration of the 'ugly and ordinary', by adapting banal motifs in their designs, depended on a sophisticated

68. Crow, G. 1989. 'The Post-War Development of the Modern Domestic Ideal', pp. 14–32. In Allan, G. and Crow, G. (eds) 1989. *Home and Family: Creating the Domestic Sphere*. Basingstoke: Macmillan.

69. Boys 1995. 'From Alcatraz to the OK Corral', pp. 50–1.

70. Woodham, J. 1996. 'Managing British Design Reform I: Fresh Perspectives on the Early Years of the Council of Industrial Design', pp. 55–65. In *Journal of Design History*, Vol. 9, No. 1.

71. Attfield 1995. 'Inside Pram Town', p. 222.

knowingness to be able to recognise that 'the familiar that is a little off has a strange and revealing power'.[72] One of the first postmodern 'street style' buildings in England to be influenced from the bottom up so to speak, was the Hillingdon Civic Centre,[73] based on the image of the gabled brick suburban house using craft techniques in an effort to provide a building 'for the people'. Although hailed in the architectural press by a new breed of 'young fogey' conservative critics as 'a key building in Britain [. . .] that has turned away from the modern movement' and hailed as 'manifestation of a fascinating change of heart',[74] its intention was lost on the public to whom it was aimed who failed to recognise their town hall because it looked more like a rather out-of-scale displaced group of suburban houses than a civic building. The sense of spatial disorientation came from the importation of a style conventionally associated with domesticity rather than city.

Although in the 1930s the suburban semi was a new form of housing that by the 1980s had become old fashioned in a ubiquitous, banal sort of way, it nevertheless disproved pre-war modernist predictions that it would become the 'slum of the future', having by then undergone several generations of upgrading and continued to provide 'desirable residences'. So much so that even now at the turn of the millennium spec-builders' vernacular remains the model for brand new estates all over the country. First-generation upgrading included back extensions to enlarge the minute kitchenettes of the smaller budget semis to take new appliances like washing machines and refrigerators that had started out as luxuries but became necessities by the 1960s. Central heating was another house improvement that also became general, while on the façade the picture window became a popular feature of modernisation. By the 1980s one of the most popular forms of upgrading was the installation of double glazing replacing windows with the omnipresent brushed aluminium window frames deplored by preservationists who by then began to turn their attention to encompass twentieth-century architecture, insisting that all renovations should be 'in keeping' with the period.[75]

72. Venturi et al. *Learning from Las Vegas*, pp. 129–30.

73. Designed in 1976 by the London firm of architects Robert Matthew Johnson-Marshall & Partners and completed in 1979.

74. Stamp, G. 1979. 'How Hillingdon Happened', pp. 80–92. In *Architectural Review*, February.

75. Turner, M and Hoskins, L. [1988] 1995. *Silver Studio of Design: A Source Book for Home Decorating*. London: Magna Books.

Figure 20. Hillingdon Civic Centre designed by Robert Matthew, Johnson-Marshall, and partners (architects), completed in 1979.

The renovations to houses that were new in the 1930s and carried out in the early 1980s, particularly to the external façade and thus visible to the public, can be interpreted as the symptoms of a particular suburban aesthetic that developed during a period in which privatisation was used as a political strategy. Under the Conservative government of Margaret Thatcher property ownership was made more accessible by means of tax incentives.[76] The personalisation of façades in the Cockfosters study indicated various forms of 'improvements' which set out to modernise what by the 1980s was an out-of-date style of house.[77] Although double glazing modernised the property it did little to personalise it. The most prominent feature used to provide the individuality that made one house stand out as different from its neighbours was the stylisation of the front door. (See illustrations Nos.

76. Quiney, Anthony, 1986. *House and Home: A History of the Small English House.* London: BBC, p. 167.

77. These examples from the study do not pretend to be representative in any way, on the contrary they are intended to show the different and multifarious treatments created through personalisation.

21, 22 and 23). The three illustrations show houses all found in the same road giving an examples of the extent and variety of styles used to enhance the façades of a basically similar semi-detached house type. No. 25 shows a white painted 'Georgian' panelled front door flanked by fluted pilasters and paned full-length side lights with matching panelled double garage doors. No. 33 has an arched filled-in porch with a solid, panelled, natural wood front door with full-length tinted-glass side and top lights, and a moulded-edge overhang on ogee brackets. No. 40's ornamental overhang extending over the entire frontage at first-floor level incorporates a 'classical' pediment over the front door, supported by two sham ionic columns on either side of the entrance. The low balustrade marked an inner private space and the rest of the site separated by the boundary marking off the public pavement from the front of the house.

The house as a site of self-expression and individuality has a long history, not necessarily confined to richer households or always obviously publicly displayed.[78] The promotion of home ownership and 'the right to buy' under the Thatcher regime proved to be a popular means of gaining a sense of independence. Increased accessibility to home ownership gave rise to a particular aesthetic of privatisation through the personalisation of the façade and the front door in particular. Privately owned property could thus be readily distinguished from public housing on estates once entirely council-owned.[79] The introduction of particular features such as pseudo-Georgian doors, bay windows, closed-in front porches, coach lamps and heraldic features such as eagles and lions became common upgrading signifiers. This was a period which saw the expansion of DIY stores making materials, tools and building components only previously obtainable by the trade from builders' merchants, much more generally available to the home improver.[80] Although some studies have analysed home owners in

78. A number of accounts of the history of the working class record the importance of articles of display in the process of self-actualisation, for example Roberts, R. 1971. *The Classic Slum.* Harmondsworth, Middlesex: Penguin, pp. 32–41; Hoggart, R. 1957. *The Uses of Literacy,* Harmondsworth, Middlesex: Penguin; Hunt, P. 1989. 'Gender and the Construction of Home Life', pp. 66–81. In Allan and Crow 1989. *Home and Family.*

79. This has been observed in numerous studies, for example: Dolan, J.A. 1999. '"I've Always Fancied Owning Me Own Lion": Ideological Motivations in External House Decoration by Recent Homeowners', pp. 60–72. In Cieraad, I. (ed.) *At Home.*

80. Sampson, A. 1971. *The New Anatomy of Britain.* London: Hodder and Stoughton, p. 427; Pawley, M. 1992. 'The Electronic Cottage' pp. 142–87. In Rivers, T. et al. *The Name of the Room.* London: BBC; Allan and Crow 1989. *Home and Family.*

Figure 21. No. 25 Hays Road with 'Georgian' style panelled door, flanked by fluted pilasters and paned full-length sidelights.

Figure 22. No. 33 Hays Road with arched filled-in porch, solid-panelled natural wood finish front door and full-length tinted-glass side and tops lights.

Figure 23. No. 40 Hays Road with ornamental overhang extending across the entire frontage, incorporating a 'classical' pediment over the front door and supported by two sham 'ionic' columns on either side of the entrance.

terms of typical consumer types, such as those interested in upgrading their own property either to indicate home ownership or as an investment with future sales in mind,[81] other studies have shown that the appropriation of the home is a much more complex process of self-actualisation which does not necessarily entail ownership.[82]

It is worth remembering that 'ordinary' was one of the characteristics which visionary architects like the Smithsons were trying to achieve, not by reproducing old forms but by providing a rational design for what they romantically envisaged as a common shared space for communality in the since maligned deck-access type of council housing

81. Dolan 1999. '"I've Always Fancied Owning Me Own Lion"'.

82. Attfield 1995. 'Inside Pram Town'; Miller, D. 1987. *Material Culture and Mass Consumption*. Oxford: Blackwell, p. 198; Miller, D. 1990. 'Appropriating the state on the council estate', pp. 43–55. In Putnam, T. and Newton, C. *Household Choices*. London: Futures; Crow, G. 1989. 'The Post-War Development of the Modern Domestic Ideal', pp. 14–32. In Allan and Crow, 1989. *Home and Family*, pp. 27–8.

inspired by the studies of London's East End carried out in the 1950s by Peter Willmott and Michael Young.[83] The design was based on their conclusions that working-class families did not want to be moved out of their neighbourhoods and preferred their front doors to give on to a shared public 'street'. The 'ordinary' in their vocabulary would appear to have referred to the familiar, the everyday. However three generations later, there is evidence that families who emigrated from London to new town corporation houses no longer felt 'out of place' and have managed to map their casual familial relations on to a garden city type of plan. For families who were still renting council houses their sense of identity derives from living in the same neighbourhood as their children and grandchildren, from their leisure activities such as CBR (Citizens Band Radio) and their home decor.[84]

What has been observed from the transformation of house into home through decorating and DIY improvements, both to owner-occupier and rented accommodation, is that occupants wanted to individualise their homes and turn them from ordinary to extraordinary – in the sense of being special to them alone though not necessarily eccentric or unusual. New décor was a way of imprinting their homes with their own identity as a way of gaining ownership, if only figuratively. There are many examples of very consumption-active inhabitants even wanting to go a bit wild and shock their friends and neighbours with their extraordinary 'way out' taste and up-to-date purchases.[85]

DIY and the Bricolage Culture Club

Consumption studies have encouraged the contradictory twin concepts of 'choice' and 'lifestyle', suggesting that either people choose what they buy according to what they consider their own sense of in-built individuality, or that what they buy is dictated by manipulative market forces that target consumer groups and entice them with products that promise entry into particular ready-made lifestyles. This caricatured interpretation of choice as entirely inwardly generated, and lifestyle as totally imposed by external forces, is intended to dispel the notion of a unidirectional process. The imponderability of the complex mechanisms driving consumption patterns was already a subject of much

83. Young, M. and Willmott, P. 1957. *Family and Kinship in East London*. London: Routledge and Kegan Paul.
84. Attfield 1999. 'Bringing Modernity Home', p. 77.
85. Ibid.

Figure 24. Welsh miner's cottage 1950s, with range and TV. (Museum of Welsh Life)

speculation, in more ways than one, well before the twentieth century with the increasing consciousness of marketing as a technique to stimulate sales rather than depending on the 'natural' pressures of supply and demand. Kathy Peiss points out how Warren Susman's turn-of-the-century American 'classic formulation' of the consumer makes a distinction between the fixed identity of 'character' and the cultivated 'personality' for its implications on consumption practices.[86] The concept of choice represents the consumer's point of view as an individual with the right and freedom to buy into a fashion or choose to desist and thus make a statement, in contradiction to the critique

86. Susman, W.I. 1984 '"Personality" and the Making of Twentieth-Century Culture' in *Culture as History: The Transformation of American Society in the Twentieth Century,* pp. 271–86, New York: Pantheon, cited by Peiss, K. 1996. 'Making Up. Making Over: Cosmetics, Consumer Culture, and Women's Identity', pp. 311–36. In de Grazia, V. (ed.) 1996. *The Sex of Things,* p. 312; and also referred to by Jean-Christopher Agnew in 'Coming up for air: consumer culture in historical perspective', pp. 19–39. In Brewer, J. and Porter, R. (eds) 1993. *Consumption and the World of Goods.* London and New York: Routledge, p. 30.

of consumerism along the lines of Veblen's 'conspicuous consumption'[87] which implied a much more manipulated consumer. But rather than exhibiting extravagant profligacy most everyday consumption practice represents a degree of control and self-conscious decision making which has been amply justified in research on consumption[88] and shopping habits.[89] And 'lifestyle', although represented by some critics as a false way of life imposed upon duped consumers by greedy commercialism, does nevertheless take as reference a possible, even if unattainable, real way of life in the first place. Pierre Bourdieu's theory of 'habitus' that explains the way individuals form their identity through their relationship to a group or class by means of sets of shared attitudes and tastes, and the French sociologist Maurice Halbwach who devised the theory of 'genre de vie' based on an earlier study of the working-class, are just two examples of the way in which lifestyle has been used to study a way of relating to the world through consumption practices. But as a number of critics have observed they do not account for social mobility nor for any kind of social difference other than class.[90]

In order to recontextualise the practice of DIY home improvement beyond the consumption phase as part of the 'ecology of personal possessions' as discussed in Chapter 6, it needs to be seen as an additional layer applied to the uncategorised 'builder's vernacular' style. For this purpose I propose to appropriate two terms used in cultural analysis – bricolage (1979) and 'culture club' (1984).[91] I see this as an appropriate use of terms originally adopted to describe urban youth subcultures that had not previously been subjected to academic analysis because they were not seen as worthy of serious scrutiny except as the butt of elitist criticism.[92] Bricolage is culled from Dick Hebdige's

87. Veblen, T. [1899] 1934. *The Theory of the Leisure Class*. New York: The Modern Library. See Chapter IV.

88. For example with reference to budget control by thrifty housewives see Benson-Porter, S. 1996. 'Living on the Margin: Working-Class Marriages and Family Survival Strategies in the United States, 1919–1941', pp. 212–43. In de Grazia 1996. *The Sex of Things*.

89. For example see Miller, D. 1998b. *A Theory of Shopping*. Cambridge: Polity.

90. For example de Grazia 1996. *The Sex of Things,* p. 153.

91. York, P. 1984. *Modern Times*. London: Futura.

92. Along the lines of the critique of the commodification of culture mounted by adherents to the Frankfurt School, see for example Storey, J. [1993] 1997. *An Introduction to Cultural Theory and Popular Culture*. London & New York: Prentice Hall Harvester Wheatsheaf, pp. 104–14.

adaptation of it from anthropology to describe 'how subcultural styles are constructed'. And 'culture club' is loosely lifted from Peter York's reportage on London youth styles.[93] It is not just that bricolage is the term used in French for DIY, that makes it so apt in the case of personalised builder's vernacular, but because Hebdige's interpretation of it describes the genre as a category of subculture where it can exist in its own right rather than as a poor copy or 'reproduction' of the real thing, in other words, as kitsch, a non-category, a no-thing. The 'style with no name' once personalised, can become highly stylish and 'wild' in a similar way to that which Hebdige applies bricolage to punk and other spectacular youth sub-cultures. Bricolage is used by anthropologists to describe the process used by particular groups to 'think' their world in a material logic of their own by means of improvisation and appropriating commodities inappropriately. Hebdige gives the example of the 'teddy boy' stealing the Savile Row suit. An example of incorrect appropriation in builders' vernacular would be the 'Georgian' door with integral fanlight incorporating the curved top glass panel that customarily would have been situated over the doorway, into the top panel of the door itself.

Peter York's use of 'the culture club' serves to describe a de rigeur style which must be adopted in order to belong to a particular sub-cultural group but has nothing to do with conforming to a fashion set from above. In the cases of both bricolage and culture club, style depends on the hybridisation of 'proper' styles through a process of amateur re- or rather dis-organisation, using disparate elements that would not necessarily be considered to 'go together', or adapted to make up a personal style of self-expression which at the same time announces membership of a particular 'culture club'. The idea of Peter York's 'culture club' adapts very well to the personalisation of spec builders' vernacular because, like all the various clubs' styles it allows infinite variation while still belonging to a particular over-arching home-centred suburban lifestyle. The possibilities of nuances between up-to-date home improvers and graduates from improvers to owners are endless. The element discussed here – the façade – is only one of the many features which has been subjected to refashioning. The interior and the garden are two other equally important elements offering even more creative opportunities. But the façade is the public face, where occupants can announce their individuality to their neighbours and passers-by.

93. Hebdige, D. 1979. *Subculture: The Meaning of Style*. London and New York: Methuen, pp. 102–6.

J.M. Richards – an architect, author of *Modern Architecture* (1940) [94] and editor of *Architectural Review* – was the one exception to advocates of modern architecture who invariably condemned suburbia. In 1946 he wrote a sensitive appreciation of suburbia[95] which he described as 'an enchanted jungle' recognising the wildness of its total disregard of 'good design'. He had been careful to specify that he was not trying to represent or perpetuate suburbia as 'some phoney "Merrie England" that has no part in the mainstream of cultural development' but to rescue the ability of the ordinary individual to use their own creativity, the quality that modernism quashed insisting that architects know best. In the introduction of the 1973 edition Richards' intention was to take the lessons of suburbia to create the space to allow individuality to flourish incorporating the new idea of encouraging 'user-participation', unlike the project of Scott Brown and Venturi or even Oliver et al. for architects to learn from suburbia. In spite of Richards' slightly condescending tone in referring to the 'amateur', taking the period in which he was writing into consideration he displayed an unusual respect for the creative home improver, of whom he wrote

> the picturesque tradition represented by the English suburban scene is preserved by the enthusiastic if somewhat inexpert efforts of the amateur. Owing to the expense of building as a hobby, the amateur architect is rare, although at one time he had a good deal to do with the founding of the villa tradition which the suburban style has adopted as its own . . . But if not with amateur architects, the present day suburb is peopled with amateur gardeners, amateur landscapists, amateur decorators, with contrivers of all sorts of effects, with handymen and with the individualists from whom the suburban jungle draws much of its vitality and for whose creative instincts it dates in a way that nothing else can . . .[96]

There are several degrees of separation between the house and the home; between the acquisition, whether by purchase or tenancy, of a piece of space for dwelling when it is still a raw commodity, and the process of transformation it undergoes in becoming a home. And within the home itself, the space is also divided up into personal and communal shared spaces and assimilated into everyday life. The acquisition and installation

94. Richards, J.M. 1940. *Modern Architecture*. Harmondsworth, Middlesex: Penguin.
95. Richards, J.M. [1946] 1973. *The Castles On the Ground: The Anatomy of Suburbia*. London: Architectural Press.
96. Ibid., pp. 66–7.

processes which territorialise and transform the commodity into an individualised domestic space requires a pliable neutral background space and an engaged producing-consumer rather than a highly designed finished product with a ready-made consumer in mind. Therefore to return to the question of why the suburban semi has managed to retain its popularity. Perhaps one of the reasons that it has remained such a desirable place is that it caters for the individual even though it was a form of mass product designed for an unidentified 'average family'. The secret of its success undoubtedly lies in its ambiguity – neither ancient nor modern, urban nor rural – a quality that has made it adaptable to a limitless range of tastes that offered its occupants infinite possibilities for self-individuation.

eight

Time: Bringing Things to Life

And indeed there will be time
To wonder, 'Do I dare?' and, 'Do I dare?' Time to turn back and descend
the stair . . .
Do I dare disturb the universe?
In a minute there is time
For decisions and revisions which a minute will reverse.

For I have known them all already, known them all –
Have known the evenings, mornings, afternoons,
I have measured out my life with coffee spoons.

(from 'The Love Song of J. Alfred Prufrock' by T.S. Eliot, 1917.)

The relational and subjective nature of time is encapsulated in the comparison between the rushing ahead to keep up with the new, and the static sense of waiting for the right moment that never comes. There are many ways in which time infiltrates the material culture of everyday life. Time implies a beginning and an end – birth and death, eternity and mortality. It is experienced through duration, frequency, longevity, change and finitude, through the relation of the body to the material world of things – as inexorably rushing towards the future or gradually evolving from the past but rarely, if ever, still. Both 'everyday' and 'life' incorporate a sense of temporality, at the same time as a sense of continuity in relation to change. Although there are conventional expectations and cultural traditions pertaining to rites of passage, personal awareness of time has a direct impact on how people form their individual subjectivity and attitudes to youth, maturity and ageing as they traverse different life stages.

The passage of time is made visible in the material world as processes of ageing – from child to adult, from new to old – in the lines on a face, in the brightness of a pristine unused newly decorated room, in

Figure 25. *Past Times* catalogue cover Summer 2000. (Innocence, Arthur Hacker, Fine Art Photographic)

the faded peeling paint on the outside of a building, or the build-up of patina on metal from exposure to the elements, in the latest up-to-date car model, in the signs of wear on a stone step trodden down for hundreds of years. Design that embodies modernity through the eternal process of renewal assumes the benefit of progress in innovation, and also accepts that in embracing change there is a risk of the inconstancy and destabilising quality of ephemerality, as discussed in Chapter 5. Conversely vernacular forms appear to have existed for ever, seeming to keep in touch with the permanent aspects of the past that provide solace and escape from the ever-changing modern world. Time does not 'stand still' nor does human life – time only stops at death. People use things to adjust their relationship to time – to keep a memory alive, to get away from the past, to get ahead or just to keep up-to-date.

There are the obvious examples of memorials which provide a material form of public mourning[1] and there are more personal objects which are cited in psychoanalytical studies like Jane Graves' 'inside' story of a jug which served as a metaphor in a process of mental healing.[2] The 'transitional object' discussed in Chapter 5 has a direct bearing on negotiating the crossing over from one life-stage to another. The methodological problem in conceptualising the motion of time in relation to a static material object as the metaphorical embodiment of a temporal aspect of life experience, can best be hypothesised in terms of the way certain types of material culture are used for keeping in touch with life and coming to terms with mortality.

Time is conceptualised as the duration of a period in which events happen or things take place, and most importantly the dimension through which human existence or, in Heidegger's sense, 'being', is experienced.[3] Some modernists like David Harvey argue that 'becoming' is a more politically engaged position since it depends on the possibility of change for the better in the future.[4] But not everyone is empowered enough to be able to make that decision. Time is sensed in relation to

1. Forty, A. and Kuchler, S. (ed.) 1999. *The Art of Forgetting*. Oxford and New York: Berg.

2. Graves, J. 1999. '"When Things Go Wrong . . . Inside the Inside": A Psychoanalytical History of a Jug'. In *Journal of Design History*, Vol. 12, No. 4, pp. 357–67.

3. Heidegger, M. [1927] [First English edition 1962] 1998. *Being and Time*. Oxford and Cambridge: Blackwell, p. 40.

4. Harvey, D. 1989. *The Condition of Postmodernity: An Enquiry into the Origins of Cultural Change*. Oxford: Blackwell.

the duration of a life cycle[5] and measured through the recurrence of natural phenomena such as the rising of the sun, the seasons, or by mechanical means based on standard clock settings. Time can be conceptualised as the matrix that holds everyday life together even though time itself is not actually material in the sense that space can be experienced physically as solid ground beneath the feet, or as intervals between the body and say a wall. Time is one of the means of orientation by which people order their day, their lives and through which they maintain a sense of being in the world in relation to what existed before their coming into it, and what may happen after they have left it. Time is experienced in many different ways through the body, the routines of everyday life, the different phases of the life cycle, unusual events, through memory and history. It is fantasised and romanticised via invented nostalgic recollections, and imagined futures that form part of the cultural representations and narratives that work their part in giving people a sense of identity – of living in their own time. At the most basic level, time is one of the dimensions that orients subjectivity in terms of an individual 'lifetime' and the agency such a self-conscious awareness of existence engenders – the opportunity (or not, as the case may be) for making 'life choices' in the anticipation of death.

Types of Time

As the reference to Heidegger above will already have announced, 'existential time' is one of the types of time adopted here for the purpose of analysing its relation to everyday life.[6] The other two types of time which are useful analytical tools to take the discussion beyond the subjective, is that of the 'ethnographic present' – a theoretical form of anthropological time, and 'historical time'. Lastly, for its particular relation to postmodernity 'time-space compression' will also be discussed although it doesn't constitute a type of time since it actually seems to negate time as a dimension. What it actually highlights is its contingency. Existential time presupposes an 'existent' with a finite lifespan and therefore a particular subjective relation to temporality

5. For an alternative to the concept of the 'life cycle' see Featherstone, M. 1995. 'The Mask of Ageing and the Postmodern Life Course' pp. 371–89. In Featherstone, M., Hepworth, M. and Turner, B.S. *The Body: Social Process and Cultural Theory*. London and Thousand Oaks, California: Sage.

6. Macquarrie, J. 1980. *Existentialism*. Harmondsworth: Penguin.

that has little to do with clock time.[7] In describing the existent's relation to temporality, John Macquarrie defines the existential consciousness of time past, present and future

> in the case of the existent past and future are intrinsically related to the present. We never catch the existent in a knife-edge present [. . .] By memory the existent has brought his past with him into the present; and by anticipation and imagination he has already laid hold on his future and projects himself into it.
>
> We would not *exist* [. . .] if we lacked this peculiar kind of temporality whereby we transcend the now and unite, to some degree, the past, present and future.[8]

This implies a form of uncomplicated agency which Macquarrie qualifies by pointing out typical imbalances produced by dwelling too much in one particular type of time – living too much in future-imagined possibilities produces unrealisable idealism, whereas dwelling in the past, as an escape from anxiety and uncertainty, prevents risking anything radical or new. While living entirely in the present suggests a total lack of agency so that all action is determined by present circumstances. Existential time provides a way of looking at how individuals form their relationship with time by observing how their subjectivity is objectified in material form.

The 'ethnographic present' invoked by Mary Douglas and Baron Isherwood in their anthropological study of mass consumption, in some way parallels 'existential time' but at a theoretical level. It layers past, present and future time in a similar synchronic time system, as a way of capturing and interpreting the cultural connections that link the past to the present and the future, that are not made evident with historic diachronic analysis which chronicles one thing after another. Douglas and Isherwood described the 'ethnographic present' as

> a special tense that aims to concentrate past, present, and future into a continuous present [. . .] It synthesises into one temporal point the events of many people, the value of the synthesis lying in the strength of the analysis of the perceived present. Whatever is important about the past is assumed to be making itself felt here and now. [. . .] current ideas about the future likewise draw present judgements down certain paths and block

7. Ibid., p. 99.
8. Ibid., p. 200.

off others. It assumes a two-way perspective in which the individual treats his past selectively as a source of validating myths and the future as the locus of dreams.[9]

Given the assertion which followed the extract quoted above, that 'the ethnographic present assumes an unchanging economic system', it is understandable that historians like John A. Walker have recommended approaching this type of anthropological time with a certain amount of caution. The caution is founded on the suspicion that the object of study is merely an exercise in spotting universal and transhistorical aspects of culture. Yet although it was indeed the case that structural anthropology sought to reveal the essential underlying models that generated similar patterns of culture across peoples transculturally,[10] one of its major contributions to academic thought has been its investigation of cultural *differences*.[11] As Walker pointed out in 1989 when he recommended anthropological theory to design historians:

Anthropology originated in the context of European colonialism. Early scholars studied foreign native cultures which were markedly different from their own. These cultures tended to be perceived as primitive, backward, fossilised, inferior, abnormal and non-historical or static. Otherness also had an exotic appeal. Modern anthropologists are now aware of the dangers of paternalism and Eurocentrism and they seek to understand and respect cultural otherness and to conduct research with their subjects in a relationship of equality not dominance. They also now realise that the presence of an outsider has an impact upon the people being studied and that this has to be taken into account when drawing conclusions about the normal functioning of the society. There are, perhaps lessons here from which design historians could benefit. They too need to show a tolerance and respect for the design tastes of others which the historians themselves may not share.[12]

9. Douglas, M. and Isherwood, B. 1978. *The World of Goods: Towards an Anthropology of Consumption*. London: Allen Lane, pp. 23–4.

10. Lévi-Strauss, C. 1963. *Structural Anthropology*, New York: Basic Books.

11. Geertz, C. [1973] 1993. *The Interpretation of Cultures*. London: Fontana.

12. Walker, J.A. 1989. *Design History and the History of Design*. London: Pluto Press, pp. 125–6.

Ten years on that lesson remains largely unheeded and although non-aesthetic objects[13] are sometimes cultivated by designers, they are more often than not regarded rather patronisingly as jokey kitsch – a fun element only to be enjoyed ironically. Kitsch is only popular in its 'cute' form – acceptable as long as its not threatening, not too ugly or offensive, as long as it has had its sting removed. But like punk, the only popular manifestation of ugliness, it is *meant* to be wild; it only works as a statement if it has not been tamed. But that only applies to design as 'things with attitude'; and Walker's remarks still apply to the broad majority of the products of mass consumption which design historians and critics have chosen to ignore as unworthy of analysis or are so inconsequential to have simply escaped their notice.

For the purposes of considering time as one of the contexts in the study of the material culture of everyday life, it is worth resurrecting the theoretical concept of the 'ethnographic present', culled from anthropology in respect of its application to the investigation of what gives different cultural groups their individuality; while also taking into consideration the perspective of the investigator. Its synthetic character is particularly useful in the context of postmodern thinking, as is the notion of 'space-time compression', explained below. The intervening twenty-two years that have elapsed since Douglas and Isherwood made their study, has seen the problematisation of the interpretation of post-colonial history through the self-conscious intervention of the historian's perspective,[14] asking awkward questions such as 'whose history?' The two disciplines have undergone similar self-searching reappraisals of the role of the investigator and the importance of recognising the diverse nature of society in the interpretation of cultural specificity. In terms of mentality, history is often referred to metaphorically as a place – another country – and requires an understanding of the particularities that are only thrown up when the dimension of 'historical time' is brought into the frame. The postmodern effect of flattening time, exemplified in Harvey's 'time-space compression' needs to be included in the caveat recommending caution, but without throwing it out as irrelevant, since it contributes to the explanation for some of the contemporary popular attitudes to history.

So before turning to 'historical time', I want to stop to consider the parallels of Harvey's postmodern theory of 'time-space

13. By 'non-aesthetic' I do not mean 'ugly' because that is too visibly interesting, but rather indifferently unnoticeable, i.e. – 'everyday'.

14. Jenkins, K. 1991. *Re-Thinking History.* London and New York: Routledge.

compression'[15] with 'existential time' and the 'ethnographic present' since each represent a different perception of time conflation and are useful in their own ways. Time-space compression is one of the features which Harvey isolates to describe the effects of postmodernity which has changed how people perceive the world. He attributes capitalism with speeding up the pace of life to such an extent as to overcome spatial barriers with the dramatic effect that 'the world sometimes seems to collapse inwards upon us'. His generalisation of the experience of the 'global village' (of communication) and the 'spaceship earth' (of economic and ecological interdependencies), presupposes a somewhat exaggerated universal awareness. His case is that the innovations in transportation that enable journeys to be made increasingly faster 'annihilates space through time'. He traces the relativity of space to nineteenth-century colonialism which had the effect of destabilising the sense of territoriality. While increased communication flow enabled 'a mere glance at the morning newspaper' to inform readers of simultaneous happenings occurring all over the world. So that now instead of linear time marked by the to and fro swing of the clock's pendulum, events could be perceived synchronically. Like Marshall Berman[16] and many other authors, Harvey's analysis of the postmodern condition includes the vast expansion of commodity production with its concomitant experience of acceleration and change made real through consumption processes. The adaptability to the fast, instantly available plethora of obsolescent goods that made them just as easily disposable[17] is evident in the postmodern experience of transience and destabilisation. Material culturists like Daniel Miller interpret consumption as a positive symptom in creating strategies for dealing with the instability of contemporary life.[18]

The time-types described so far all deal with time as multi-layered and can best be conceptualised and analysed in the form of time intervals of concurrence, that is – synchronically. But leaving aside existential (subjective) time, and for the moment just taking on board theoretical time-types which can contribute to the study of the material culture of everyday life at a more abstract level, the ethnographic present and time-space compression, would both appear to have theorised the

15. Harvey 1989. *The Condition of Postmodernity*, pp. 240–2.

16. Berman, M. 1983. *All That Is Solid Melts Into Air: The Experience of Modernity*. London: Verso.

17. Ibid., p. 286.

18. Miller, D. 1987. *Material Culture and Mass Consumption*. Oxford: Blackwell.

same effect of synchronic time, but from very different programmatic starting points. The first can be applied at a detailed empirical level of research to investigate subjective culturally-specific experiences, while the latter was directed at producing a totalising theory based on a critique of capitalist production. I would contend that existential time – how temporality is experienced at a personal individual level, and how it is objectified in material productions in which the layering effect is quite specific – can usefully be theorised through the format of the 'ethnographic present'. To this can be added how such experience is actualised through material processes of production and consumption in social and individual acts of self-creation.

'Other' Times – History and 'the Past'

To many, history is represented by public institutions like the National Trust which not only are seen to preserve cultural heritage and national identity, but also to have become translated into a material confirmation for the popular aversion to 'modern' design. This taste for 'heritage' has produced a genre of style that can be applied anachronistically to almost anything from street furniture to carrier bags. Its appeal lies in the reference to vague nostalgic 'other' times rather than to any pretence at accurate historic reproduction. There was a spate of critical literature on the commodification of 'heritage'[19] and some counter arguments from a popular culture stance.[20] The main intention in introducing the phenomenon here is not to engage in aesthetic critique or to review the debates concerning the manner History has represented the past,[21] but to draw attention to the magical transformational qualities attributed to the notion of 'heritage' in arresting modernisation. This is exemplified in the recent objections mounted by campaigners against the design of a proposed Road Chef motorway service station reported in the *Hampshire Chronicle* on 10 December 1999:

Opponents of an M3 service station near Shroner Wood have described approval of its design as 'a tragedy'. [. . .] The service area, some four miles north of Winchester city centre, will be constructed in modern materials and will have a rolling metal roof. [. . .] Itchen Valley Parish

19. Hewison, R. 1987. *The Heritage Industry.* London: Methuen.
20. Wright, P. 1985. *On Living in an Old Country.* London and New York: Verso.
21. See for example, Bann. S. (ed.) 1990. *The Inventions of History.* Manchester and New York: Manchester University Press.

Council chairman, Alison Matthews, was one of the opponents who claimed design restrictions had not been respected. 'There was an assurance that the service station would fit into the surrounding area, but it is nothing like what we expected' she said. 'We wanted the buildings to have a traditional appearance and the look of a National Trust property.'

What is more revealing than the assumption that conjured up the historic country house as the model for a motorway service station, was the way in which an imagined past was recruited as a panacea for the unacceptable face of modern life. No doubt the same objectors against the service station would protest even more vociferously if they were to be banned from bringing their cars into the very city centre they were defending from contamination by what they considered visual pollution of a building four miles away. The point I am trying to make with this anecdote is the way 'history' is embedded in contemporary culture as a material idealisation of the past. Historic time in this context has nothing to do with how we might know the past, or with conventional History – the recorded chronicle of important events and personages that have been instrumental in shaping the present of a country, institution or cultural form. Nor does it even have much to do with the more reflexive 'post-modern' formulation of history that recognises it as a discourse – an interpretation shaped by the sources, methods and theories chosen to direct the study of the past in relation to particular interest groups and therefore specific cultural identities. This tendency has redirected some historians' attention to the hidden side of history and attempted to redress the balance by enquiring into the history of the working class, of women, the disenfranchised and the poor. Although some academics are informed by popular concepts of imagined pasts[22] in attempting to engage with the perspective of their objects of study using oral history techniques, the project is invariably mediated by the historian who interprets the testimony. Nevertheless, the political strategy to destroy the credibility of history has been vigorously refuted by a number of eminent historians who at the same time recognise the necessity for contemporary historians to 'be more self-aware of their rhetorical strategies.'[23]

22. For example Williamson, J. 1978. *Decoding Advertisements: Ideology and Meaning in Advertising.* London and Boston: Marion Boyars, see Chapter 7: 'Time: Narrative and History', pp. 152–66; Samuel, R. 1995. *Theatres of Memory.* London: Verso.

23. This quotation from Stephen Bann refers specifically to art historians but is equally applicable to other branches of history. In *The Inventions of History*, p. 222.

Modern Times, Historic Time and Modernity

Unlike the synchronicity implied by the above-mentioned theoretical models – the anthropological 'ethnographic present', the philosophical 'existential time' and post-modern 'time-space compression' – 'historic time' assumes a retrospective knowledge of the past and a diachronic time structure that links the present with the past but cannot bring it back to life. I am not referring to what can be known about the past in the form of interpretations by professional historians – historians' time. The way subjects make connections with their past is not necessarily articulated but can be observed in the form of material manifestations in the construction of their personal material worlds. Historic time in the context of everyday life might be to do with a sense of identity acquired by adhering to tradition, or conversely by departing from it in a bid for change. The latter depends on a knowing subject who to some extent feels in command of their own life and is more in tune with modern time than past time. Judith Williamson, in referring to the way advertisements trigger a sense of historic time, calls this an 'imaginary relationship to past *personal* time'.[24]

What I refer to here as historic time has little to do with the fruits of professional historians' research since it refers to popular notions of the past in the form of 'other' times. There was no need for accuracy of architectural detail in the out-of-town supermarkets built to evoke Victorian town halls in the 1980s, nor in the attempt to retain a sense of the picturesque rural idyll invoked by the notion of a 'National Trust' style service station. It is the converse of the sense of 'living in the now' and engaging with the present that separates the present off from the past, such as would be experienced through the ephemerality of engaging in a fashion that won't last and not knowing what will come next. It is much more to do with a search for identity through a sense of a shared 'history' with a family, a nation or a group of like-minded individuals. That kind of 'historic time' however has little to do with History because it takes place within a closed narrative in which there is no danger of a surprise ending.[25] It has more to do with evocation than History since there no link with the reality of the present. The 'past' is comforting in its familiarity – it lends a sense of belonging, but is also intriguing in its capacity to stimulate desire, the longing for

24. Williamson 1978. *Decoding Advertisements*, p. 164.
25. Ibid., p. 152.

a past that cannot really be brought to life, an evasion of mortality.[26] Historic time that engages with the present rather than with 'the past', unlike 'home', is not a popular resort, except in a metaphorical sense to indicate a degree of separation from what 'is best forgotten', the 'putting-behind' place for 'reality' with its prescience of death of which T.S. Eliot, that inveterate modernist, wrote: 'human kind cannot bear very much reality. Time past and time future. What might have been and what has been point to one end, which is always present'.[27] Time past is unreachable in any 'authentic' experiential form, while the longing for it – nostalgia – can only produce an inauthentic reconstruction. Recent research on memorials has sought to investigate the way in which they materialize social remembering and affect the way the past is perceived.[28]

That existential time to which Eliot refers is the only dimension in which anything can happen, but requires a subject to actually make something happen. Jürgen Habermas points out the particularity of a modernity which bears no relation to history and can only 'create its normativity out of itself'.[29] 'Actuality can be constituted only at the point where time and eternity intersect.'[30] With reference to modern time-consciousness Habermas describes Walter Benjamin's 'now-time' as a 'solution to the paradoxical task of obtaining standards of its own for the contingency of a modernity that had become simply transitory'. The concept of historic time assumes some kind of historical continuum and therefore can only conceive of modernity located in the present as the only point in time in which it *is* possible to make a decisive break from the past, to exercise agency and effect change. This modernist version sees the present as the 'forge of history' and 'the matrix of the future'[31] and has little interest in conceiving of history as a museum or a memory.

26. Stewart, S. [1984] 1996. *On Longing: Narratives of the Miniature, the Gigantic, the Souvenir, the Collection.* Durham and London: Dukes University Press.

27. Eliot, T.S. 'Burnt Norton' [1935]. In *Collected Poems 1909–1962*, 1975. London: Faber and Faber, p. 190.

28. Forty and Kuchler 1999. *The Art of Forgetting.*

29. Habermas, J. 1987. Lecture I: 'Modernity's Consciousness of Time' pp. 1–22. *The Philosophical Discourses of Modernity: Twelve Lectures.* Cambridge: Polity, p. 7.

30. Ibid., p. 9.

31. Poggioli, R. 1968. *The theory of the avant-garde: Cambridge, Mass.*, p. 73. cited in Harvey 1989. *The Condition of Postmodernity*, p. 359.

Encountering the 'Past' in the Heritage Museum

The popularisation of the past objectified in the burgeoning revival of preservationism in the 1980s was institutionalised with the National Heritage Acts (1980 & 1983) [32] which facilitated 'the means whereby property could be transferred to the State in lieu of capital transfer tax and estate duty'[33] and established the National Heritage Memorial Fund. Under the newly established conservative government it became part of an attempt to revive the patriotic spirit of the Second World War in the form of a memorial that could be shared by the nation in common. In addition to maintenance and preservation, the remit for stewardship was now to include the exhibition and display of Heritage sites so as to facilitate public access to the famous historic houses, stretches of unspoilt countryside, archaeological sites, monuments and other property considered worthy of being given the status of 'national heritage'. The trustees of the National Heritage Memorial Fund, in charge of dispensing grants who were chosen for their 'great common sense in the world of art', evaded the issue of defining what should qualify as 'national heritage' by ' let[ing] it define itself' and just responding reactively to requests as they came in.[34] The perception which appeared to rule was one of a nation in decline, of mouldering country houses and a disappearing industrial heritage that had to be saved for posterity. The popular appeal of 'heritage' gave rise to a genre of invented styles loosely based on evocative historic periods – Victorian, Deco, Fifties – used for marketing in mass media and styling all types of commodities from clothes, beauty products, and kitchen fitments to themed entertainments such as the medieval banquets at Hatfield House, or the Lancaster Georgian Festival.

New strategies in museum display techniques were purposely developed to enhance the visitor's experience of an encounter with the past. Changes in museum display techniques moved away from categorisation and took objects out of glass cabinets to be rearranged in more interesting configurations to engage and stimulate visitors' interest. The historical reconstruction was a technique increasingly used to give a 'realistic' representation using the three dimensional mise-en-scène. The techniques include the 'frozen moment' which might show a

32. Kirby, S. 1989. 'Policy, Politics: charges, sponsorship, and bias', pp. 89–101. In Lumley, R. (ed.) 1990. *The Museum Time Machine. London and New York: Comedia*, p. 89.

33. Wright 1985. *On Living in an Old Country*, p. 44.

34. Ibid., pp. 46–7.

Figure 26. Re-enactment scene of knights in armour, Nottingham Robin Hood Fair.

workshop with tools in disarray and signs of recently absented characters about to return any minute, or the tableau using figurines, replicas and facsimiles, sound effects and the voices of informants' oral history accounts to build an atmosphere as well as to impart information directly from informants' testimony.[35] There was also the re-enactment using costumed museum staff or volunteers to create 'living museums'.[36] The scene could have been of a Victorian cook busy in the kitchen where the visitor would be greeted by the enticing smell of baking and invited to taste the biscuits, or where for a few minutes, the museum visitor could become a pupil in a late nineteenth-century school room. These kind of dramatisations that use relational arrangements of museum artefacts are intended to transform them into everyday objects

35. For example the social history museum – *The People's Story* in Edinburgh.
36. Lumley 1990. *The Museum Time Machine.*

and imbue them with a sense of history.[37] Displays of this kind are meant to draw the viewer in at a more visceral level than the 'difficult' intellectual engagement required to study uncontextualised numbered objects in glass cases referenced to explanatory textual labels. The appeal to empathy that facilitates the identification with unfamiliar circumstances in the teaching of history to schoolchildren, has been the subject of considerable debate amongst educationists because of the fear that it fictionalises history, but has proved to be very popular and widely used in social history, local and regional museums.

Historical re-enactments in which people dress up and participate in 'living history' has become a popular form of leisure pursuit enabling enthusiasts to indulge in ancient forms of battle, music, dance and feasting, spinning, weaving and crafts. Part of the interest lies in the making of the dress, weapons and other everyday appurtenances using 'authentic' methods and materials of manufacture. Historians and cultural critics have been very critical of the 'invention' of traditions and the mythological 'construction of history' in a bid to formulate accurate interpretations[38] or as an attack on strategies that exploit history for ideological or commercial purposes. For example critiques of consumerism have attacked advertisements for selling inaccurate representations of the past, and museums for imposing dominant views of history. The need for more rigorous examination of historians' ideological motives, as well as a new critical awareness of the responsibility for the nation's heritage recognised the need for rigorous examination of historians' ideological motives, as well as a critical awareness of the responsibility for the nation's heritage.

The so-called 'new museology' was an attempt to put into practice a self-awareness and sensitivity on the part of museums in relation to issues of cultural property and the interpretation of history through the medium of material artefacts. The connotations of political and national identity[39] involved in the ownership of cultural artefacts is an issue periodically brought to public attention through the media, exemplified in the claim made by Greece for the return of the Elgin

---

37. Denker, E.P. 1997. 'Evaluating Exhibitions: History Museums and Material Culture', pp. 381–400. In Smart Martin, A. and Ritchie Garrison,J. (eds.) 1997. *American Material Culture: The Shape of the Field*. Winterthur, Delaware: Henry de Pont Winterthur Museum.

38. For example Hobsbawm, E. and Ranger, T. (eds) [1983] 1992. *The Invention of Tradition*. Cambridge: Cambridge University Press.

39. Coombes, E. A. 1988. 'Museums and the Formation of National and Cultural Identities', pp. 57–68. In *The Oxford Art Journal*, Vol. 11, No. 2.

marbles held by the British Museum. Encounters with the past through museum and other educational sources which increasingly make use of similar devices to those used in theme parks and the popular media to produce an experiential engagement, mediate the way history is perceived.[40] Although novelty has been a central marketing device used in design, historical themes and references to 'traditional' and 'classic' have also proved popular for some time.[41] The amazing proliferation of new museums during the 1980s[42] must be held responsible in some way for diffusing a form of popular historical imagination reflected in so much of contemporary material culture. It also indicates the structure of feeling which gave rise to an interest in the past made manifest in the Heritage phenomenon. Since its formal institutionalised recognition,[43] one of the central debates among academics and museum professionals involved in the collection and display of 'heritage' has been the tussle between the interests of education versus the commercial necessity to market history as entertainment. Much of the critical literature on 'heritage' has been condemnatory on the grounds of its propagation of inauthentic or biased representations and the commodification of history which fails to give a truthful interpretation.[44] The fact is that design which recalls the past has proved extremely popular cannot be ignored; yet few writers have attempted to explain the phenomenon in terms of popular culture. And as for the specialist literature on the history of design, the impact of the taste for archaism has been ignored as an aberration, except by a few writers who have either neutrally explained it away in economic terms,[45] or have ironically revelled in 'culture as commodity'.[46] In museology circles the

40. Sorensen, C. 1989. 'Theme Parks and Time Machines', pp. 60–73. In Vergo, P. (ed.) *The New Museology*. London: Reaktion.

41. Woodham, J. 1997. *Twentieth-Century Design*. Oxford and New York: Oxford University Press. See Chapter 9: 'Nostalgia, Heritage and Design', pp. 205–19.

42. According to Norman Palmer 'At no other time in our history has there existed so intense an interest in the preservation of our cultural patrimony. In England, new museums are appearing at a rate of one a fortnight'. In 'Museums and Cultural Property', pp. 172–204. In Vergo 1989. *The New Museology*, p. 172.

43. Greenhalgh, P. 1989. 'Education, Entertainment and Politics: Lessons from the Great International Exhibitions', pp. 74–98. In Vergo 1989. *The New Museology*.

44. Hewison 1987. *The Heritage Industry*.

45. Woodham 1997. *Twentieth-Century Design*.

46. York, P. 'Culture and commmodity: style wars, punk and pageant', pp. 160–8. In Thakara, J. (ed.) 1988. *Design After Modernism*. London: Thames and Hudson.

Figure 27. 'Heritage' style bollards.

growing sensitivity and self-reflectiveness on the importance of formu-
lating policy that would protect the quality and integrity of the
scholarship of curatorial museum practices was outlined in several
reports on Britain's national museums.[47] One of the concerns in the
exhibiting of material culture was to consider how value is assigned to
objects making them historically significant beyond antiquarian,
connoisseurial and aesthetic élitism in respect of their ideological and
political dimensions.

Patrick Wright's admonition not to 'sneer at the theme parks' was
based on an attempt to get on the other side of the display – that of
the audience. In a defence of continuing public access to National Trust
houses Wright noted in 1989:

> It has to be [a] key priority to take on that question of audience and use.
> The problem is that the analysis that has been produced so far has simply
> been read out of the display and its representations. If one doesn't go
> further it is going to be difficult to ground a critical discussion in anything
> other than disdain. What we need now is to differentiate and move
> beyond the refusal which says it's all fake, it's all constructed, and get
> into a situation where the arguments are based on the ability to support
> and develop the kinds of practice which are valuable while also consist-
> ently de-polemicising where necessary.[48]

47. *The National Museums and Galleries of the United Kingdom*, 1988. London: HMSO.
48. Wright, P. and Putnam, T. 'Sneering at the Theme Parks', pp. 48–55. In *Block* 15,
Spring 1989, p. 55.

From Wright's position as a freelance expert he could mount a critical exposé of the institutional politics of bodies such as the National Trust, while at the same time, and in distinct contrast, observe the way history permeates everyday life of ordinary people. His radical political stance against the 'death of history' in the face of a country in decline, saw the Heritage movement propagated at the height of the Thatcher period as 'right-wing radicalism which treats people as objects [. . .] the proles as battered ornaments still waiting to be dug out of the ever-collapsing junk-shop of modern history'.[49] His archaeological metaphor revealed his aversion to the historicism shared by modern designers but was also concerned with the structure of feeling that placed history as such an important aspect of the formation of individual identity. The debate on heritage has moved on considerably since then and there is much more awareness of the problems of authenticity and the need to include the history of everyday life through displays of its artefacts.[50]

The diffusion of nostalgic 'good old days' images whether through visits to National Trust properties, 'time-capsule' museum exhibits, advertisements, or gifts from one of the sixty outlets of the Past Times chain of gift shops[51] have all added to the common bank of historic 'memories'. One of the most memorable of the first TV advertisements to use a 'past times' mini-narrative was set in a sepia inter-war village with an adult voice-over recalling a memory from his childhood. It followed a boy pushing his bike up a steep cobbled street and into his granddad's warm inviting cottage where he sat down to have tea at a table set with a fresh Hovis loaf, a product still available 'today' – thus associating the Hovis brown bread brand with a timeless tradition of quality. The ubiquitous presence of past times in the styling of gifts, interior design goods, kitchen utensils, in period dramas on television and in films, all undoubtedly mediate the popular perception of history. Identifying with such stories and objectifications like the family photograph album self-recording important events creates an intimate and meaningful sense of personal history. It is such experiences that interact with memory and make up the texture of a consciousness of historic time. The subjective nature of a personal sense of the past is

49. Wright 1985. *On Living in an Old Country*, p. 248.

50. Phillips, D. 1997. *Exhibiting Authenticity*. Manchester and New York: Manchester University Press, p. 66. Re. new approaches to English Heritage by the recently appointed Director Sir Neil Cossens see Field, M. 2000, 'Dark satanic mills get the cool treatment', p. 4, *Independent on Sunday*, 2 April.

51. Woodham 1997. *Twentieth-Century Design*, p. 218.

not the same as History, nevertheless, in considering everyday life; historical consciousness is an essential ingredient which cannot be ignored in the actualisation of individuality.

Memory – 'the Mummification of Desire' and the New Antiquarianism

The 'Material Memories' conference[52] held at the Victoria and Albert Museum in April 1998 is just one of the recent events which have brought 'memory' into the academic arena as a means of discussing the past at a more subjective level than history normally allows. The aim was to investigate the way that different kinds of memory – from the personal to the public, and the political to the aesthetic – is invested, invented, recollected or forgotten through a range of different kinds of material forms. These were loosely grouped under the somewhat unsatisfactory term 'Design, suggesting a genre of manufactured artefacts', when in fact the conference was set to look at a much broader gamut of objects for a different purpose to that normally assigned to researching design history.

Postmodernism's critical interrogation of history which has cast a sensitive self-conscious inflection in how the past should or can be studied and what history has to tell us about the present, was apparent in the gathering of papers offered at the Material Memories conference. The context of the museum setting as a repository for the past, in this instance spread well beyond the Victoria and Albert Museum – the nineteenth-century building in South Kensington – to encompass for example, a well-known modern architect's former residence now in the care of the National Trust,[53] and the *Titanic* – the famous passenger liner that sank on its maiden voyage in 1912 and now lies at the bottom of the sea.[54] The emphasis was on evocation as a dialogic process that places objects as instigators of subjective interpretations, rather than as vehicles for communicating fixed meanings. The underlying methodological object of the exercise, according to the cover notes on the

52. Kwint, M., Breward, C. and Aynsley, J. (eds) 1999. *Material Memories: Design and Evocation*. Oxford and New York: Berg.

53. Naylor, G. 1999. 'Modernism and Memory: Leaving Traces', pp. 91–106. In Kwint et al. *Material Memories*.

54. Gronberg, T. 1999. 'The *Titanic*: An Object Manufactured for Exhibition at the Bottom of the Sea', pp. 237–52. In Kwint et al. 1999. *Material Memories*.

conference's ensuing publication,[55] was to study 'the physical within the intellectual' and thereby ' "test" the concept of material culture'. This indication of a rather literal understanding of 'material culture' as an opposition between mind and body (culture/nature) along Cartesian lines, and suggesting an interpretation of matter as factual and therefore 'testable' in a systematic scientific manner, was not carried through in the range of papers which offered a multiplicity of perspectives demonstrating the 'undisciplined' nature of the field. How such a 'test' should or could be done was not disclosed and becomes rather lost in the further unreconciled contradiction presented by the propositions 'that objects "speak" to us through the memories we associate with them',[56] and 'the silence of such objects, which ultimately defy all attempts to represent them in language.'[57] This interpretation of material culture infers an elaboration on an empirical exercise in object analysis that allots primacy to biological or economic 'truth', and then by adding a subjective gloss, attends to meaning as if it were some sort of value-added extra.

In his introductory chapter to *Material Memories* – 'The Physical Past' – Marius Kwint suggests that memory is more accurate than history. He appears to attribute history with a will of its own by charging it with the task of 'admit[ting. . .] its illusory and constructed nature, and stop pretending that it refers to a real process which is amenable to systematic analysis and even prediction'. He then goes on to propose that if we are to gain 'a truer understanding of the significance and causality of the past we should reckon more with memory'.[58] Although he admits to overstating his claim, there is an underlying lack of shift from the philosophical position that history is teleological; a denial which is a requirement of the postmodern critique he invokes to base his argument upon. It is only by challenging the philosophical foundation on which the conventions of disciplinary history are based and rethinking the relationship between people and objects that the history of material culture can be re-examined in a new way. Even though the inclusion of subjectivity in historical practice is not a given, it is far from new in academic thought, which for some time now has accepted

55. Kwint et al. 1999. *Material Memories*.

56. Kwint et al. 1999. *Material Memories*, back cover notes.

57. Kwint, M. 1999. 'Introduction: The Physical Past', pp. 1–16. In Kwint et al. 1999. Material Memories, p.16.

58. Ibid., p.1.

the concept of the decentred subject, that is – the validity of different points of view that a recognition of cultural diversity requires.[59]

Theorisation within social anthropology and archaeology have taken a much more radical approach by rejecting dualism and pursuing the study of the interaction between the object world and social reproduction – that which the social anthropologist, Daniel Miller refers to as the objectification of social relations.[60] The archaeologist, Julian Thomas also approaches materiality in terms of the dynamic interaction between object and subject, contending that

> Physical and mental activity are coextensive, and thinking is one aspect of the way in which human beings skilfully negotiate their world. Yet Cartesianism suggests that we can distinguish a biological organism which is somehow more fundamental than the mind which has been added to it. It is quite possible to argue the opposite: that rather than the mind being a separate entity grafted onto a biological organism, the very notion of the human body as an animal requires a systematic forgetting of the kind of entity which it is. That is, the enterprise of 'human biology' involves covering over of the body's character as a site of experience, interpretation and self-formation.

> The oppositions between mind and body and culture and nature are products of Enlightenment thought. For archaeology, the consequence has been a failure to appreciate the character of the material world which human beings live in and through.[61]

There are also more ways than one of thinking about past time, as illustrated by the 'time types' described above. The context and the purpose of recollecting, recording, reconstructing or memorialising the past does, of course, introduce a degree of contingency which negates the possibility of reaching a single accurate version – what among historians used, at *one time,* to be called an 'authoritative' interpretation. There is a danger in mistaking memory for history however. Memory is a very personal and intimate form of recollection, although it can and is experienced collectively in ritualised public expressions of shared

59. For example the disciplinary field of Women's Studies which developed from feminist critique.

60. Miller 1987. *Material Culture and Mass Consumption.*

61. Thomas, J. 1996. 'A précis of *Time, Culture and Identity'* ,pp. 6–46. In *Archaeological Dialogues* 1, p. 9.

cultural traditions. In historical practice there is a place for considering the anecdotes, personal recollections and gossip which may be the only remains of the structure of feeling that animated a past culture, often conjured up through the means of material objects.[62] But this should not be confused with the responsibility of those in charge of History and museums to safe-keep evidence of, record, and explain events of importance with a sense of responsibility to truth above aesthetics. This includes the transmission of different points of view that may well be inconclusive and keep the interpretation open for discussion.

But to go back to the interpretation of the past through the media of material objects. Marcia Pointon's essay of a paper given at the Material Memories conference,[63] on a Victorian bracelet made of human hair – a common-place type of nineteenth-century jewellery, exemplifies the memorialisation of a loved one in an intimate object of personal adornment. She describes how 'hair jewellery materialises grief as secular reliquary and micro-museum' and interprets it as 'the "mummification" of desire' – that which is experientially inaccessible. The representation of memory as desire suggests a romantic nostalgic yearning for an unattainable time, place, person, and an accepting confrontation to death through a ritualised reminder, typical of the Victorian attitudes to sex and death. The case also encapsulates some of the problems involved in using memory as a framework for the analysis of material culture because it evokes pathos and sentimentality, an academic form of nostalgia for the past which could become a kind of cosy retreat from the problems challenged by the questions of history. It has its place in mourning the past as dead, in facing up to the needs of the present and the realisation of the inaccuracy of memory, its selective tendency to blank out the unpleasant. Memory has just as strong a tendency to 'construct' or invent the past as history and could just be a way of getting back to historicism of avoiding the confusions of postmodernity. Maybe the best way to regard the angst-ridden pre-millennium doubt that all history is 'constructed' makes us think about how to look back over the past for what it has to tell us about our present. Memory has a place but it is only a partial and somewhat

62. The sound archivist of the Essex Country Record Office, where I deposited some Harlow New Town residents' recorded responses to their houses and furnishings, commented on the different kind of recollections elicited from interviewees by objects, to the more usual 'life history' type of interviews.

63. Pointon, M. 1999. 'Materialising Mourning: Hair, Jewellery and the Body', pp. 39–57. In Kwint et al. 1999. *Material Memories*, p. 56.

sentimental view of the past – a sign maybe that we should beware of not creating a 'new antiquarianism'.

There is no way of conceptualising the world without a sense of time. Although it is clearly understood in terms of clock-time, it is so difficult to define that even physicists have trouble pinning it down objectively except to assert that time cannot exist without matter. So though it has physical and relational effects, it is not clear that it is a phenomenon in its own right as such. Psychologists have been remarkably slow to investigate how subjects experience time passing. Their research to date has mainly relied on a common-sense notion of time as 'neutral' and have worked with clock time as a base, reinforcing the notion of it as 'linear and straightforward'. There is now increasing interest in researching 'subjective time' which is perceived as fragmented, contradictory and culturally specific.[64] The aim of this chapter is not to conclude with some universal positivist definition, but rather to sketch out some of the 'time types' that make it more possible to understand how time is experienced from the point of view of academics within different disciplines as well as from within the context of everyday life where culture is reproduced at a less conscious level. These time types are meant to elucidate the elusive 'structures of feeling' that partially form the context of everyday life. At the conceptual level individuals consciously negotiate their relationship to time through life-choice decisions. But the material world of coffee spoons, clothes, and household goods also keep individuals in touch with life as a sense of time-passing in a day-to-day manner that is not necessarily articulated but just as, if not more, telling.

64. Burkeman, O. 1999. 'Time and emotion'. In the *Guardian*. December 21, 1999, p. 10–11.

The Body: The Threshold
Between Nature and Culture

The materialism of contemporary societies is widely deplored. But why do the critics not stress that consummate fashion also helps detach human beings from objects? Under the regime of use value, we no longer become attached to things; we readily trade in our houses, our cars, or our furniture. The age that imparts social sanctity to merchandise is an age in which people part from their objects without pain. We no longer love things for themselves or for the social status they confer, but for the services they render, for the pleasures they provide, for a perfectly exchangeable use value. In this sense, fashion makes things less real; it takes away their substance through the homogenous cult of utility and novelty. What we own we will replace; the more objects become our prosthesis, the less we care about them. Our relation to them stems now from an abstract, paradoxically disembodied love.[1]

This last chapter brings together the two former contexts discussed in Part III – space and time – by looking at how they are united in the socio-physical entity of the human body. Part of the aim in so doing is to see to what extent the theme of 'containment'[2] as a cultural process is ensconced within the body, and if so, how that embodiment is effected. Containment has been defined as 'a particular kind of eccentric order'[3] used to characterise the objectification of the contradictory nature of modernity, the impulse to re-integrate the increasingly fragmentary tangled texture of contemporary everyday life. In Chapter

1. Lipovetsky, G. 1994. *The Empire of Fashion: Dressing Modern Democracy.* Princeton, New Jersey: Princeton University Press.
2. Introduced in Chapter 3 and developed in Chapter 6.
3. Chapter 6.

6 the dwelling place or home was used as a metaphor of containment. Here the body is posited as the threshold between the interior subjective self (the individual) and the exterior object world (society). Put another way the body can be regarded as the traffic junction between (human) nature – that which has become absorbed into everyday life and appears unamenable to change – and culture – that which is constructed, contingent and ephemeral. Thus we are not looking at the body as the nexus of a static state of formed individuality, but a form of containment which in postmodern terms has increasingly been referred to as a 'subject position' – open to change, that is *subject to* a myriad contexts, conditions and experiences that go towards forming and reforming the self in relation to others. Deborah Lupton's study of food as a cultural artefact defines the

> fragmented and contingent rather than the unified self, adopting the term 'subjectivity' to describe the manifold ways in which individuals understand themselves in relation to others and experience their lives. Subjectivity [. . .] incorporates the understanding that the self, or more accurately, selves, are highly changeable and contextual, albeit within certain limits imposed by the culture in which an individual lives, including power relations, social institutions and hegemonic discourses.[4]

The body is a different genre from that of things, even though in its most objectified (alienated) sense it can become a 'thing'. The body is constituted within social relations in that persons can only establish their individual identity through their interrelation with others. Class, age, gender and sexuality are all inscribed on the body contributing to the formation of self in terms of individuation, individuality and subjectivity. Much of the negotiation in respect of the interrelation between the individual and others is carried on through material things at the most mundane level of everyday life through bodily concerns defined by means of dress, alimentation, dwelling, technological appliances for work and leisure; but particularly in the process of consumption where many of the adjustments to the social construction of identity can be seen to be formed and transformed. The fine modulations of gesture and demeanour, of particular interest to anthropologists, can be generalised under the term of 'embodiment' which includes the

---

4. Lupton, D. 1996. *Food, the Body and the Self.* London and Thousand Oaks, California: Sage, p. 13.

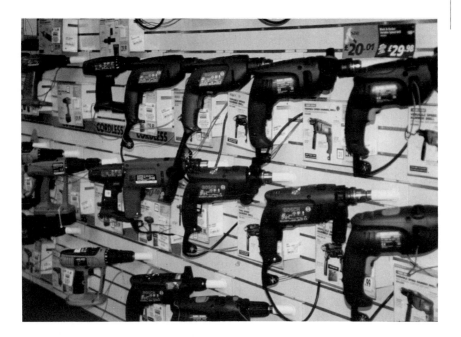

Figure 28. Electric powered hand drills display in DIY store.

nuanced non-verbal expressions of identity that are both informed and performed through the body.

Embodiment

The way the body relates to modern consumption in forming the self has been theorised by Pasi Falk by positing 'the consuming body' as the link between body, self and culture (or society).[5] His schema, based on consumption as 'the primary realm of self-construction, offering material for both its social and personal dimensions, and for both sides of individuation – as separation and self-completion',[6] is very literal in its translation of the way in which the sensory body consumes desire.[7]

5. Falk, P. 1994. *The Consuming Body*. London and Thousand Oaks, California: Sage.
6. Ibid., p. 7.
7. There are a number of texts which emanate from within literary studies and art history derived from linguists and critical theory which treat the body and dress as language and emphasise its meanings in terms of representation and visuality. For example Warwick, A. and Cavallaro, D. 1998. *Fashioning the Frame: Boundaries, Dress and the Body*. Oxford and New York: Berg.

He looks to Georges Battaille's critique of the productivist economy to explain the 'wasteful' economy in which expenditure of the 'cursed part' (excess) produces culture. Falk's enquiry sets off with a rather *literal* interpretation of the consuming body casing the mouth as 'an organ of *sensory* and sensual experience and of *censorship:* either you swallow it up or spit it out'.[8] However, he ends with Jean Baudrillard's theory of representation to explain the contradictory fabrication of the real through the media and spectacle so that there is no return to the physical body or to the material thing. Although all these approaches are helpful in their own way, particularly in tracing the genealogy of taste and how changes have been affected by the interrelatedness of cultural and technological mechanisms, they seem to evade the nitty-girtty of thingness to explain how people use material things like dress to come to terms with their own bodies (embodiment)[9] and relate to the world at large. And there are few references to physical deterioration either through illness, disability or ageing as an aspect of living in and with the body from day to day.

The question addressed here is centred on the body, conceptualised as the threshold between the self and things (as opposed to language or images – representation), and its relationship to the everyday material world for how it can help to reveal the dynamic process of self-construction. Thus the body is posited as the point at which the object/subject relation is managed, in order to observe the role of things as props in effecting the separation necessary between the inside (the self) and the outside (others) to embody a real sense of individuality. And, taking on Lipovetsky's notion of 'an abstract, paradoxically disembodied love' as indifference towards things, one step further, to consider it as a form of transcendence over the thing world. Thus the creation of material culture as a world of things given social meaning through the mechanism of fashion, might in part be seen as a means of overcoming attachment to enable sacrifice, to confront mortality and to risk the renunciation of reliance on things as a means towards self-sufficiency both physically and psychically. At the centre of this question there is a paradox that I would contend gives material culture its dynamism – that only by embracing things (embodiment) is it possible to renounce them (disembodiment), and in so doing is there a direct engagement with life and death.

8. Ibid., p. 90.
9. Poole, R. 1990. 'Embodiment', pp. 264–5. In Bullock, A., Stallybrass, O. and Trombley, S. (eds) *The Fontana Dictionary of Modern Thought.* London: Fontana.

'The body' is a much more complex entity than the biological form that defines the human person. The contradictory dictionary definition that it both refers to 'the main part' of the human frame that excludes the limbs, as well as to 'the whole', suggests some of the ramifications implied by the term. Disciplinary and sub-disciplinary conventions have theorised a diverse range of 'bodies'. Sociology is said only recently to have discovered the body as a focus of attention, giving more importance to the unconscious than corporeal embodiment.[10] Whereas social anthropology has been particularly active in developing important studies of the body as the locus of culture.[11] Embodiment is a widely used term in cultural studies and social anthropology which explains how culture is *incorporated* into the body, to become naturalised in the form of taste, demeanour and appearance. Theories of consumption are particularly appropriate to the study of material culture in recognising the importance of things external to the body in constituting a sense of embodiment and the subjectivity which informs the process of individuation. Bourdieu's definition of 'embodiment' as a form of 'incorporation' is most appropriate in this connection because it describes a process which is inscribed in and through the body rather than translated in linguistic terms.

Even though based on what is now considered a rather static classificatory study of taste as social denominator,[12] Bourdieu's attention to the significance of banal bodily gestures as interpretative cultural factors in the analysis of social distinction, provides a useful definition of embodiment in describing the unselfconscious discriminatory system that operates in the context of the everyday. His definition of 'embodiment' describes it as part of the cultural 'practice' – the habitus[13] – 'beyond the grasp of consciousness'. He observes that the embodied workings of the habitus are particularly deep-seated so that

10. Frank, A.W. 1995, 'For a Sociology of the Body: an Analytical Review', pp. 36–102. In Featherstone, M., Hepworth, M. and Turner, B.S. *The Body: Social Process and Cultural Theory.* London and Thousand Oaks, California: Sage, p. 38.

11. For example Douglas, M. 1966. *Purity and Danger: An analysis of concepts of pollution and taboo.* London: Routledge and Kegan Paul; Bourdieu, P. [1972] 1982. *Outline of a Theory of Practice.* Cambridge: Cambridge University Press; Bourdieu, P. 1984. *Distinction: A social critique of the judgement of taste.* London: Routledge and Kegan Paul.

12. Bourdieu, P. 1984. *Distinction*, p. 175.

13. Bourdieu, P. [1972] 1982. *Outline of a Theory of Practice*, pp. 87–95.

nothing seems more ineffable, more incommunicable, more inimitable, and, therefore, more precious, than the values given body, *made* body by the transubstantiation achieved by the hidden persuasion of an implicit pedagogy, capable of instilling a whole cosmology, an ethic, a metaphysic, a political philosophy through injunctions as insignificant as 'stand up straight'. [14]

Taste, a class culture turned into nature, that is, *embodied,* helps to shape the class body. It is an incorporated principle of classification which governs all forms of incorporation, choosing and modifying everything that the body ingests and digests and assimilates, physiologically and psychologically. It follows that the body is the most indisputable materialisation of class taste, which it manifests in several ways. It does this first in the seemingly most natural features of the body, the dimensions (volume, height, weight) and shape (round or square, stiff or supple, straight or curved) of its visible forms, which express in countless ways a whole relation to the body, i.e. the way of treating it, caring for it, feeding it, maintaining it, which reveals the deepest dispositions of the habitus.[15]

Alexandra Warwick and Dani Cavallaro's theory of the body as an ambiguous boundary rejects embodiment, and thereby corpo*reality,* setting up dress as a metaphor in the formation of identity which never quite achieves objectification and remains in a constant state of flux.[16] The problem with this type of psychoanalytical-philosophical explanation, though entirely plausible in theoretical terms, is that while it helpfully analyses a number of important theories of the body in relation to individuation so that they can be applied by artists and designers working in and around dress media, it does not explain the phenomenon in terms of materiality. Nor does it address the material culture of the body in everyday life unless it envisages the process of self-fashioning as an ongoing life project. The last section of this chapter will consider the way in which the ageing body adapts to change by looking at a case study of a group of people who have refashioned their way of life by moving home in the latter part of it and in the process managed to shed some of the accumulation of possessions acquired in their lifetime.

14. Ibid., p. 94.
15. Ibid., p. 190.
16. Warwick and Cavallaro 1998. *Fashioning the Frame.*

Disembodiment

Contrary to the traditional critique of consumerism based on Marx's theory of commodity fetishism[17] further developed by the Frankfurt School's critical theory [18] and evident in later thinkers like Barthes,[19] Bourdieu[20] and Baudrillard[21] who have dealt with how people relate to the world through things, Lipovetsky presents his thesis of 'consummate fashion' as a form of liberation rather than alienation.[22] His provocative and contentious stance merits much more serious discussion than will be dedicated to it here.[23] The primary reason for its introduction is to pursue just one aspect of his thesis – that of *dis*embodiment – the renunciation of attachment to things. Yet disembodiment in the imaginary context of a world of consummate fashion – that is a working democracy – relies on the unrealistic possibility of a totally realised subject who is able to make those liberating types of choices and manages to free themselves entirely from the clutter which inevitably accumulates over a lifetime.

17. Marx, K. [1867] 1990. *Capital: A Critique of Political Economy,* Volume I. Harmondsworth, Middlesex: Penguin. See Chapter 1, 4: 'The fetishism of the commodity and its secret', pp. 163–77.

18. Strinati, D. 1995. *An Introduction of Theories of Popular Culture.* Manchester: Manchester University Press. See Chapter 2: 'The Frankfurt School and the Culture Industry', pp. 51–85.

19. Barthes, R. [1957] 1981. *Mythologies.* London: Paladin. See 'Myth Today', pp. 109–59.

20. Bourdieu 1984. *Distinction.*

21. Baudrillard, J. 1981. *For a Critique of the Political Economy of the Sign.* St Louis, Mo: Telos.

22. In *The Empire of Fashion* Lipovetsky asserts that fashion is democratic and that conservatism is 'antithetical to the spirit and logic of fashion. While consummate fashion functions according to a logic of hedonism, seduction, and novelty, neoconservatism rehabilitates moralism, repression and tradition' (p 218).

23. I do not agree with Lipovetsky's theory as a universal structural premise and suspect that were it to be put to the test would soon prove to be far flimsier than would appear from his robust presentation. Nevertheless it does provide a substantive foundation for the investigation of the relationship between people and things in the process of self-individuation that goes beyond the 'manipulated consumer' notion of 'I shop therefore I am'. He is not alone in proposing a form of transcendence through the process of consumption – Daniel Miller mounts a polemic of the stereotypical housewife as the consumer *par excellence* and the 'vanguard of history' in *Acknowledging Consumption* (Miller, D. (ed.), London: Routledge, 1995, pp. 34–9) who, he suggests, can overcome so-called economic imperatives to effect autonomous forms of cultural diversity.

It is to be assumed that Lipovetsky's reference to 'the West'[24] confines his analysis to modern industrial societies where there is a surfeit of goods and consumers with the means, not just to acquire them, but with a degree of control over the *choice* they make from the array on offer. Similarly it is only under circumstances of excess, or at least sufficiency, that one can consider objectification – that is the materialisation of a world view outside or beyond the body – not in the Marxian sense of alienation perceived as disorientation, but from a stronger sense of experienced separateness. This can be translated into two very common everyday responses that might arise in the course of shopping – one in which the underlying impulse is generated by a search for the self as a means of overcoming alienation and expressed as 'this is/is not me/us/mine', and the more objective search for the use-value defining type of consumption which depends on a sense of separation between the self and the rest expressed as 'this suits *me*' where the product must match up with the already realised subject. The latter assumes a disembodied subject but one that can only be achieved through an engagement with the material world.

Among the many theoretical 'bodies' one of the most notable is the 'disciplined body' delineated by Michel Foucault's discourse theory of power/knowledge that focused on the regulation of the body and populations as 'constitut[ing] the two poles around which the organisation of power over life was deployed'.[25] Using the body as the starting point Foucault's genealogical study of the embodiment of discipline has been explained as the deep-seated naturalisation of an individualised personalised sense of desire that drives the 'micro-mechanisms of power that [. . .] have played an increasing part in the management of people's lives through direct action on their bodies: they operate not through a code of law, but through a technology of normalisation, not by punishment, but by control, at levels and in forms that go beyond the state and its machinery'.[26] Lipovetsky's theory of fashion as a form of body politics that can overturn the concept of the technology of the body as both Bourdieu and Foucault have formulated it – as the inculcation of hierarchical power structures – presents an alternative interpretation that recognises the way individuals can evolve

24. Lipovetsky 1994. *The Empire of Fashion*, p. 4.

25. Foucault, M. 1984. *The History of Sexuality. Volume I: An Introduction*. Harmondsworth, Middlesex: Penguin, p. 139.

26. Sheridan, A. 1980. *Michel Foucault: The Will to Truth*. London and New York: Tavistock, p. 181.

through a recognition of the transitory superficiality of things. This takes the discussion from out of the body on to the 'effects' – material things attached to the body by way of property or possession and the contextual 'body' which holds them in place.

Things as Prostheses

A prosthesis is an artificial external body-part and however intimately attached to the body cannot in any way be perceived as carnal. And just as a prosthesis is intended to replace a missing or faulty organic part of the body, so design, whether tools, clothes, houses, cars, toothbrushes or gadgets, can similarly be conceived of as in some way supplementing the body and co-extensive to it – all the better to be able to make things and meanings, weather the storm, travel or maintain itself. For example powered hand tools introduced a new technology to supplement muscle power, to improve dexterity and precision in craft production. Much more 'handy' than a factory machine tool, its compactness and affordability detached it from a fixed location in a factory or workshop and placed it into the hands and therefore control of individuals who were thus offered independence over their own 'means of production'.

Reyner Banham's romantic interest in technology, and American industrial design in particular, alerted him to a genre of 'portable technology' which he instanced in the outboard motor, the walkie-talkie, the transistor radio and the various 'gadgets' in the tradition of the pioneering frontiersman's Stetson hat and Franklin stove with which he was able to survive, 'tame' and transform the wilderness. Dubbed 'The Great Gizmo' he described it as

> a small self-contained unit of high performance in relation to its size and cost, whose function is to transform some undifferentiated set of circumstances to a condition nearer to human desires. The minimum of skill is required in its installation and use, and it is independent of any physical or social infrastructure beyond that by which it may be ordered from catalogue and delivered to its prospective user. [27]

Banham's article, written in 1965, is representative of the design theory that arose during a time when there was much discussion about the

---

27. Banham, R. [1965] 1981. 'The Great Gizmo', pp. 108–14. In Sparke, P. (ed.) *Reyner Banham: Design By Choice*. London: Academy Editions, p. 110.

benefits and disadvantages of technology. Banham's romantic notion of the untamed paradise, identified the Cortez camper as the ultimate in gizmo-type technology because it provided a way of exploring what was left of the 'wild West' without spoiling it. Similarly the mystique of a 'powered hand' in the ideological context of the 'alternative society' was in its ability to provide a sense of self-sufficiency complying with the stand against the incursion of 'high tech' by those who saw it as too invasive. More to the point, that it may destroy the little bit of wildness left in the West. Needless to say it was a movement which developed in the first world where there was more than a sufficiency of 'progress' that brought such amenities. The concern with sustainability was not just on the grounds of environmental ethics which emerged in the wake of the oil crisis of 1972 when the realisation dawned that some natural resources are non-renewable. It was also to do with the recognition that it was possible to make a conscious choice of lifestyle that rejected consumerism and conventional values ('the rat race') by turning to a simpler self-sufficient way of life often now referred to as 'downshifting'.

Although Banham's love affair with Americana has been caricatured as an attraction for 'boys' toys',[28] his acknowledgement of the importance of portability deserves to be emphasised for the intimate link he makes between the body and designed objects. He concluded his article with a plea for a more sustained investigation of the history of portable gadgetry 'since Sigfried Giedion first tickled the topic'.[29] Banham then went on to ruminate on whether 'Gizmology' might be a suitable name for such a field of enquiry, when in fact the original impetus for his interest in the subject came from 'a single very precise and concrete image – a man carrying a portable welding plant across the Utah salt-flats with one hand'. Rather than the genre, it was the 'unique and discrete object' which fascinated him. His almost naive faith in modern design ascribed it with the power to come up with, somewhere in a catalogue, the precise gadget for 'whatever you want to do'. The portable mechanical contrivance that acts like a machine but is controlled by

---

28. Buckley, C.1987. 'Made in Patriarchy: towards a feminist analysis of women and design', pp. 3–15. In *Design Issues*, Vol. 3, No. 2.

29. Banham 1965. 'The Great Gizmo, p.114. In Sparke 1981. *Reyner Banham: Design By Choice;* see Giedion, S. 1948. *Mechanization Takes Command,* New York: Oxford University Press, 'Mechanization of the Smaller Tools' pp. 553–60 and 'Imitation of the Hand' pp. 560–1.

the hand is not unlike the cross between artificiality and the body combined in the operation of a prosthesis. There is much more mileage in pursuing the possibilities of the prosthesis as the material metaphor of modern design in contradistinction to the 'thing with attitude'. But here it is confined to making the case for extending the view of the relationship between the body and things so that design may be conceived of as an amenable artificial disposable body-part. What can also be discerned in discussing tools as 'design' (and design as tools) is the way the distinction between production and consumption becomes blurred particularly once the construction of individuality is brought into the equation.

The Body as Machine

But going back in history it is possible to see why there is such a persistent legacy of the class-determined fragmentation of the body – both the body as society separating the workers from the middle and upper classes, and as the human body separating the hand (manual work) from the head (mental work). It would seem inconceivable not to include Marx in this section dealing with materiality and the body, but specifically because of his analysis of the social changes wrought by the economic system that introduced new technologies in the form of machine tools. It was the factory organisation system that he identified as 'alienating' workers from the fruits of their labour by taking control over their bodies.[30] And under the same system, the role given to commodities was that of enticer, a different object to that which delivered 'use value'. To Marx the commodity was not to be trusted because of its 'mysterious powers' to transform itself by virtue of its 'exchange value'.

30. Without adhering too strictly to the critique of the consumerism induced by capitalism as interpreted by Marx, *Capital* still remains a classic text with valuable insights into the social effects of alienated labour more than a century ago. See too Marx, K. 'Alienated Labour' 1844 (from Economic-Philosophical Manuscripts). In Clayre, A. 1977. *Nature and Industrialisation*. Oxford: Oxford University Press, pp. 245–50. For interpretations which show that mass production by means of industrialisation was not actually as all embracing as suggested, see for example Samuel, R. 1977. 'Workshop of the World: Steam power and hand technology in mid-Victorian Britain', pp. 6–72. In *History Workshop*, Vol 3, Spring; Berg, M. 1985. *The Age of Manufactures*. London: Fontana Press.

A commodity appears at first sight an extremely obvious, trivial thing. But its analysis brings out that it is a very strange thing, abounding in metaphysical subtleties and theological niceties. So far as it is a use-value, there is nothing mysterious about it, whether we consider it from the point of view that by its properties it satisfies human needs, or that it first takes on these properties as the product of human labour. It is absolutely clear that, by his activity, man changes the forms of the materials of nature in such a way as to make them useful to him. The form of wood, for instance, is altered if a table is made out of it. Nevertheless the table continues to be wood, an ordinary, sensuous thing. But as soon as it emerges as a commodity, it changes into a thing which transcends sensuousness. It not only stands with its feet on the ground, but, in relation to all other commodities, it stands on its head, and evolves out of its wooden brain grotesque ideas, far more wonderful than if it were to begin dancing of its own free will.[31]

Lipovetsky's concept of 'disembodied love' – easy-come-easy-go attitude to commodities – Banham's 'portable technology', or the idea of design as prosthesis, have little to do with the period to which Marx refers. But his understanding of the commodity – of a thing that takes on human characteristics as in the table that develops a brain – continues to have some purchase on design theory to this day. His concept of fetishisation discussed elsewhere,[32] works at a much more sophisticated level than the interpretation rendered by the good design movement whose principles required a purely functional object, an indestructible classic product detached from the fashion system and extracted from exchange value, thereby barring it from entry into the commodity system, that vital ingredient that Marx detected as its 'last finish'.[33] The pro-Morris (arts and crafts) lobby, which has insisted in skilled hand production of one-off or small batch pieces, is a contradiction in terms, in that to produce a high quality piece requires the skill handed down from generation to generation and acquired via the kind of repeated production process which does not lend itself readily to new design. Apart from refusing to acknowledge fashion, craft-type design has

31. Marx 1990. *Capital*, p.163.

32. Attfield, J. 1999. 'Beyond the Pale: Reviewing the relationship between Material Culture and Design History' in *Journal of Design History*, Vol. 12, No. 4, p. 376.

33. Attfield J. forthcoming. 'The Real Thing: Tufted Carpet's Entry Into the Vernacular' in Schoeser, M and Boydell, C. (eds) *Disentangling Textiles*. Middlesex: Middlesex University Press.

continued to interpret the advent of technology and mass consumption as a degrading influence. What has now become a marker of 'fine craft' has been avant-garde aesthetics rather than function or skill.

The introduction of the machine and 'the division of labour' that occupied Marx was seen to fragment the body by separating the hand from the head and thus art from craft. Critics of modernism like Roger Coleman have traced the degradation of skill back to the Renaissance when a hierarchical separation was made between art and craft.[34] The emphasis here is on 'embodiment' as a form of materiality which rather than assuming the theoretical classic economic 'division of labour' syndrome, looks for the links people make through things at the level of materiality, for example by means of portable technology where it is questionable whether any such division is actually experienced. This is not to suggest that the 'division of labour' analogous to class hierarchy is not an actuality even today, although maybe not as pronounced in societies where there is an abundance of available consumer goods as in earlier periods of history. Marx observed that the division of labour was 'purely technical' in the 'automatic factory' where all that the unskilled worker need be taught from childhood upwards was 'to adapt his own movements to the uniform and unceasing motion of an automaton',[35] doing away with the necessity to use the same worker for the same function, nevertheless

> it hangs on in the factory as a tradition handed down from manufacture,[36] and is then systematically reproduced and fixed in a more hideous form by capital as a means of exploiting labour-power. The lifelong speciality of handling the same tool now becomes the lifelong speciality of serving the same machine. Machinery is misused in order to transform the worker, from his very childhood, into a part of a specialised machine.[37]

A similar criticism has also been levelled against the way in which some methods of modern design have treated the body of the consumer, reducing it to a standard unit to serve the functional needs of the product and the production processes of the manufacturer. Indeed, it follows that once products were manufactured for the mass market such a process would necessarily reduce consumers to a homogenous

34. Coleman, R. 1988. *The Art of Work: An Epitaph to Skill*. London: Pluto.
35. Marx 1990. *Capital*, p. 546.
36. 'Manufacture' in this context refers to manual skilled craft work.
37. Ibid., p. 547.

undifferentiated mass.[38] The science of ergonomics was devised in order to make the design process more systematic by means of a set of standardised average measurements of the human body (anthropometrics) applied to the design of objects and environments.[39] Much of the research to improve design according to the modern principle of functionalism, which understandably has been criticised so widely, was prosecuted in the interest of human efficiency, personified in the 'user' rather than in respect of individuals with initiative, or consumers with desires of their own. This lack is also evident in the way the culture of mechanisation used in the organisation of the work process with the development of scientific management and the continuous assembly line to cut down on wasted energy and time loss, was also applied to industrially designed consumer goods.[40] It is significant that some of major developments in ergonomic design, as well as such techniques as the 'American system' of manufacture which depended on 'interchangeable parts' thus enabling standardisation of production, were actually first used in design for war.[41] F.W. Taylor, one of the foremost figures in 'scientific management' – the rationalisation of work processes where every second was counted and every extraneous movement eradicated – described his method as a 'military type of organisation'. His method evolved into the system known as 'Taylorism' used in the Ford car factory that culminated in the first decade of the twentieth century in the production of the popular Model T.[42]

In mid-century Britain the term 'ergonomics' was adopted for what in the United States was already known as 'human engineering', revealing the manipulative face of functional design which only took into account the instrumental role of the user. This assumption that design improvements were ultimately for the purpose of making the body an efficient machine-part, is clearly illustrated in the case cited by Hywel Murrel at a Design History Society conference in 1982. A

38. Needless to say the practice of bespoke production whereby clothes, furniture, buildings etc. are made to individual specification still operates for those who can afford it.

39. Woodham, J. 1997. *Twentieth-Century Design.* Oxford and New York: Oxford University Press, pp. 180–1.

40. Giedion 1948. *Mechanization Takes Command,* pp. 86-101.

41. For example in the manufacture of muskets in the eighteenth century. See Heskett, J. 1980. *Industrial Design.* London: Thames and Hudson, pp. 50–2.

42. Ibid., p. 67.

professor in applied psychology and early expert in ergonomics involved
in its development in Britain during and after the War, he described
the success of its application in the redesigned interior of the Comet
tank. He recalled that

> the benefits [. . .] were probably [still] regarded cautiously when ergo-
> nomics were introduced into design towards the end of the war. At this
> time possible ways of improving the extremely low rate of fire of the
> Comet tank were being studied. This vehicle, with an internal headroom
> of 5ft 8in, was issued to the Guards Armoured Brigade (a Guard, almost
> by definition, is usually over 6ft tall). A film of the firing operation
> revealed the physical contortions of those inside the turret (the first usage
> of such a technique in designing), as well as the fact that the designers
> concerned had never attempted to fire a tank gun. The new stowage
> arrangements devised more than trebled the rate of fire.[43]

It could be said, as many advocates of modern design theory have
done, that rationalising the work process by treating the human body
or body-part as a constituent of the production operation as if it were
any tool or machine, is justified in the aim of extracting from it the
maximum amount of work with the minimum of strain in the interest
of economy. Giedion, like Marx before him, was critical of the hierarchical structure imposed by military-type rationalisation according
to an economic imperative, pointing out the deficiency of Taylorism
that did not demand '*personal* initiative [. . .] but automatization [so
that] human movements become levers in the machine'.[44]

Marketing domestic appliances to the consumer in the first half of
the twentieth century adopted similar tactics in addressing the 'home
worker' envisaged as a female stereotype of the universal 'housewife',
and presenting domestic appliances as 'labour saving devices'. Christine
Frederick, an American exponent of labour saving based her book,
Household Engineering; Scientific Management in the Home (1920), on
Taylorism despite the illogicality of making an analogy between the
domestic kitchen in a middle-class house dependent on a sole housewife, and a factory where the work was carried out according to a

43. Murrell, H. 1985. 'How Ergonomics Became Part of Design' pp. 72–6. In Hamilton,
N. (ed.) *From Spitfire to Microchip: Studies in the History of Design from 1945*. London: The
Design Council, p. 72.
   44. Giedion 1948. *Mechanization Takes Command,* p. 99.

division of labour.[45] Some feminists like Caroline Haslett embraced the possibilities of emancipation offered by the new devices and the power sources made readily available through increased distribution in the inter-war period, declaring, 'the machine has really given women complete emancipation. With the touch of a switch she can have five or six horsepower at her disposal; in an aeroplane she has the same power as a man.'[46]

An Ambivalent Love Affair – the Gendered Object and the Fashioned Body

Recent studies in materiality have concentrated on consumption as the exchange system that transacts the construction of identity. But the body is the site where the transactions are ultimately made, that establish what I have called elsewhere 'the interrelations of gender and objects – two of the most fundamental components of the cultural framework which holds together our sense of social identity'.[47] In considering the body as a figure of containment, the relation between sex and things cannot be ignored as one of the most formative dynamics of the object/subject relation.[48] It is clear that the female body has been stereotyped as 'nature' in the nature/culture binary, and, as Beverley Gordon has observed of the nineteenth-century domestic interior and women's dress – the 'body and interior space were often seen and treated as if they were the same thing'.[49] Gordon has also noted that in the late twentieth century the domestic environment is no longer as strongly inflected as feminine, or even necessarily gendered at all. In short, that identity formation is generally much more fluid and changeable when viewed in historical perspective.

45. Worden, S. 1995. 'Powerful Women: Electricity in the Home 1919–40' pp. 131–50. In Attfield, J. and Kirkham, P. (eds) *A View From the Interior: Women and Design*. London: The Women's Press, p. 139.

46. Worden points this out in Ibid., p. 138.

47. Kirkham, P. and Attfield, J. 1996. 'Introduction', pp. 1–11. In Kirkham, P. (ed.) *The Gendered Object*. Manchester: Manchester University Press, p. 1.

48. There is a vast literature on this subject to which some recent additions have made valuable contributions. For example de Grazia, V. (ed.) 1996. *The Sex of Things: Gender and Consumption in Historical Perspective*. Berkeley: University of California Press.

49. Gordon, B. 1996. 'Woman's Domestic Body: The Conceptual Conflation of Women and Interiors in the Industrial Age', pp. 281–301. In *Winterthur Portfolio*, Vol. 31, No. 4, Winter, p. 281.

The increasing accessibility to an expanding range of consumer goods, which in Britain can be dated to the 1960s, provided one of the means through which such identity transactions could be negotiated, particularly through the intermediary of the body – the threshold between nature and culture. In Elizabeth Wilson's biographical 'Memoirs of an Anti-heroine' she recalled the distinctive quality of the 'sixties' when 'You needed shopping in order to construct your image, you needed shopping and the media.'[50] Her description also characterises the self-conscious act of 'changing your image' typical of the new-found freedom to 'chose' from a range of goods on offer.

Going beyond the study of the historical stereotype of the gendered body as socially 'constructed' and morally fashioned, feminists like Judith Butler have questioned the very 'category of woman',[51] challenging the notion that a straightforward correlation can be made between sex and gender,[52] and even more awkwardly that 'the singular notion of identity is a misnomer'.[53] However her critique of 'the constraints of representational discourse', recruited in pursuit of feminist political interests by resetting them within a more dynamic framework where there is more room for manoeuvre, applies here too because it translates identity into the kind of materiality which does not presume to be satisfied by representation that defines by exclusion (i.e. female because not male). There are parallels in this study of material culture that seeks for a way of looking at how people form their identity through a sense of objectified agency that grounds social acts in matter (such as dress) and thus make it 'real', with Butler's reconfigurative (rather than deconstructive) discussion of gender in relation to identity. Her critique of 'construction' does not presume exclusion, on the contrary, as she points out

50. Wilson, E. 1989. 'Memoirs of an Anti-heroine', pp. 1–10. *Hallucinations: Life in the Post-Modern City*. London: Hutchinson Radius, p. 9.

51. Butler, J. 1990. *Gender Trouble: Feminism and the Subversion of Identity*. London and New York: Routledge, p. 2.

52. There are a number of other correlations between gender issues and material culture which are relevant to the discussion of the body as a social entity through which issues of identity could usefully be discussed beyond the limits of this project. For example see Haraway, D.J. 1991. *Simians, Cyborgs and Women – The Reinvention of Nature*. London: Free Association Books; Colomina, B. 1992. 'The Split Wall: Domestic Voyeurism', pp. 72–128. In Colomina, B. *Sexuality and Space*. Princeton: Princeton Architectural Press.

53. Butler 1990. *Gender Trouble*, p. 4.

the reconceptualisation of identity as an *effect*, that is, as *produced* or *generated*, opens up possibilities of 'agency' that are insidiously foreclosed by positions that take identity categories as foundational and fixed. For an identity to be an effect means that it is neither fatally determined nor fully artificial and arbitrary.[54]

What Butler does not discuss, however, is how that '*effect*' is put into practice since 'effect' suggests the end of a process, not just in terms of termination but as an outcome. Dress and fashion are obvious vehicles for exploring the way in which individuals formulate their identity in material ways. The expanding field of fashion theory has produced relevant studies of the role of the body and clothing in self-creation but only at a theoretical level, so fails to follow the process through in personal terms.[55] And although recent writings on the way which 'fashion'[56] constructs masculinity have appeared,[57] most of the literature on the type of design referring to the dynamic relationship between sex and things, whether as the gendered object where a thing is given sexual connotations (fetishism), or conversely where a body is treated as an object (reification), refers mainly to women because of the continuing assumption that the consumer is female. The reference to fetishism and reification is not intended to reduce the social to objects since the project of focusing on 'material culture' is in order to break away from the either/or dualism and attempt a more dynamic study of object/subject relations. As Jane Graves writes in her psychoanalytical history of a jug: 'Objects are neither people nor nature, yet they contain elements of both. They function as a disturbing interface, an ambivalent love affair.'[58]

54. Ibid., p. 147.

55. Warwick and Cavallaro 1998. *Fashioning the Frame*.

56. 'Fashion' is used here, as in earlier sections of the book, in a generalised sense to refer to a type of designed products directly associated with consumption where the purchase, along with the product simultaneously offers a lifestyle with which the purchaser is meant to be able to identify.

57. For example Breward, C. 1999. *The Hidden Consumer: Masculinities, fashion and city life 1860–1914*. Manchester: Manchester University Press; Kirkham 1996. *The Gendered Object*; Kuchta, D. 1996. 'The Making of the Self-Made Man: Class, Clothing and English Masculinity, 1688–1832', pp. 54–78. In de Grazia *The Sex of Things*.

58. Also see Graves, J. 1999. '"When Things Go Wrong ... Inside the Inside": A Psychoanalytical History of a Jug', pp. 357–67. In *Journal of Design History*, Vol. 12, No. 4, p. 364.

The act of self-creation in the face of a characteristic as seemingly biological (natural) as gender identity, explained by Butler as cultually determined by the genealogy of the naturalisation of sex and of bodies in general posits the body as mute prior to culture, 'awaiting significa-tion'. While Graves suggests that the process of internalisation effected through objects, also works in the self-creation of identity. Where it is particularly visually apparent is in the use of dress for its performative qualities where it shows up in sharp distinction from the kind of conven-tional dress that blends into the background. In this order of high drama, the transgressive statements to defy biology made by cross-referencing are inscribed on the body via dress and comportment to produce specific effects such as androgyny.[59] The adoption of subcultural codes as 'looks' are now common practice in high fashion conveyed through a narrative and presented in pageant form in 'cat-walk' shows. Theatricality and dressing up are also combined with formal ritual to establish and maintain class identity through such staged ceremonies as coronations, whether of established royalty or used to construct social elites like the traditional annual San Antonio Coronation of Texan debutantes enacted to preserve a Euro-American aristocracy.[60]

There is an underwritten history of spectacular subcultural dress practices[61] which has formed part of urban youth lifestyle,[62] expressed through a repertoire of images representing identities that could be taken up, traded in, discarded, played with at will and recognisable as belong-ing to particular groups, clubs or gangs. The ironical referencing to over-determined gender identity as in camp culture where a mask is figura-tively adopted to superficialise and thus inflect the inauthenticity and

59. Garber, M. 1993. *Vested Interests: Cross Dressing and Cultural Anxiety.* London: Thames and Hudson; Wilson, E. 1992. 'Fashion and the Postmodern Body' pp. 3–16. In Ash, J. and Wilson, E. *Chic Thrills: A Fashion Reader.* London: Pandora.

60. Haynes, M.T. 1998. *Dressing Up Debutantes: Pageantry and Glitz in Texas.* Oxford and New York: Berg.

61. Polhemus, T. 1994. *Street Style: from sidewalk to catwalk.*London: Thames and Hudson. There also are some mentions in passing in many social history accounts to particular styles of dress taken up by young people of all classes purposely to identify with specific gangs or groups. For example Elizabeth Rouse's reference in the chapter on 'Youth' (pp. 282–311) in *Understanding Fashion* (1989, Oxford and London: BSP Professional Books); York, P. 1985. *Modern Times.* London: Futura; Roberts. R. 1971. *The Classic Slum.* Harmondsworth, Middlesex: Penguin.

62. Chambers, Ian. 1986. *Popular Culture: The Metropolitan Experience.* London and New York: Routledge.

insubstantiality of identity is an exaggerated form of image-making said to be used to fashion femininity and identity through everyday dress.

The Material Culture of Disembodiment

Although by taking into account changes in the demographic profile, fashion product marketing in the 1990s has been directed at 'the older woman' as a likely subject, the ideal fashionable subject is primarily young. So much so that the emphasis on youthfulness in fashion models became the focus of scandal when a 1993 fashion shoot of Kate Moss, even though she was not under sixteen – the legal age of consent for heterosexuals – was interpreted as having paedophiliac connotations.[63] And therefore fashions, cosmetics and remedies are sold on the idea that they will perpetuate this state or at least arrest 'signs of ageing'. Old bodies are seen as pathetic if they are seen at all, so that there is a mismatch between the anxiety instilled by the ideal image and the inevitable and inescapable reality of the physical change perpetrated by time. Changing attitudes and an increasing awareness of health has made the public much more interested in matters concerning food, medication, air pollution, fitness and generally anything that enables greater control over their own body. Not least has been the demand for housing specially designed for older persons in the last stage of their life.

There have been some initiatives taken by the Royal College to study design specially aimed at the older person. And during the 1980s when product differentiation took hold, among the marketing acronyms to identify particular lifestyles the 'woopy' was devised to describe the 'well-off older person', a new type of consumer devised for a range of products targeted at that age group. There was obviously no point in bothering much with a low income older person since they did not represent a likely group of consumers for 'added value' goods.

The recognition that older persons were actually getting younger,[64] in the sense of still being active on retirement and wanting smaller trouble-free accommodation with some sort of support system but where they could still be independent without the worries of maintaining a

63. Jobling, P. 1999. *Fashion Spreads: Word and Image in Fashion Photography Since 1980.* Oxford and New York: Berg, pp. 96 and 115.

64. Featherstone, M. 1995. 'The mask of Ageing and the Postmodern Life Course', pp. 371–89, In Featherstone, M. et al. *The Body: Social Process and Cultural Theory.* London and Thousand Oaks, California: Sage.

house and garden, produced a new type of housing. Sheltered accommodation comprises small one- or two-bedroom flats with a centralised alarm system in case of emergency and a warden. There is usually some kind of communal space such as a common room with a kitchenette for social activities and a shared garden. A pilot study of a small group of sheltered accommodation residents through an investigation of their experience of moving in the latter part of their lives, produced some surprising conclusions with regard to their attitudes to material possessions.[65] Even though most of them brought some of their belongings with them, most spoke about having to get rid of things that could not be accommodated in smaller quarters. On the whole there seemed to be little regret about having to get rid of the majority of their belongings.

One resident, Mr Cross, when asked what he had brought with him said 'nothing' and proudly announced that all the furnishings were bought new when they moved in, although it is quite possible that, like the majority of the residents, some items of sentimental value had been retained. Yet in spite of choosing brand new décor and furniture the choice of reproduction style and 'faded' chintz print fabrics gave a traditional effect which did not announce 'new', but on the contrary could easily have been mistaken for 'old' suggesting some desire for a link with the past. In the absence of a fireplace a small shelf had been fixed over the convection heater to hold a clock and other type of objects usually found on a mantleshelf. The most personal feature of the living room apart from the large shelf fitment charged with ornaments, floral arrangement, decanters and photographs, were the only pictures adorning the walls – the gallery of family photographic portraits. These represented what Mr Cross described as his only occupation since his retirement – 'baby-sitting' for his many grandchildren. Photographs

---

65. The material presented here is based on a set of interviews with some of the residents of David Wood House, a block of forty-nine flats, purpose-built as sheltered accommodation for residents over the age of fifty-five. It forms part of a comparative pilot study carried out with Joanne Turney, of people's attitudes to moving residence through a study of their homes as an aspect of material culture. David Wood House was built by a private developer in 1993 and acquired by the local Town Council. The bias of the study was to respondents who were willing to be interviewed and therefore tended to be the ones who were more positive about the experience of moving and adapting to a different kind of accommodation. The response from some of the residents when approached about collaborating in the project made it apparent that for a few of those not willing to be interviewed, it had been a difficult and painful experience.

Figure 29. Sheltered accommodation living-room interior furnished in new 'old' style.

and ornaments housed in some sort of shelf fitment were found in all the flats visited. And when asked about treasured possessions these always seemed to consist of small decorative items such as holiday souvenirs or decorative objects with particular familial associations, such as Mrs Tucker's 'Buddha'.

> I wouldn't part with that for a king's ransom. My uncle brought that from India when I was a baby. And it was in [. . .] my mother's home and I was the only one who ever polished it. I was attached to that Buddha from my earliest remembrance. And I've never been without it.

Figure 30. Mrs Tucker's ornament display with her Buddha in pride of place.

In the case of Mr and Mrs Tucker, the move from a family house into a small two-bedroom flat in David Wood House was the perfect solution to what had become a problem – the maintenance of their old house in the face of increasing disability and deteriorating health. Their attitude to possessions was in the main pragmatic and practical. It was, however, quite clear that there was intense attachment to a number of the small items on the part of Mrs Tucker. Apart from the Buddha which held pride of place in the centre of the shelf fitment, there was 'my little blue glasses, they all mean a lot to me because of the people who gave me those, [they] have sentimental value'. She related how one of the blue glasses got lost in the move and her son had bought her another one for her birthday. But it was not a replacement because 'the one I lost was the one that he'd bought as a boy and I was very attached to it'.

While the loss of her son's gift was still felt by Mrs Tucker, the couple's attitude to the things they had had to get rid of on moving was in direct contrast. 'It was difficult to choose, but we didn't have time to feel upset about it, we had to be really ruthless, because it's no good being sentimental. The children came first and took whatever was of use to them.' They described how different members of the family chose books, tools, furniture, 'knick knacks, towels and things' commenting that 'it's only right to keep things in the family. They had first pick.' The rest was sold and given away. 'We didn't have any problems [. . .] getting rid of things. We had to get rid of a lot of stuff [. . .] We had to be ruthless, because we knew we were moving. We all save things in case they are useful [. . .] "Do we need it?", if we don't get rid of it. The Salvation Army did quite well.'

It would seem from the group of people interviewed, of which only two cases are referred to above, that the smaller space of the sheltered accommodation reflects a certain kind of concentration related to a conscious change made to adapt to a smaller space and a smaller portion of time left of life. In spite of the Tuckers' declaration that 'you can't take possessions with you' and their 'ruthless' determination to become detached from most of their possessions, nevertheless strong attachments and genuine sentiment was installed in small items that took on intense significance and were given pride of place within their more circumscribed domestic space.

It would seem that the ability to 'choose', a characteristic ascribed to our consumer society and usually critically associated to profligacy, has social uses which are not necessarily to do with acquiring. In observing the Tuckers' rationalisation of their attachment to things, what counted was the legacy to their children. In referring to 'possessions'. Mrs Tucker declared, 'You can't take them with you. But we enjoy them while we've got them. What the children do with them that's up to them. As long as Buddha goes to my daughter. . .'

In the *Today* news programme broadcast on BBC Radio Four on 10 December 1999, a bishop and a geneticist discussed a proposed experiment to attempt to create some form of human life for the first time. Ethical objections from religious groups were discussed with the bishop declaring that the putting together of certain proteins and other ingredients did not constitute human life since to achieve human status an organism had to include 'choice, mind and feelings'. It was notice-able that 'choice' came first in the list of specifications. A possible interpretation could be that today, envisaging the state of being bio-logically human is synonymous with being a consumer. It is obviously ridiculous to suggest that to be a consumer is a natural condition in spite of the perception that toddlers now seem to be demanding logo-ed trainers as soon as they can talk. In any case I doubt that the bishop had such an interpretation in mind and only mention it here to make the point that choice is *not* just to do with consumption but with self-determination. In the cases mentioned above it would seem to do with choosing to become detached (disembodied) from their material possessions. The most important links to life with all the respondents interviewed was their attachment to their families expressed in a variety of ways through the medium of their material world.

Conclusion

Holly came from Miami, FLA
Hitch-hiked her way across the USA
Plucked her eyebrows on the way
Shaved her legs and then he was a she
She says, Hey babe
Take a walk on the wilde side
She said, Hey honey
Take a walk on the wild side

Lou Reed's song *A Walk on the Wild Side* recorded in 1972,[1] encapsulates the narcissistic use of appearance transformation to achieve self-emancipation through the transcendence of biological destiny. It can also be seen as representative of the kind of manifestations that formed part of a transgressive underground movement alongside the wave of critical theory that emerged from the period now characterised as the cultural revolution and exemplified in texts like Guy Debord's *Society of the Spectacle*.[2] The wilder side of experimental identity creation that breached gender codes and the etiquette of good taste in looks and behaviour infiltrated the mainstream via popular culture disseminated through the media.

The characters in the song are based on people associated with Andy Warhol, one of the best-known artists of the New York pop art scene, who recognised the exploitative evanescent instant power of the mass

---

1. 'A Walk On the Wild Side' by Lou Reed (© Copyright; 1971 by Dunbar Music Inc. & Oakfield Avenue Music Ltd for the World and © Copyright 1973 by Sunbury Music Ltd. London for British Commonwealth (excluding Canada and Australasia)) is one track from the album *Transformer* produced by David Bowie in 1972.
2. Debord, G. 1967. *La Société du Spectacle,* Paris: Buchet-Chastel. Published in English as *Society of the Spectacle*. Detroit: Black and Red, 1977.

media. Susan Sontag's 'Notes on Camp'[3] of 1964 trace the esoteric underground aestheticism of camp as a metaphor of life as theatre, and foreshadowed the changes of sensibility which were to be defined as the postmodern condition. Camp according to Sontag was 'the glorification of "character" as a state of continual incandescence, a person being one very intense thing', beyond the 'good-bad axis of ordinary aesthetic judgement', treating life as art so that 'another kind of truth about the human situation, another experience of what it is to be human – is being revealed'.[4] The emergence of camp from the underground marked the popularisation of one of the counter-cultural symptoms representative of the awareness of multiple possibilities typified in the new-found confidence through 'reinventing' the self as a conscious act of pure agency. 'Too much' was the term used to characterise camp, referring to the exaggerated forms of dress and demeanour used to express the extraordinariness of 'being special, glamorous'.

Such acts of exaggerated individuality as those mentioned above require a high degree of narcissism and self-conscious assertion. They explain the social changes wrought by modernity which have enabled individuals to experience a sense of self much more acutely than in the 'everyday' where the process of individuation takes place but remains unnoticed. The intentionality of the visual trangressive statement is as dramatically evident as design made to hit the eye – the 'thing with attitude' while it still retains the sparkle of newness, before it loses its fashionability. Yet although the everyday is by its very nature not a spectacular place, and pervasive media infiltration stokes the desire to encounter the authentic 'wild side' of life its wider availability only makes it more vicarious. Yet the everyday is where life is lived both vicariously and concretely, and ultimately where individuality is realised albeit unseen.

The making and unmaking of different life-stages of identity are manifested through social relations, enacted and embodied through a material world and designed in the form of things and practices in the context of personal and public space, experienced through the dimension of time and sensorially through the body. Social theory has

3. Sontag, S. 1964. 'Notes on Camp', pp. 275–92. In Sontag, S. 1994. *Against Interpretation*. London: Vintage.

4. Sontag 1964. 'Notes on Camp', pp. 286–7.

5. Falk, P. 1994. *The Consuming Body*. London and Thousand Oaks, California: Sage, p. 52.

responded to the modern concept of individuality – 'the free subject' –
in terms of materiality, citing 'the body as a means of expression.'[5] But
the material world also has effects on people, it stores memories and
interrupts the flow of time to restore a sense of continuity as well as to
reflect change and contain complex and apparently irreconcilable
differences.

Bibliography

Agius, P. 1978. *British Furniture 1880–1915*. London: Antique Collectors Club.

Alderson, S. 1962. *Britain in the Sixties: Housing*. Harmondsworth, Middlesex: Penguin

Allan, G. and Crow, G. (eds) 1989. *Home and Family: Creating the Domestic Sphere*. Basingstoke: Macmillan.

Amery, C. 1991. *A Celebration of Art and Architecture*. London: The National Gallery.

Ames, K.L. 1992. *Death in the Dining Room and Other Tales of Victorian Culture*. Philadelphia: Temple University Press.

Anderson, B.S. and Zinsser, J.P. 1988. *A History of their Own: Women in Europe from Prehistory to the Present* (2 vols.). London: Penguin Books.

Andrews, M. 1997. *The Acceptable Face of Feminism: The Women's Institute Movement*. London: Lawrence and Wishart.

Appadurai, A. (ed.) 1986. *The Social Life of Things: Commodities in Cultural Perspective*. Cambridge: Cambridge University Press.

Apter, E. and Pietz, W. (eds) 1993. *Fetishism as Cultural Discourse*. Ithaca: Cornell University Press.

Arendt, H. (ed.) 1968. *Illuminations: Walter Benjamin Essays and Reflections*. New York: Schocken.

Ash, J. and Wilson, E. 1992. *Chic Thrills: A Fashion Reader*. London: Pandora.

Ashwin, C. 'Craft makes a comeback', *Times Higher Education Supplement*, 1 May 1987.

Ashwin, C., Chanon, A. and Darracott, J. 1988. *Education Crafts: A Study of the Education and Training of Craftspeople in England and Wales*. London: Crafts Council.

Attfield, J. 1984. 'A tale of two cultures' and 'Design for learning', p. 13. *The Times Higher Education Supplement*, 10 August 1984.

Attfield, J. 1985. 'Feminist Designs on Design History' in *Feminist Art News* Vol. 2, No.3: pp. 21–3.

Attfield, J. 1989. 'A foot note with some point to it', p. 6. In *The Weekend Guardian,* Saturday–Sunday 8–9 April.

Attfield, J. 1990. '"Then we were making furniture, and not money": A case study of J.Clarke, Wycombe Furniture Makers', pp. 54–7. In *Oral History,* Vol. 18, No. 2.

Attfield, J. 1992. 'The role of design in the relationship between furniture manufacture and its retailing 1939-1965 with initial reference to the furniture firm of J. Clarke' (unpublished doctoral thesis) Brighton: University of Brighton.

Attfield J. 1995. 'Women Designing: Redefining Design in Britain between the Wars' (review) in *Journal of Design History,* Vol. 8, No. 1, pp. 64–7.

Attfield, J. 1996. ' "Give 'em something dark and heavy": The Role of Design in the Material Culture of Popular British Furniture 1939–1965', pp. 185–201. *Journal of Design History,* Vol. 9, No. 3.

Attfield, J. 1997. 'A case for the study of the coffee table: Design as a practice of modernity' pp. 267–89. *Journal of Material Culture,* Vol. 2, No. 3, November.

Attfield, J. (ed.) 1999. *Utility Reassessed: The role of ethics in the practice of design.* Manchester and New York: Manchester University Press.

Attfield, J. 1999. 'Beyond the Pale: Reviewing the relationship between Material Culture and Design History' in *Journal of Design History,* Vol. 12, No. 4, pp. 373–80.

Attfield J. forthcoming. 'The Real Thing: Tufted Carpet's Entry Into the Vernacular' in Schoeser, M. and Boydell, C. (eds) *Disentangling Textiles.* Middlesex: Middlesex University Press.

Attfield, J. and Kirkham, P. (eds) 1995. *A View From the Interior. Women and Design.* London: The Women's Press.

Auslander, L. 1996. *Taste and Power: Furnishing Modern France.* Berkeley: University of California Press.

Bachelard, G. 1969. *The Poetics of Space.* Trans. Donald Nicholson-Smith. Oxford: Blackwell.

Baker, S. 1995a. '"To go about noisily": Clutter, writing and design' in *Emigre,* No. 35.

Baker, S. 1995b. 'Thinking things differently', pp. 70–7. In *Things, No. 3.*

Baker, S. 1996. 'Clutter, disorder and excess: The obstinacy of objects'. Unpublished paper circulated to delegates of the *Clutter* symposium.

Banham, J. (ed.) 1997. *Encyclopedia of Interior Design.* London and Chicago: Fitzroy Dearborn.

Bann. S. (ed.) 1990. *The Inventions of History.* Manchester and New York: Manchester University Press.

Barnett, P. et al. 1985. *Craft Matters: 3 attitudes to contemporary crafts.* Southampton: John Hansard Gallery.

Barthes, R. [1957] 1981. *Mythologies.* London: Paladin.

Barthes, R. 1984. *The Fashion System.* New York: Hill & Wang.

Baudrillard, J. 1981. *For a Critique of the Political Economy of the Sign.* St Louis, Mo: Telos.

Baudrillard, J. 1996. *The System of Objects.* London: Verso.

Baxandall, M. 1988. *Patterns of Intention: On the Historical Explanation of Pictures.* New Haven and London: Yale University Press.

Baynes, K. (ed.) 1969. *Attitudes in Design Education.* London: Lund Humphries.

Benjamin, A. (ed.) 1992. *The Problems of Modernity: Adorno and Benjamin.* London: Routledge.

Benson, J. 1994. *The Rise of Consumer Society in Britain 1880–1980.* Harlow: Longman.

Benton, T. & C. with Sharp, D. 1975. *Form and Function: A Source Book for the History of Architecture and Design 1890–1939.* London: Granada.

Berg, M. 1985. *The Age of Manufactures.* London: Fontana Press.

Berman, M. 1983. *All That Is Solid Melts Into Air: The Experience of Modernity.* London: Verso.

Bird, J., Curtis, B., Putnam, T., Robertson, G. and Tickner, L. (eds) 1993. *Mapping the Futures: Local cultures, global change.* London and New York: Routledge.

Birdwell-Pheasant, D. and Lawrence-Zúñiga, D. (eds) 1999. *House Life: Space, Place and Family in Europe.* Oxford and New York: Berg.

Bittker, S. 1989. 'Report of a Survey of Recent Crafts and Design Graduates of Scottish Art Colleges', pp. 219–28. In *Journal of Design History*, Vol. 2, Nos. 2 & 3.

Boumphrey, G. 1940. *Town and Country Tomorrow.* London: Thomas Nelson and Son.

Bourdieu, P. [1972] 1982. *Outline of a Theory of Practice.* Cambridge: Cambridge University Press.

Bourdieu, P. 1984. *Distinction: A social critique of the judgement of taste.* London: Routledge and Kegan Paul.

Bourdieu, P. 1993. *The Field of Cultural Production.* Cambridge: Polity.

Boyne, R. and Rattansi, A. (eds) 1990. *Postmodernism and Society.* London: Macmillan.

Brettle, J. and Rice, S. *Public Bodies – Private States.* Manchester: Manchester University Press.

Breward, C. 1995. *The Culture of Fashion: A New History of Fashionable Dress.* Manchester: Manchester University Press.

Breward, C. 1999. *The Hidden Consumer: Masculinities, fashion and city life 1860-1914.* Manchester: Manchester University Press.

Brewer, J. and Porter, R. (eds) 1993. *Consumption and the World of Goods.* London and New York: Routledge.

Briggs, M.S. 1934. *Middlesex Old and New.* London: Allen and Unwin.

Britton, A. and Margetts, M. 1993. *The Raw and the Cooked.* London: Crafts Council.

Bronner, S. J. (ed.) 1989, *Consuming Visions: Accumulation and display of Goods in America 1880–1920,* London & New York: W.W. Norton & Co.

Broude. N. and Garrard, M.D. 1982. *Feminism and Art History.* New York: Harper & Row.

Bryden, I. & Floyd, J. (eds) 1999. *Domestic Space: Reading the nineteenth-century interior.* Manchester: Manchester University Press.

Brydon, A. and Niessen, S. (eds) 1998. *Consuming Fashion: Adorning the Transnational Body.* Oxford and New York: Berg.

Buchanan, R. 1998. (Review of) Woodham, J.M. 1997. *Twentieth Century Design.* Oxford University Press, pp. 259–63. In *Journal of Design History,* 11 (3).

Buck, L. and Dodd, P. 1991. *Relative Values: or What's Art Worth?* London: BBC Books.

Buckley, C. 1986. 'Made in Patriarchy: Towards a feminist analysis of women and design'. *Design Issues* Vol. 3, No. 2 (Fall 1986), pp. 3–14.

Bullock, A., Stallybrass, O. and Trombley, S. (eds) *The Fontana Dictionary of Modern Thought.* London: Fontana.

Burchill, J. 'Material Boys' p. 3. *The Guardian Weekend.* 3 October, 1998.

Burman, B. (ed.) 1999. *The Culture of Sewing: Gender, Consumption and Home Dressmaking.* Oxford and New York: Berg.

Burman, S. (ed.) 1979. *Fit Work For Women.* London: Croom Helm.

Burnett, J. 1978. *A Social History of Housing 1815-1970.* Cambridge: Cambridge University Press.

Butler, J. 1990. *Gender Trouble: Feminism and the Subversion of Identity.* London and New York: Routledge.

Campbell, C. 1996. 'The Meaning of Objects and the Meaning of Action', pp. 93–106. In *Journal of Material Culture.* Vol. 1, No. 1.

Campbell, K. 1976. *Home Sweet Home: Housing designed by the London County Council and Greater London Council Authority 1888-1975.* London: Academy.

Carrier, J.G. 1995. *Gifts and Commodities: Exchange and Western Capitalism since 1700.* London: Routledge.

Cescinsky, H. 1925. 'America: Glimpses into Furniture Factories', pp. 386–7. In *Cabinet Maker,* May 23, 1925.

Cescinsky, H. [1931] 1967. *The Gentle Art of Faking Furniture*. London: Chapman & Hall.

Chambers, Ian. 1986. *Popular Culture: The Metropolitan Experience*. London and New York: Routledge.

Cieraad, I. (ed.) 1999. *At Home: An Anthropology of Domestic Space*. New York: Syracuse University Press.

Clarke, A.J. 1999. *Tupperware: the promise of plastic in 1950s America*. Washington D.C. and London: Smithsonian Institution Press.

Clayre, A. 1977. *Nature and Industrialisation*. Oxford: Oxford University Press.

Clifford, J. [1988] 1994. *The Predicament of Culture: Twentieth-Century Ethnography, Literature, and Art*. Cambridge, Massachusets: Harvard University Press.

Cocks, A.S. 1980. *The Victoria and Albert Museum: The Making of the Collection*. Leicester: Windward.

Coleman, A. and the Design Disadvantaged Team of Land Use Research, 1985. *Utopia on Trial: Vision and Reality in Planned Housing*. London: Kings College London.

Coleman, R. 1988. *The Art of Work: An Epitaph to Skill*. London: Pluto.

Coleridge, N. 1989. *The Fashion Conspiracy*. London: Heinemann.

Conway, H. *Design History: A Students' Handbook*. London: George Allen & Unwin

Colomina, B. 1992. *Sexuality and Space*. Princeton: Princeton Architectural Press.

Colomina, B. 1994. *Privacy and Publicity: Modern Architecture as Mass Media*. Cambridge, Massachusetts and London: MIT Press.

Coombes, A.E. 1988. 'Museums and the Formation of National and Cultural Identities', pp. 57–68. In *The Oxford Art Journal*, Vol. 11, No. 2.

Cowley, J. 1979. *Housing for People or for Profit?* London: Stage 1.

Craik, J. 1994. *The Face of Fashion: Cultural Studies in Fashion*. London: Routledge.

Cranz, G. 1989. *The Politics of Park Design: A History of Urban Parks in America*. Cambridge, Massachusetts: MIT.

Csikszentmihalyi, M. and Rochberg-Halton. E. 1981. *The Meaning of Things: Domestic Symbols and the Self*. Cambridge: Cambridge University Press.

Cummings, N. (ed.) 1993. *Reading Things*. London: Chance Books.

Dant, T. 1999. *Material Culture in the Social World*. Buckingham and Philadelphia: Open University Press.

Davidoff, L. and Hall, C. 1987. *Family Fortunes: Men and Women of the English Middle Class 1780-1850.* London: Hutchinson.

Debord, G. 1967. *La Société du Spectacle,* Paris: Buchet-Chastel.

de Certeau, M. 1988. *The Practice of Everyday Life.* trans. Steven Rendall. Berkeley: University of California Press.

Deetz, J. 1996. *In Small Things Forgotten: The Archaeology of Early American Life.* New York: Doubleday.

de Grazia, V. (ed.) 1996. *The Sex of Things: Gender and Consumption in Historical Perspective.* Berkeley and Los Angeles: University of California Press.

Descombes, V. 1986. *Objects of All Sorts: A Philosophical Grammar.* Oxford: Blackwell.

Dilnot, C. 1984. 'The State of Design History – Part I: Mapping the Field', pp. 4–23. In *Design Issues.* Vol 1, No. 1, Spring.

Dittmar, H. 1992. *The Social Psychology of Material Possessions: To Have Is To Be.* Hemel Hempstead, Hertfordshire: Harvester Wheatsheaf.

Doordan, D.P. 1995. *Design History: An Anthology.* Cambridge, Massachusetts: The MIT Press.

Dormer, P. 1990. *The Meanings of Modern Design: towards the Twenty-first Century.* London: Thames and Hudson.

Dormer, P. (ed.) 1997. *The Culture of Craft: Status and Future.* Manchester: Manchester University Press.

Douglas, M. 1966. *Purity and Danger: An analysis of concepts of pollution and taboo.* London: Routledge and Kegan Paul.

Douglas, M. and Isherwood, B. 1978. *The World of Goods: Towards an Anthropology of Consumption.* London: Allen Lane.

Droog Design 1991–1996, Utrecht: Utrecht Centraal Museum.

du Gay, P., Hall, S. et al. 1997. *Doing Cultural Studies: The Story of the Sony Walkman.* London: Sage.

Eatwell, J., Milgate, M and Newman, P. (eds) 1989. *The New Palgrave: The Invisible Hand.* London and New York: W.W.Norton.

Edwards, C.D. 1993. *Victorian Furniture: Technology and Design.* Manchester: Manchester University Press.

Edwards, C.D. 1994. *Twentieth Century Furniture: Materials, Manufacture and Markets.* Manchester: Manchester University Press.

Elias, N. 1978. *The Civilising Process: The History of Manners.* Oxford: Blackwell.

Elinor, G. et al. 1987. *Women and Craft,* London: Virago.

Eliot, T.S. 1963. *Collected Poems 1909-1962.* London: Faber and Faber.

Factors in Industrial and Commercial Efficiency, HMSO, 1927.

Falk, P. 1994. *The Consuming Body*. London and Thousand Oaks, California: Sage.

Falk, P. and Campbell, C. (eds) 1997. *The Shopping Experience*. London and Thousand Oaks, California: Sage.

Fastnedge, R. 1955. *English Furniture Styles From 1500-1830*. Harmondsworth, Middlesex: Penguin.

Featherstone, M. 1991. *Consumer Culture and Postmodernism*. London and Thousand Oaks, California: Sage.

Featherstone, M., Hepworth, M. and Turner, B.S. 1995. *The Body: Social Process and Cultural Theory*. London and Thousand Oaks, California: Sage.

Fine, B. and Leopold, E. 1993. *The World of Consumption*. London: Routledge.

Forty, A. 1986. *Objects of Desire: Design and Society 1750-1980*. London: Thames and Hudson.

Forty, A. and Kuchler, S. (eds) 1999. *The Art of Forgetting*. Oxford and New York: Berg.

Foucault, M. 1984. *The History of Sexuality* Volume I: An Introduction. Harmondsworth, Middlesex: Penguin.

Foucault, M. 1985. *The Order of Things: An Archaeology of the Human Sciences*. London: Tavistock.

Frampton, K. 1980. *Modern Architecture: A critical history*. London: Thames & Hudson.

Friedman, A.T. 1998. *Woman and the Making of the Modern House: A Social and Architectural History*. New York: Harry N. Abrams.

Fry, T. 'A Geography of Power: Design History and Marginality', pp. 204–18. In *Design Issues*, Vol. 6, No. 1, Fall 1989.

Furniture Working Party Report, HMSO, 1947.

Garber, M. 1993. *Vested Interests: Cross Dressing and Cultural Anxiety*. London: Thames and Hudson.

Gardner, C. and Sheppard, J. 1989. *Consuming Passion: The Rise of Retail Culture*. London: Unwin Hyman.

Garland, M. 1962. *Fashion*. Harmondsworth: Penguin.

Geertz, C. [1973] 1993. *The Interpretation of Cultures*. London: Fontana.

Geertz, C. 1983. *Local Knowledge: Further Essays in Interpretive Anthropology*. New York: Basic Books.

Gell, A. 1998. *Art and Agency*. London: Clarendon Press.

Giddens, A. 1991. *Modernity and Self-Identity: Self and Society in the Late Modern Age*. Cambridge: Polity.

Giddens, A. 1992. *The Transformation of Intimacy*. Cambridge: Polity.

Giedion, S. 1948. *Mechanization Takes Command.* New York: Oxford University Press.

Gloag, J. 1934. *English Furniture.* London: Adam & Charles Black.

Gloag, J. 1944. *The Missing Technician in Industrial Production.* London: George Allen and Unwin.

Gloag, J. 1945. *Plastics and Industrial Design.* London: George Allen and Unwin.

Gloag, J. 1947a. *Self Training for Industrial Designers.* London: George Allen and Unwin.

Gloag, J. 1947b, *The English Tradition in Design.* Harmondsworth: Penguin.

Gloag, J. 1966. *A social history of furniture design from B.C.1300 to A.D. 1960.* New York: Bonanza Books.

Glynn, P. 1978. *In Fashion: Dress in the twentieth century.* London: George Allen & Unwin

Goffman, E. 1959. *The Presentation of Self in Everday Life.* Garden City, New York: Doubleday.

Gordon, B. 1996. 'Woman's Domestic Body: The Conceptual Conflation of Women and Interiors in the Industrial Age', pp. 281–301. In *Winterthur Portfolio,* Vol. 31, No. 4, Winter.

Gorz, A. 1982. *Farewell to the Working Class: An Essay on Post-Industrial Socialism.* London: Pluto.

Graves, J. 1998. 'Clutter'. In *Issues in Art, Architecture and Design,* Vol. 5, No. 2.

Graves, J. 1999. '"When Things Go Wrong. . . Inside the Inside": A Psychoanalytical History of a Jug'. In *Journal of Design History,* Vol. 12, No. 4, pp. 357–67.

Greenberg, J.R. and Mitchell, S.A. 1983. *Object Relations in Psychoanalytic Theory.* Cambridge, Massachusetts and London: Harvard University Press.

Gronberg, T. 1997. (Review of) Reed, C. (ed.) 1996. *Not At Home: The Suppression of Domesticity in Modern Art and Architecture.* In *Journal of Design History,* Vol. 10, No. 1, pp. 97–9.

Gronberg, T. 1998. *Designs on Modernity: Exhibiting the City in 1920s Paris.* Manchester: Manchester University Press.

Habermas, J. 1987. *The Philosophical Discourses of Modernity: Twelve Lectures.* Cambridge: Polity Press.

Habermas, J. 1989. *The Structural Transformation of the Public Sphere.* Cambridge: Polity Press.

Hall, S. (ed.) 1997. *Representation: Cultural Representations and Signifying Practices.* London and Thousand Oaks, California: Sage.

Halle, D. 1993. *Inside Culture: Art and Class in the American Home.* Chicago: Chicago University Press.

Hamilton, N. (ed.) *From Spitfire to Microchip: Studies in the History of Design from 1945*. London: The Design Council.

Haraway, D.J. 1991. *Simians, Cyborgs and Women – The Reinvention of Nature*. London: Free Association Books.

Hardyment, C. 1995. *Slice of Life: The British Way of Eating Since 1945*. London: BBC Books.

Harling, R. 1973. *Dictionary of Design and Decoration*. London and Glasgow: Collins.

Harris, S. and Berke, D. (eds) 1997. *Architecture of the Everyday*. New York: Princeton Architectural Press.

Harrod, T. 1997. *Obscure Objects of Desire*. London: Craft Council.

Harrod, T. 1999. *The Crafts in Britain in the Twentieth Century*. New Haven and London: Yale University Press.

Harvey, C. and Press, J. 1991. *William Morris: Design and Enterprise in Victorian Britain*. Manchester University Press.

Harvey, D. 1989. *The Condition of Postmodernity*: *An Enquiry into the Origins of Cultural Change*. Oxford: Blackwell.

Haug, W.F. [1971] 1986. *Critique of Commodity Aesthetics: Appearance, Sexuality and Advertising in Capitalist Society*. Oxford: Polity.

Haynes, M.T. 1998. *Dressing Up Debutantes: Pageantry and Glitz in Texas*. Oxford and New York: Berg.

Hebdige, D. 1979. *Subculture: the Meaning of Style*. London and New York: Methuen.

Hebdige, D. 1987. 'The Impossible Object: Towards a sociology of the sublime', pp. 47–76. In *New Formations,* Vol. 1, No. 1.

Hebdige, D. 1989. 'Designs for Living'. In *Marxism Today*, October 1989, pp. 24–7.

Heidegger, M. [1927] 1998. *Being and Time*. Oxford: Blackwell.

Heskett, J. 1980. *Industrial Design*. London: Thames and Hudson.

Hewison, R. 1987. *The Heritage Industry*. London: Methuen.

Hill, R. 'How the country craftsmen became contemporary applied artists'. *Guardian,* 15 January 1987.

Hitchcock, H-R. and Johnson, P. 1966 [1932] *The International Style*. New York and London: Norton and Co.

Hobsbawm, E. 1994. *Age of Extremes: The Short Twentieth Century 1914-1991*. London: Michael Joseph.

Hobsbawm, E. and Ranger, T. (eds) [1983] 1992. *The Invention of Tradition*. Cambridge: Cambridge University Press.

Hodder, I. 1986. *Reading the Past: Current Approaches to Interpretation in Archaeology*. New York: Cambridge University Press.

Hoggart, R. 1957. *The Uses of Literacy,* Harmondsworth, Middlesex: Penguin.

Howson, H.F. 1979. *London's Underground*. London: Ian Allan.

Hunte, E.V. 1997. *Eternally Yours: visions of product endurance*. Rotterdam: 010 Publishers.

Jackson, A. 1973. *Semi-Detached London*. London: Allen and Unwin.

Jackson, S. and Moores, S. (eds) 1995. *The Politics of Domestic Consumption: Critical Readings*. London and New York: Harvester Wheatsheaf.

Jameson, F. 1984. 'Postmodernism, or the cultural logic of late capitalism', pp. 53–92. In *New Left Review*, No.146, July/August.

Jencks, C. 1977. *The language of post-modern architecture*. London: Academy.

Jenkins, K. 1991. *Re-thinking History*. London and New York: Routledge.

Jobling, P. 1999. *Fashion Spreads: Word and Image in Fashion Photography Since 1980*. Oxford and New York: Berg.

Jones, M. (ed.) 1990. *Fake? The Art of Deception*. London: British Museum.

Kaufmann, J-C. 1998. *Dirty Linen: couples and their laundry*. London: Middlesex University Press.

Keat, R. and Abercrombie, N. (eds) *Enterprise Culture*. London and New York: Routledge.

Kenny, A. [1973] 1993. *Wittgenstein*. Harmondsworth, Middlesex: Penguin.

Kingery, W.D. (ed.) 1996. *Learning From things: Method and theory of Material Culture Studies*. Washington and London: Smithsonian Institution.

Kingston, S. 1999. 'The Essential Attitude' pp. 338–51. In *Journal of Material Culture*. Vol. 4, No. 3.

Kirkham, P. (ed.) 1996. *The Gendered Object*. Manchester University Press.

Kirkham, P., Porter, J. and Mace, R. 1987. *Furnishing the World: The East London Furniture Trade 1830–1980*. London: Journeyman.

Kwint, M., Breward, C. and Aynsley, J. (eds) 1999. *Material Memories: Design and Evocation*. Oxford and New York: Berg.

Latour, B. 1991. *We have never been modern*. New York: Harvester Wheatsheaf.

Lee, M.J. 1993. *Consumer Culture Reborn: The cultural politics of consumption*. London: Routledge.

Lefebvre, H. 1987. 'The Everyday and Everdayness' pp. 7–11. In *Yale French Studies*. Vol. 73, Fall.

Lefebvre, H. 1996. *The Production of Space*. Trans. Donald Nicholson-Smith. Oxford: Blackwell.

Leslie, E. 1996. 'The exotic of the everyday: Critical theory in the parlour', pp. 83–101. In *Things*, No. 4.

Lethaby, W.R. 1923. *Home and Country Arts.* London: Home and County.

Lewis, R. and Maude, A. 1949. *The English Middle Classes.* London: Phoenix House.

Lipovetsky, G. 1994. *The Empire of Fashion: Dressing Modern Democracy.* Princeton: Princeton University Press.

Lowenthal, D. 1985. *The Past Is Another Country.* Cambridge: Cambridge University Press.

Lubar, S. and Kingerly, W.D. (eds) 1993. *History from Things: Essays on Material Culture.* Washington D.C.: Smithsonian Institution Press.

Lucie-Smith, E. 1975. *World of the Makers: Today's master craftsmen and craftswomen.* New York:Two Continents Publishing Group.

Lüdtke, A. (ed.) 1995. *The History of Everyday Life: Reconstructing Historical Experiences and Ways of Life.* New Jersey: Princeton University Press.

Lumley, R. (ed.) 1990. *The Museum Time Machine.* London and New York: Comedia.

Lunt, P.K. and Livingstone, S.M. 1992. *Mass Consumption and Personal Identity: Everyday Economic Experience.* Buckingham and Philadephia: Open University Press.

Lupton, D. 1996. *Food, the Body and the Self.* London and Thousand Oaks, California: Sage.

Lyotard, J.F. 1984. *The Post-Modern Condition,* Manchester: Manchester University Press.

Lyotard, J.F.1985. *Les Immatériaux* (exhibition catalogue) Paris.

MacCarthy, F. 1972. *All Things Bright and Beautiful.* London: George Allen & Unwin.

MacCarthy, F. 1979. *A History of British Design 1890–1970.* London: George Allen & Unwin.

Macdonald, S. 1970. *The History and Philosophy of Art Education.* London: University of London Press.

Mackay, H. (ed.) 1997. *Consumption and Everyday Life,* London and Thousand Oaks, California: Sage.

MacKenzie, M. 1991. *Androgynous Objects.* Melbourne: Harwood.

Macquarrie, J. 1980. *Existentialism.* Harmondsworth, Middlesex: Penguin.

Macquoid, P. 1904–1908. *History of Furniture in 4 Volumes: The Age of Oak, The Age of Walnut, The Age of Mahogany and The Age of Satinwood.* London: Lawrence & Bullen.

Margolin, V. 1989. *Design Discourse: History, Theory, Criticism.* Chicago: University of Chicago Press.

Margolin, V. and Buchanan, R. (eds) 1995. *The Idea of Design: A Design Issues Reader.* London: MIT Press.

Marling, K.A. (ed.) 1997. *Designing Disney's Theme Parks*. Paris and New York: Flammarion.

Marx, K. [1867] 1990, *Capital: A Critique of Political Economy, V*olume I. Harmondsworth, Middlesex: Penguin.

Mauss, M. [1950] 1990. *The Gift*. London: Routledge

Mayes, J.L. 1960. *History of Chairmaking in High Wycombe*. London: Routledge & Kegan Paul.

McCracken, G. 1988. *Culture and Consumption: New Approaches to the Symbolic Character of Consumer Goods and Activities*. Bloomington: Indiana University Press.

McGuigan, J. 1992. *Cultural Populism*. London: Routledge.

McGuiree, R.H. and Paynter, R. (eds) 1991. *The Archaeology of Inequality*. Oxford: Blackwell.

McRobbie, A. (ed.) 1989. *Zoot Suits and Second-Hand Dresses*. Basingstoke, Hampshire: Macmillan.

McRobbie, A. (ed.) 1997. *Back to Reality? Social Experience and Cultural Studies*. Manchester and New York: Manchester University Press.

McRobbie, A. 1998. *British Fashion Design: Rag Trade or Image Industry?* London: Routledge.

Maguire, P.J. and Woodham, J.M. (eds) 1997. *Design and Cultural Politics in Postwar Britain*. London: Leicester University Press.

Mayes, J.L. 1960. *History of Chairmaking in High Wycombe*. London: Routledge & Kegan Paul.

Miller, D. 1987. *Material Culture and Mass Consumption*. Oxford: Blackwell.

Miller, D. 1994. *Modernity: An Ethnographic Approach*. Oxford: Berg.

Miller, D. (ed.) 1995. *Acknowledging Consumption*. London: Routledge.

Miller, D. 1997. *Capitalism: An Ethnographic Approach*. Oxford and New York: Berg.

Miller, D. (ed.) 1998a. *Material cultures: Why some things matter*. London: UCL Press.

Miller D. 1998b. *A Theory of Shopping*. Oxford: Polity.

Miller, D. 1998c. 'Groans from a bookshelf: New books in Material Culture and Consumption'. *Journal of Material Culture* Vol. 3, No. 3, pp. 379–88.

Miller, T. and McHoul, A. *Popular Culture and Everyday Life*. London and Thousand Oaks, California: Sage.

Moles, A.A. 1988. 'Design and Immateriality: What of It in a Post Industrial Society?', pp. 25–32. In *Design Issues,* Vol. 4, No. 1–2 (Special Issue 1988).

Moody, E. 1966. *Modern Furniture*. London: Studio Vista.

Morris, B. 1991. *Western Conceptions of the Individual*. Oxford and New York: Berg.

Mukerji, C. 1983. *From Graven Images: Patterns of Modern Materialism*. New York: Columbia University Press.

Muthesius, S. 1988. 'Why do we buy old furniture? Aspects of the authentic antique in Britain 1870–1910', pp. 231–54. In *Art History*, Vol. 11, No. 2, June.

Newman, O. 1973. *Defensible Space: People and Design in the Violent City*. London: Architectural Press.

Neustatter, A. 1999. 'Happy ever after' pp. 4–5. *The Guardian*, 22 October.

Norman, D.A. 1998. *The Design of Everyday Things*. London: MIT Press.

Oliver, P., Davis, I. and Bentley, I. 1981. *Dunroamin: The Suburban Semi and its Enemies*. London: Barrie & Jenkins.

Orvell, M. 1989. *The Real Thing: Imitation and authenticity in American culture 1880-1930*. Chapel Hill, University of South Carolina Press.

Pahl, R.E. 1984. *Divisions of Labour*. Oxford: Blackwell.

Palmer, A. 1997. 'New Directions: Fashion History Studies and Research in North America and England'. *Fashion Theory*, Vol. 1, No. 3, pp. 301–2.

Parker, R. 1984. *The Subversive Stitch: Embroidery and the making of the feminine*. London: The Women's Press.

Parker, R. and Pollock, G. 1981. *Old Mistresses: Women, Art and Ideology*, London: Routledge & Kegan Paul.

Pearce, S.M. (ed.) 1994. *Interpreting Objects and Collections*. London and New York: Routledge:

Percy, C. and Triggs, T. 1990. 'The Crafts and Non-verbal Learning', pp. 37–9. In *Oral History*. Vol. 18, No. 2, autumn.

Pesce, G. 1995. '18 questions on architecture today'. In *Domus*, No. 768, February.

Pevsner, N. 1940. *Academies of Art*. London: Cambridge University Press.

Pevsner, N. 1956. *The Englishness of English Art*. London: Architectural Press.

Phillips, A. 1988. *Winnicott*. London: Fontana Press.

Phillips, D. 1997. *Exhibiting Authenticity*. Manchester and New York: Manchester University Press.

Physick, J. 1982. *The Victoria and Albert Museum: The history of its buildings*. London: Phaidon.

Piper, D.W. (ed.) 1973. *Readings in Art and Design Education*, 2 volumes: *1. After Hornsey, 2. After Coldstream*. London: Davis Poynter.

Poe, E.A. 1986. 'The Purloined Letter'. In *The Fall of the House of Usher and other writings*. Harmondsworth, Middlesex: Penguin, p. 331.

Pointon, M. 1986. *History of Art: A Students' Handbook*. London: Unwin Hyman.

Polhemus, T. 1994. *Street Style: from sidewalk to catwalk*. London: Thames and Hudson.

Polhemus, T. and Proctor, L. 1978. *Fashion and Anti-Fashion*. London: Thames and Hudson.

Prown, J.D. 1982. 'Mind in Matter: An Introduction to Material Culture Theory and Method'. *Winterthur Portfolio*, Vol. 17, No. 1, pp. 1–9.

Putnam, T. 1990. 'The Crafts in Museum: Consolation or Creation', pp. 40–3. In *Oral History*, Vol. 18, No. 2.

Putnam, T. and Newton, C. (eds) 1990. *Household Choices*. London: Futures.

Pye, D. 1968. *The Nature and Art of Workmanship*. Cambridge: Cambridge University Press.

Quimby, I.M.G. (ed.) 1978. *Material Culture and the Study of American Life*. New York: W.W.Norton.

Quiney, Anthony, 1986. *House and Home: A History of the Small English House*. London: BBC.

Raban, J. 1974. *Soft City*. London: H. Hamilton.

Rabinow, P. (ed.) 1984. *The Foucault Reader*. Harmondsworth, Middlesex: Penguin.

Race, E. 1953. 'Design in Modern Furniture', pp. 62–5. In Lake, F. (ed.) *Daily Mail Ideal Home Book 1952–53*. London: Daily Mail Ideal Home.

Ramaker, R. and Bakker, G. 1998. *Droog Design: Spirit of the Nineties*. Rotterdam: 010 Publishers.

Ranson, B. 1989. 'Craftwork, Ideology and the Craft Life Cycle', pp. 77–92. In *Journal of Design History*, Vol. 2, Nos. 2 & 3.

Rapoport, A. 1969. *House, Form and Culture*. Englewood Cliffs, NJ: Prentice Hall.

Rapoport, A. 1977. *Human Aspects of Urban form: Towards a Man-Environment Approach to Urban Form and Design*. Oxford and New York: Pergamon Press.

Ravetz, A. 1986. *The Government of Space: Town Planning in Modern Society*, London and Boston: Faber and Faber.

Rawsthorn, A. 'Lutyens, Starck and the barrow boys: design and the economy in a post-Thatcher world', pp. 14–16. In *Issue*, Spring 1991.

Reed, C. (ed.) 1996. *Not At Home: The Suppression of Domesticity in Modern Art and Architecture*. London: Thames and Hudson.

Rees, A.L. and Borzello, F. 1986. *The New Art History*, London: Camden Press.

Reynolds, H. 1997. *Couture or Trade?* Chichester, West Sussex: Philmore.

Riccini, R. 'History From Things: Notes on the History of Industrial Design' in *Design Issues,* Vol. 14, No. 3, Autumn 1998, pp. 43–64.

Richards, J.M. 1940. *Modern Architecture.* Harmondsworth, Middlesex: Penguin.

Richards, J.M. [1946] 1973. *The Castles On the Ground: The Anatomy of Suburbia.* London: Architectural Press.

Riggins, S.H. 1994 *The Socialness of Things.* Berlin: Mouton De Gruyter.

Rivers, T., Cruickshank, D., Darley, G. and Pawley, M. 1992. *The Name of the Room.* London: BBC.

Roach, M.E. and Bubolz Eicher, J. 1965. *Dress, Adornment, and the Social Order.* New York: John Wiley.

Roberts, R. 1971. *The Classic Slum.* Harmondsworth, Middlesex: Penguin.

Rouse, E. 1989. *Understanding Fashion.* Oxford and London: BSP Professional Books.

Roux, C. 'You're sitting on a work of art'. In *The Guardian,* 6 April, 1999, pp. 10–11.

Rowbotham, S. 1973. *Hidden From History.* London: Pluto.

Saisselin, R.G. 1985. *Bricabracomania: The Bourgeos and the Bibelo.* London: Thames and Hudson.

Sampson, A. 1971. *The New Anatomy of Britain.* London: Hodder and Stoughton.

Samuel, R. 1977. 'Workshop of the World: Steam power and hand technology in mid-Victorian Britain', pp. 6–72. In *History Workshop,* Vol. 3, Spring.

Samuel, R. 1994 and 1998. *Theatres of Memory,* Vols I and II. London and New York: Verso.

Scarry, E. 1985. *The Body In Pain: The Making and Unmaking of the World.* New York: Oxford University Press.

Schlereth, T.J. (ed.) 1985. *Material Culture: A Research Guide.* Lawrence: University Press of Kansas.

Schlereth, T.J. 1992. *Cultural History and Material Culture: Everyday Life, Landscapes and Museums.* Charlottesville: University Press of Virginia.

Schwartz, H. 1996. *The Culture of the Copy: Striking Likenesses, Unreasonable Facsimiles.* New York: Zone.

Searle, A. 1999. 'Cheap tricks, bad jokes, black magic', pp. 12–13. In the *Guardian,* 13 July.

Sennett, R. 1977. *The Fall of Public Man.* Cambridge: Cambridge University Press.

Severa, J. and Horswill, M. 1989. 'Costume as Material Culture'. In *Dress* Vol. 15, p. 53.

Sheridan, A. 1980. *Michel Foucault: The Will to Truth*. London and New York: Tavistock.

Shields, R. (ed.) 1992. *Lifestyle Shopping: The Subject of Consumption*. London and New York: Routledge.

Silverstone, R. (ed.) 1997. *Visions of Suburbia*. London: Routledge.

Silverstone, R. and Hirsch, E. (eds) 1992. *Consuming Technologies: Media and information in domestic spaces*. London: Routledge.

Simmel, G. [1902] 1957 'Fashion'. In *The American Journal of Sociology*, Vol. 62, No. 6, pp. 541–8.

Slater, D. 1997. *Consumer Culture and Modernity*. Cambridge: Polity.

Smart Martin, Ann and Ritchie Garrison, J. (eds) 1997. *American Material Culture: The Shape of the Field*. Winterthur, Delaware: Henry du Pont Winterthur Museum.

Smithson A. & P. 1970. *Ordinariness and Light: Urban theories 1952–1960 and their application in a building project 1963–1970*. London: Faber and Faber.

Sontag, S. 1994. *Against Interpretation*. London: Vintage.

Sparke, P. (ed.) 1981. *Reyner Banham: Design By Choice*. London: Academy Editions.

Sparke, P. 1982. *Ettore Sottsass Jr*. London: Design Council.

Sparke, P. 1983. *Consultant Design: The history and practice of the designer in industry*. London: Pembridge Press.

Sparke, P. 1986. *An Introduction to Design and Culture in the Twentieth Century*. London: Allen & Unwin.

Sparke, P. 1995. *As Long As Its Pink: The Sexual Politics of Taste*. London: Harper Collins.

Sparke, P.1998. *A Century of Design: Design Pioneers of the 20th Century*. London: Michael Beazley.

Sparkes, I. 1973. *The English Country Chair*. Buckinghamshire: Spur.

Spyer, P. (ed.) 1998. *Border Fetishisms: Material Objects in Unstable Spaces*. London: Routledge.

Stallybrass, P. and White, A. 1986. *The Politics and Poetics of Transgression*. London: Methuen.

Steedman, C. 1998. 'What a Rag Rug Means' in *Journal of Material Culture*. Vol. 3, No. 3, pp. 259–82.

Steele, V. 1985. *Fashion and Eroticism*. New York: Oxford University Press.

Stewart, S. [1984] 1996. *On Longing: Narratives of the Miniature, the Gigantic, the Souvenir, the Collection*. Durham and London: Dukes University Press.

Storey, J. [1993] 1997. *An Introduction to Cultural Theory and Popular Culture*. London & New York: Prentice Hall Harvester Wheatsheaf.

Strasser, Susan, 1989. *Satisfaction Guaranteed: The Making of the American Mass Market*. New York: Pantheon.

Strinati, D. 1995. *An Introduction to Theories of Popular Culture*. Manchester University Press.

Sullivan, L. 1896. 'The Tall Office Building Artistically Considered', p. 13. In Benton, T. & C. with Sharp, D. (eds) 1975. *Form and Function*. London: Granada.

Sutton, G. 1967. *Artisan or Artist? A History of the Teaching of Art and Crafts in English Schools*. Oxford: Pergamon.

Swales, V. 1996. 'Clutter: disorder in the spaces of design, the text and the imagination' (review) p. 5. In *Design History Society NewsLetter*, No. 70.

Swengley, N. 'Very Arty Crafty' in the *Observer*, 5 July 1987, pp. 40–3; *Craft Workshops in the English Countryside*, 1978. Salisbury: CoSira.

Thakara, J. (ed.) 1988. *Design After Modernism: Beyond the Object*. London: Thames and Hudson.

Thomas, J. 1998. 'Where are we now? Archaeology theory in the 1990s' in Ucko, P.J. *Theory in Archaeology: A world perspective*. London and New York: Routledge.

Thomas, N. 1991. *Entangled Objects: Exchange, Material Culture, and Colonialism in the Pacific*. Cambridge, Massachusets, and London: Harvard University Press.

Thompson, E.P. 1963. *The Making of the Working Class*, Harmondsworth: Penguin.

Thompson, M. 1979. *Rubbish Theory: The Creation and Destruction of Value*. Oxford: Oxford University Press.

Thompson, P. 1988. *The Voice of the Past: Oral History*. Oxford: Oxford University Press.

Tilley, C. (ed.) 1990. *Reading Material Culture*. Oxford: Blackwell.

Tilley, C. 1999. *Metaphor and Material Culture*. Oxford: Blackwell.

Tomlinson, A. (ed.) 1990. *Consumption, Identity and Style: Marketing, meanings and the packaging of pleasure*. London: Routledge.

Tsëelon, E. 1995. *The Masque of Femininity*, London: Sage.

Tunbridge, J.E. and Ashworth, G.J. 1996. *Dissonant Heritage: The Management of the Past as a Resource in Conflict*. Chichester and New York: Wiley.

Turner, C. 1955. *The Parker-Knoll Collection*. Northampton: Vernon.

Turner, M. (ed.) 1983. *The Decoration of the Suburban Villa 1990-1940*, Middlesex: Middlesex Polytechnic (exhibition catalogue).

Turner, M and Hoskins, L. [1988] 1995. *Silver Studio of Design: A Source Book for Home Decorating*. London: Magna Books.

Urban Task Force 1999. *Towards an Urban Renaissance: Final Report of the Urban Task Force.* London: Department of the Environment, Transport and Regions.

Vaneigem, R. [1967] 1983. *The Revolution of the Everyday.* London: Left Bank Books and Rebel Press.

Varnedoe, K. and Gopink, A. 1991. *High and Low: Modern Art and Popular Culture.* New York: The Museum of Modern Art.

Veblen, T. [1899] 1934. *The Theory of the Leisure Class.* New York: The Modern Library.

Venturi, R., Scott Brown, D. and Izenour, I. [1972] 1982. *Learning from Las Vegas: The forgotten symbolism of architectural form.* Cambridge, Massachusetts: MIT.

Verbeek, P.P. and Kockelkoren, P. 1998. 'The Things That Matter'. *Design Issues,* 14 (3): 28–42.

Vergo, P. (ed.) 1989. *The New Museology.* London: Reaktion.

Walker, J.A. 1989. *Design History and the History of Design.* London: Pluto.

Walker, J.A. and Chaplin, S. 1997. *Visual Culture: An Introduction.* Manchester: Manchester University Press.

Warwick, A. and Cavallaro, D. 1998. *Fashioning the Frame: Boundaries, Dress and the Body.* Oxford and New York: Berg.

Weiner, A. 1992. 'Inalienable Wealth'. *American Ethnologist,* Vol. 12, pp. 52–65..

Weiner, A. 1992. *Inalienable Possessions: the Paradox of Keeping While Giving.* Berkeley: University of California Press.

Weiner, A.B. and Schneider, J. (eds) 1988. *Cloth and Human Experience.* Washington: Smithsonian Institution Press.

White, J.N. 1989. 'The First Craft Centre of Great Britain; Bargaining for a Time Bomb', pp. 207–14. In *Journal of Design History,* Vol. 2, Nos. 2 & 3.

Whiteley, N. 1993. *Design for Society,* London: Reaktion.

Williams-Davies, J. 1989. 'The Preservation and Interpretation of Traditional Rural Crafts at the Welsh Folk Museum', pp. 215–18. In *Journal of Design History,* Vol. 2, Nos. 2 & 3.

Williams-Ellis, C. 1929. *England and the Octopus.* London: Geoffrey Bles.

Williams, R. 1973. *The Country and the City.* St Albans, Hertfordshire: Paladin.

Williamson, J. 1978. *Decoding Advertisements: Ideology and Meaning in Advertising.* London and Boston: Marion Boyars.

Williamson, J. 1985. 'The Making of a Material Girl', pp. 46–7. *New Socialist,* No. 31, October.

Wills, G. 1974. *Craftsmen and Cabinet-makers of Classic English Furniture.* London: John Bartholomew

Wills, G. and Midgley, D. (eds) 1973. *Fashion Marketing: An anthology of viewpoints and perspectives*. London: George Allen & Unwin.

Willis, P. 1993. *Common Culture*. Milton Keynes: Open University Press.

Wilson, E.1985. *Adorned in Dreams: Fashion and Modernity*. London: Virago.

Wilson, E. 1989. *Hallucinations: Life in the Post-Modern City*. London: Hutchinson Radius.

Wilson, E. 1991. *The Sphinx in the City: Urban Life, the Control of Disorder and Women*. London: Virago.

Wilson, E. and Taylor, L. 1989. *Through the Looking Glass: A History of Dress from 1860 to the Present Day*. London: BBC Books.

Winnicott, D. 1971. *Playing and Reality*. London: Tavistock.

Winnicott, D. 1987. *Home is Where We Start From: Essays by a Psychoanalyst*. Harmondswoth, Middlesex: Penguin.

Wittgenstein, L. [1953] 1968. *Philosophical Investigations*. Oxford: Blackwell.

Wolff, J. 1981. *The Social Production of Art*. London: MacMillan.

Woodham, J. 1996. 'Managing British Design Reform I: Fresh Perspectives on the Early Years of the Council of Industrial Design' pp. 55–65. In *Journal of Design History*, Vol. 9, No. 1.

Woodham, J.M. 1997. *Twentieth Century Design*. Oxford and New York: Oxford University Press.

Worden, S. 1980. 'Furniture for the Living Room' [unpublished PhD thesis] Brighton: University of Brighton

Worden, S. 1989. 'The Development of the Fireside Chair 1928-1940' pp. 5-9. In *Antique Collecting*, Vol. 24, No. 2.

Wright, P. 1985. *On Living in an Old Country*. London and New York: Verso.

Wright, P. and Putnam, T. 'Sneering at the Theme Parks', pp. 48–55. In *Block* 15, Spring 1989.

Wykes-Joyce, M. 1961. *Cosmetics and Adornment*. London: Peter Owen.

York, P. 1985. *Modern Times*. London: Futura.

Young, M. and Willmott, P. 1957. *Family and Kinship in East London*. London: Routledge and Kegan Paul.

Zeldin, T.1994. *An Intimate History of Humanity*. London: Sinclair Stevenson.

Index

UNIVERSITY OF WOLVERHAMPTON
LEARNING RESOURCES

[library stamp — illegible]